PENGUIN REFERENCE

THE PENGUIN GUIDE TO PLAIN ENGLISH

Harry Blamires, a graduate of University College, Oxford, was formerly Dean of Arts and Sciences at King Alfred's College, Winchester. He was Visiting Professor of English Literature at Wheaton College, Illinois, in 1987. The University of Southampton has awarded him a D.Litt. in recognition of his achievements as a writer. His total output of some thirty books includes fiction and theology, but he is widely known for his works of literary history and criticism. These include *A Short History of English Literature* (Routledge) and *Twentieth-Century English Literature* (Macmillan). For over three decades students in the USA and the UK have benefitted from his classic guide to Joyce's *Ulysses*, *The New Bloomsday Book*. More recently, in *The Cassell Guide to Common Errors in English*, he has shown how lively and entertaining the exploration of current usage can be.

HARRY BLAMIRES

The Penguin Guide to Plain English

Express Yourself Clearly and Effectively

PENGUIN BOOKS

PENGUIN BOOKS

Published by the Penguin Group
Penguin Books Ltd, 80 Strand, London WC2R 0RL, England
Penguin Putnam Inc., 375 Hudson Street, New York, New York 10014, USA
Penguin Books Australia Ltd, Ringwood, Victoria, Australia
Penguin Books Canada Ltd, 10 Alcorn Avenue, Toronto, Ontario, Canada M4V 3B2
Penguin Books India (P) Ltd, 11 Community Centre, Panchsheel Park, New Delhi – 110 017, India
Penguin Books (NZ) Ltd, Cnr Rosedale and Airborne Roads, Albany, Auckland, New Zealand
Penguin Books (South Africa) (Pty) Ltd, 24 Sturdee Avenue, Rosebank 2196 South Africa

Penguin Books Ltd, Registered Offices: 80 Strand, London WC2R 0RL, England

www.penguin.com

First published 2000
5

Set in 9.75/12 pt Monotype Joanna
Typeset by Rowland Phototypesetting Ltd, Bury St Edmunds, Suffolk
Printed in England by Clays Ltd, St Ives plc

Contents

PART 2 Arranging Words Correctly

INTRODUCTION

What is Plain English?

'Sir, 'tis my occupation to be plain' says Kent to the king in Shakespeare's *King Lear*, as he all but despairs of persuading his master to face facts. And Kent is Shakespeare's chosen vehicle to represent the values of common sense and reason in a world toppling into lunacy. Kent's is the voice of healthy discernment in recognizing the difference between truth and falsehood, genuineness and corruption. Plainness is his pride. And in Shakespeare's *Richard III* this is how the villain Gloucester protests against misrepresentation of his character:

> Cannot a plain man live and think no harm,
> But that his simple truth must be abused
> By silken, sly, insinuating Jacks?

He postures as the plain man up against the showy, greasy tricksters who specialize in nods and winks and innuendoes. The 'plain' is again opposed to the bogus and the deceptive. And although we sometimes nowadays use the word 'plain' as the converse of 'beautiful', it remains a connotatively rich one. 'Plain living and high thinking are no more' Wordsworth complained in criticism of the worship of wealth and show corrupting contemporary life. Yet plainness does not generally imply austerity. When the words 'plain' and 'English' are taken into the expression 'plain English cooking', we are more likely to encounter roast beef and Yorkshire pudding, apple pie and cream, than the menu of the ascetic.

We are looking then for usage which is genuine and direct, unspoiled by any hint of the bogus or the pretentious, English which is clear and open as the day, which claims no special attention to itself but rather melts away into what it conveys. That should be the standard usage of speakers and writers. But we only need to open a newspaper or turn on the radio to realize that the prevailing verbal usage of our age falls short in numerous ways. That is the reason for the method of approach adopted in this book. Tidily explaining to readers how the English language should be used by a neat progression through the parts of speech, and the construction of clauses and sentences, can be illuminating. But it is not quite the same process as checking up at the coalface on the English that is actually used and uncovering where it goes wrong. I have taken heed of a wise popular saying, 'If it ain't broke, don't mend it.' That advice has always seemed to me to be peculiarly applicable to the business of writing books with an instructive purpose. And that is why I have believed that the most practically helpful starting-point for giving advice about how to write good English is from the mass of bad English with which we are surrounded.

I now have a collection of some 7,000 bad sentences, accumulated over the years from the press, the radio, commercial publicity and junk mail. Bringing this material to light enables us to discern where people go wrong in their use of English, not just occasionally but time after time. Where a bad practice turns up day after day in the newspaper, on the air and in the morning mail it ought to get proportionate attention and space in a book which specifically concentrates on the English we actually read, actually hear, actually use.

That is why this book abounds in examples. It does not take up a dogmatic position in relation to traditional grammar or to the revisionist grammars of the last few decades. It does not lay into the latest slang or get over-excited about split infinitives. It explores the English now in use with determined emphasis on the guide-lines we must follow if what we say and what we write is to be exactly what we mean.

For we are about a much more positive task than that of mere detection and correction of error. That in itself is not an inspiring activity. Nor does it win friends. 'Filthy famished correctioner' Shakespeare's Doll Tearsheet screams at the interfering Beadle. But correction can be salutary. 'Whom the Lord loveth He correcteth,' the Book of Proverbs tells us. And the positive aim here is to reveal how gratifying, indeed how stimulating it is to achieve that sustained level of correctness which marks 'plain English'. There is great satisfaction for all those who do not have to worry that what they write, or what they say when they speak in public, may not stand up to scrutiny on some point of style or usage.

For most people it is not a matter of mastering a lot of grammatical rules. It is rather a matter of learning to keep a clear head. Having read 'Glancing to the right, the church spire is visible above the rooftops', the grammarian will talk about the 'hanging participle', while the clear-headed reader will anyway protest mentally 'But the church spire is not glancing to the right.' In the same way, having read 'As the inheritor of an illustrious name in hunting, the threat to the sport came as a great shock', the grammarian will quite properly talk about 'misconnecting an appositional phrase', but the clear-headed reader can see anyway that it is nonsense to talk of a 'threat' as having 'an illustrious name in hunting', and will not need to refer to the grammatical rule book. Correct use of English depends so much on straight thinking and sheer common sense that it is possible in discussion of the subject to be selective and economic in the use of grammatical terminology. That is the policy in this book.

Some light can be shed on what constitutes 'plain English' if we take a preliminary look at a few of the obvious qualities it must have. Utterance that is plain is utterance that cannot be misunderstood. And utterance that cannot possibly be misunderstood will be precise. To be precise is to get exactly the right word. Precision ought not to be regarded as the preserve of pedants. Getting nearly the right word renders prose uncomfortable for the educated reader. Here we have an advertisement where a touch of cleverness misfires through failure to be precise.

> Five Alive, one of the most popular fruit drinks on the market, has developed a new tasty recipe that's an ideal accompaniment for any breakfast table.

Reading with proper attention, we sense at once that the word 'accompaniment' is ill-chosen. Tomato sauce might be a suitable accompaniment for fish and chips, and a piano might provide a suitable accompaniment for a singer, but a breakfast table does not need to be accompanied by a recipe. The writer's desire not to say the simple and direct thing, that 'the recipe makes a tasty drink for breakfast', instead of dragging in the notion of accompanying a table, merely makes for imprecision.

Plain English is never wasteful of words. If a thing can be said briefly, then so it should be. Great poets recognize this. Few sentences say as much as Shakespeare's 'To be or not to be; that is the question.' Not that compression so extreme fits all occasions. But the pointless piling-up of words degrades the words it wastes. Nevertheless, the notion that brief conversational idioms should be translated in print into long-winded utterance is widespread. Here is a report on the result of a test taken by nurses.

> The assessments were all successfully undertaken. The anticipated learning outcomes of each group member were substantially exceeded and are currently being expressed as part of the outcome profile for each of them.

Translated into English, this would read: 'They all did better than expected and their results are being recorded.'

The converse error of excessive thrift in the number of words used is perhaps much rarer. But it is possible to write without being long-winded and yet to produce wording that is stilted and strained. Here is a comment on the disposal of a locomotive by a railway preservation society.

> It is a year since its custodianship transferred to another society.

The use of the word 'custodianship' here sounds awkwardly affected. Why not: 'It is a year since it was handed over into the keeping of another society'?

There is of course a place for artificial vocabulary which confers a degree of dignity on what is said. But there are contexts where the avoidance of the most familiar and natural vocabulary merely seems emptily pretentious. Here is a piece from an article about a particular breed of dogs.

> It was apparent that with the enormity of their size, their slobbering habits and also their general dislike of the heat it was obvious that their preference would be an outside environment, which was certainly more practical for us.

We overlook the elementary error of repeating 'it was apparent' in 'it was obvious'. What concerns us here is the use of such expressions as 'the enormity of their size' (a bad error anyway, since 'enormity' does not mean magnitude but dreadfulness) and 'their preference would be an outside environment'. What it all amounts to is that 'because they are big and slobber and dislike heat, they would be better kept outside'. And that is how it should be put.

It should go without saying that plain English will be accurate in its use of words. Ensuring that your sentence makes the point you want to make clearly is a matter of clarifying your meaning mentally before you pen a word. Inaccuracy is not found only in long, awkward paragraphs. A brief and at first sight simple sentence, which to the superficial glance raises no problems, may not stand up to careful scrutiny in this respect. Here is a sentence from an article about collecting Old Master drawings.

> The history of collecting Old Master drawings in this country is of unrivalled distinction.

The reader wonders how a 'history' can be so distinguished. From the sentence that follows this one we learn of aristocratic collectors who indulged in this hobby. In short, the writer did not mean that the 'history' had unrivalled distinction, but that from earliest times collectors were distinguished people. What was really meant was: 'Distinguished aristocrats were early collectors of Old Master drawings in our country.'

In this matter of accuracy, the good writer will learn to play safe. We must fully understand every word we use and take no risks. Venturing outside the range of our understanding is dangerous. Sometimes avoiding what is simple and straightforward lures us into error. A misjudged attempt at distinctiveness in vocabulary can fail disgracefully. Even highbrow critics are not exempt from the temptation to be just a little too clever. Thus we find a literary reviewer writing:

> After a while exaggerated comic scenes mount up meaninglessly, and even the funniest feel belaboured.

Clearly what the writer wanted to convey was that the comic scenes seemed 'laboured', which means laboriously put together. The somewhat archaic verb to 'belabour' means to thrash, so the critic's sentence really means that the comic scenes seemed thrashed, which makes no sense at all.

There is another way of avoiding what is straightforward, when we pick up some ready-made but contrived expression where a simple sequence of familiar words would be better.

> He was awkward, stubborn and lazy to the extent that his parents finally lost patience with him.

This is a case in point. It is difficult to think of a sentence using the expression 'to the extent that' which would not be better without it. Nothing is gained here from avoiding the straightforward wording: 'He was so awkward, stubborn and lazy that his parents finally lost patience with him.'

Plain English will use words that are appropriate to the context. There will not be words which seem incongruously out of place. Even a fairly simple statement of fact may be marred in this respect. Here is a police officer reporting on the discovery of a dead body:

> At 7.0 p.m. last night officers attended some waste ground.

The word 'attended' may be standard in 'police-speak', but it is surely out of place here. It has too formal a ring and in any case conveys the wrong meaning. We might speak of 'attending' a wedding reception in a hotel, but not of 'attending' the hotel. To speak of attending 'waste ground' is a clumsy way of avoiding something very simple: 'Officers went to some waste ground.' Plain English will not furrow the brow of the reader by a hint of inappropriateness in the relation of word to word.

We cannot write plain English unless we keep a clear head. Here is a sentence from an article in a quality paper on the subject of body-piercing.

> With a tongue-stud, there are two main veins underneath the tongue and you have to make sure that you keep away from them.

There is a strange illogicality here. The two main veins underneath the tongue are there whether you are going to fix a stud in the mouth or not. 'With' is a problematic word in this respect. We shall see many instances of its misuse later in the book. What the writer means is: 'If you fit a tongue stud, you have to make sure that you keep away from the two main veins underneath the tongue.'

Plain English is easy on the ear. It reads fluently. There are occasions in poetry and in other imaginative literature when the writer may wish to exploit the unsettling, percussive power of words. But generally speaking, prose should flow smoothly. It should not unsettle the reader's response by jerkiness or by seemingly cluttered wording.

> 'School from Hell' headlines stereotyped children from the Ridings School in Halifax, young reporters from the Save the Children-backed Newcastle Children's Express News Agency told journalists at a recent seminar.

The thirteen-word pile-up as the subject of the verb 'told' unsettles the reader's attention. 'Young reporters from the Newcastle Children's Express News Agency' is surely long enough as the subject of the verb. To bolt on to that the words 'Save the Children-backed' is to apply a packed bale of straw to the camel's already fully loaded back. Where the situation is as desperate as this, use brackets: 'young reporters from the Newcastle Children's Express News Agency (backed by Save the Children) told journalists'.

If utterance is plain, it will not be complex. Whatever intricacies there may be in the message conveyed, the wording will not overtax our minds to sort it out. Here is a piece from a marketing journal about the European Monetary Union.

> The respondents, however, in spite of their doubts about the single currency, foresaw many benefits, including the elimination of the risks involved with currency exchange, the equalization of currencies, the reduced administration costs (e.g. in billing) and the psychological benefits attached because of a strengthening of the bonds between countries and it being evidence of a united European economic power.

The complexity here is not gross, but it is enough to make the sequence seem awkward. The reader senses a lack of cohesion. Too many bits seem to have been stuck together. Indeed, the passage asks to be broken up into its constituent parts. 'The correspondents had doubts about the single currency, but they foresaw many benefits. The risks taken in exchanging currencies would be removed, currencies would be equalized, administrative costs would be reduced, and, psychologically, bonds between countries would be strengthened by the existence of a united European economic power.'

Two general lessons could be learned from this little exercise. Where argument or reasoning is involved, a watch should be kept on paragraphing, to ensure that the force of individual points is not lost in the process of heaping them together. The second point is that replacing nouns by verbs often simplifies and clarifies meaning ('elimination' is replaced by 'could be removed', 'equalization' by 'equalized' and 'strengthening' by 'strengthened'). That kind of shift in usage will be thoroughly explored later in the book.

Plain English will never be muddled. Here is a travel article tempting us to visit the island of Corfu.

> From Odysseus through to the English poet and novelist Lawrence Durrell, the island has long been lauded for its glorious beaches, great rock formations along the west coast, picturesque villages and spectacular birdlife. Add to that the acres of silvery, ancient olive groves, and it is hard to believe that you are nearly at the end of the twentieth century.

We do not have doubts about what the writer is wanting to tell us here. But we wish she had actually said it, instead of leaving us to keep up a running process of mental correction as we read. 'From Odysseus to

Durrell, people have lauded Corfu' would make sense. 'From Odysseus to Durrell, the island has been lauded' does not. The word 'that' in 'Add to that', placed where it is, ought to refer to the long lauding of the island. But it doesn't. The writer has changed tack. Moreover, she immediately changes tack again. Adding olive groves to villages and birdlife does not make it difficult to believe that we are where we are in history. What the writer means is that the (unmentioned) tranquillity and remoteness of the scenery seem to belong to a past century. Clear articulation of a train of thought will leave no gaps in logic which the reader's mind has to jump over. The connecting expressions 'Add to that', 'and it is hard to believe' and 'Otherwise' all need to be replaced: 'From Odysseus through to the English poet Lawrence Durrell, people have long lauded the island for its glorious beaches, great rock formations along the west coast, picturesque villages and spectacular birdlife. Moreover, there are acres of silvery, ancient olive groves, and the peaceful atmosphere makes it hard for the visitor to remember that we are nearly at the end of the twentieth century.'

Finally, plain English has a directness which ensures that its meaning will never seem more complex than it is. It will never become convoluted by tangled syntax. Here we have an observation about the introduction of a new High Intensity Cruising Licence for vessels which have no permanent mooring, on our inland waterways.

> In an about-face British Waterways changed from claiming the new licence was due to the majority of continuous cruisers flouting the rules, causing mooring congestion at popular visitor moorings, and cost enforcement issues, to saying that this was part of the process to resolve the funding and arrears of maintenance problems.

To begin with, by 'the new licence was due to' the writer really means 'the introduction of the new licence was due to'. Too big a pile-up of participles and gerunds (ending in '-ing') is almost always clumsy. The basic construction chosen ('changed from claiming . . . to saying'), when complicated by 'due to flouting' and 'causing congestion' sinks under its own weight. The direct presentation of the items awkwardly joined would make reading far easier. 'BW has done a U-turn. They said the new licence was introduced because continuous cruisers flouted the rules, caused congestion at popular mooring sites and made enforcement of the regulations expensive. They now say that the new scheme helps towards the general costs of maintenance.' In the original there are three finite verbs only ('changed', 'was' and 'this was') surrounded by an entanglement of non-finite forms ('claiming', 'flouting', 'causing', 'saying', 'to resolve', 'funding'). In our corrected version there are eight finite verbs ('has done', 'said', 'was introduced', 'flouted', 'caused', 'made', 'say' and 'helps'). The change not only makes the passage more straightforward and easier to follow. It also makes the prose tauter and more vigorous.

THE PLAN OF THIS BOOK

We have dipped our toes into the sea of carelessness that contemporary usage exemplifies. We have noticed dominant tendencies – tendencies to inflation, to inexactitude, to muddle and to illogicality. In all these directions, and in many others, variable degrees of erroneousness will be fully explored in the following chapters, as we systematically take stock of current usage.

Part 1 The Words at Our Disposal

The focus of the earlier chapters of the book is upon our vocabulary. The English vocabulary is vast and varied. We must learn to be confident about which is the right word and which is the wrong word in any context. To that end the chapters in Part 1 are devoted to thorough exploration of words now commonly misused or over-used and to problems that can arise in maintaining accuracy in meaning when juxtaposing word with word. We then take a look at the peculiar character of the English language, examining the development of its extraordinarily rich vocabulary and considering some of the problems as well as the advantages that its resources present.

Part 2 Arranging Words Correctly

Part 2 has a series of chapters more concerned with the build-up of sentences, the proper arrangement of words in rational utterance and the need for congruity and coherence in this respect. It is in this section that attention is given to the constructions that tend to trip us up, to the proper techniques for arguing a case, to the demands of sound logic, and to what it is that distinguishes good style from bad. The aim throughout this section is to ensure clear understanding of the various pitfalls besetting the would-be writer of good English today, and to show how they may be avoided.

Part 3 Changing Fashions in Usage

Finally, in Part 3 the emphasis is upon verbal fashions and trends affecting current usage. Here the book explores the innovations of recent decades, samples trendy verbal practices, and looks into some of the liberties taken in current usage. There is emphasis throughout upon the evident need for new discipline to restore vitality to our utterance. The last chapter, in particular, focuses on contemporary usage in various spheres of business and public life.

PART 1

The Words at Our Disposal

CHAPTER 1

The Words to be Used

SOME RISKY CONTEXTS

When are we most likely to feel a little dissatisfied with what we have just said? Which are those occasions when we feel for the right word and don't quite find it? When are we most likely to say 'You know what I mean?' One such occasion may arise when we are trying to explain a situation to someone else, or trying to argue a point. The process of explaining or arguing is one of the contexts in which the use of words is likely to present problems. By 'explaining or arguing' I do not have in mind any very abstruse reasoning processes. After all, we are involved in modest reasoning processes when we say 'That sunset seems to promise a fine day tomorrow.' And we may get involved in a fairly awkward search for the right words in the right order when a passing motorist asks us the way to a given street in a town riddled with one-way signs.

We have seen that to choose the right word is to choose the precise word, the appropriate and straightforward word. That ought to mean choosing the obvious word, the word that comes first to mind. But unfortunately that is not the case. What comes first to mind is often the currently most frequently used word. Now of course there is no point in trying to avoid use of the most frequently used word simply in order to be different. But fashionable habits establish some words widely and firmly in current usage to the neglect of others. And that has unfortunate consequences. In the first place, a given word is over-used while other words are too little used. In the second place, differences in connotation, sometimes slight, sometimes subtle, are thus lost. And thirdly, current speech is riddled with usages which excessive exploitation has rendered inaccurate. We shall consider various spheres of discourse in which the damage done to the connotation of crucial words makes difficulties for us.

Of course, things can go wrong in a more complex way than in the mere choice of words. Later on in the book we shall have to return to consider the contexts in which errors abound, with an eye on more complex problems of sentence structure and syntax.

Reasoning

cause, reason, reasonably

Nowhere is it more necessary to select words carefully than in dealing with matters of cause and effect. In this respect a current bad habit is the careless use of the word 'reason'. In the contexts with which we are concerned 'reason' is best used of human motivation. If a man is hurrying to catch a train, the 'reason' for his haste may be that he wants to be home in time for dinner. If he meets an old friend who detains him, that is not the 'reason' why he misses the train, it is the 'cause' of his missing it. Thus when we read: 'Acne is on the increase among women . . . The reason is thought to be stress', we recognize that this should be: 'the cause is thought to be stress'. The error is a common one.

> The common reason for money to go unclaimed is shareholders failing to inform registrars of change of address . . . Another reason is cheques, delivered to the wrong address, lapsing because they are not cashed within six months.

This gives us two 'causes', not reasons. In correcting the passage it would be far better, as so often is the case, to base the wording neither on the noun 'reason' nor on the noun 'cause' but on use of the word 'because': 'Money often goes unclaimed because shareholders fail to inform registrars of change of address . . . It also may go unclaimed because cheques are delivered to the wrong address, are not cashed within six months and so lapse.'

> The company's difficulties were due to no other reason than inefficiency.

Similarly this would better be: 'Inefficiency was the sole cause of the company's difficulties.'

If 'reason' is a word that over-use has weakened, even more so is the word 'reasonably'. It is one of those adverbs which we throw about in conversation with little sense of precision. If we were more disciplined in our choice of words we should recall that the distinction between what is 'reasonable' and what is 'unreasonable' is a crucial one. But conversational freedom allows the word 'reasonably' to mean something like 'moderately' ('I'm reasonably certain about it') until its connotation deteriorates finally into something like 'rather' and we find in print: 'The details are reasonably sketchy at the moment.'

mean

In dealing with matters of cause, result and effect, there is now a tendency to fall back too often on the word 'mean'. Throughout this book usage of the word in its strictest connotation is bound to be frequent. We must repeatedly observe that a given word 'means' this and does not 'mean' that. It is by a natural and logical development that we arrive at such conversational usages as 'That sky means there's rain ahead' or even the more idiomatic 'That fellow means business.' However, popular usage now drags the verb into contexts where it merely draws attention to the paucity of vocabulary in the writer's grasp.

> The hillside location of this hotel means there are wonderful views of the town and harbour.

The writer is here concerned, not with a matter of meaning, but with a matter of cause and effect. It would be much better to say: 'Because of its hillside location, this hotel has wonderful views of the town and harbour.' There is a similar causal function in the word 'mean' in:

> Recent developments in surgical practice mean that patients are not required to stay in hospital overnight.

Clearly it would be more precise to say: 'As a result of recent developments in surgical practice patients are not required to stay in hospital overnight.' And the following advice, given to young women about their appearance when they are going to be interviewed, stretches the idiomatic usage further.

> If in doubt, dress 'up' rather than 'down' – even if the job you're going for doesn't mean looking smart.

Our objection to the usage is that it over-uses a much over-used verb, and also that it is imprecise, when what is really meant is: 'even if the job you're going for doesn't require you to look particularly smart'. It is after all the possible 'requirement' presented by the employer or the post that is at issue.

involve / involvement

The verb to 'involve' is also being used to cover a variety of rational connections, causal and otherwise. Its connotation has developed interestingly. The Latin root ('volvere') meant to roll something about and is behind both our words 'revolve' and 'involve'. 'Involvere' came to mean to overwhelm or cover, used of clouds sweeping over the sky. So in English usage in the eighteenth century the poet William Cowper began his powerful poem about a castaway at sea with the lines:

> Obscurest night involved the sky,
> The Atlantic billows roared . . .

From meaning to roll things up, to enwrap, to envelop or entangle we can see how it has become the useful word we now know too well.

> The retirement package involved continued rent-free residence.

Here the word 'involve' is used to mean 'include'.

> The expedition would involve spending three weeks in an exposed position on the mountain.

Here the word 'involve' is used to mean 'necessitate'.

> Accepting the new post would have involved my whole family.

Here the word 'involve' is used to mean 'affect'.

> We could not consider the board's proposal without involving the whole work force.

Here the word 'involve' means 'consult'. This is a far cry from the notion of rolling up clouds in a stormy sky. It is a pity to weaken an already weakened word further. That is what we should say to ourselves before lightly using the word.

The popularity of the verb to 'involve' has now been matched by the popularity of the noun 'involvement'. If a project 'involves' collecting information, then collecting information is a necessary part of the project. People 'involved' in a project are significantly concerned and associated with it. When we read of the hope that a pretty but neglected waterway 'will see an increased local involvement' we recognize the same usage, but what can we make of the following?

> The case for one member, one vote involvement in future leadership elections is not just to provide democratic legitimacy but also as an incentive to join.

The writer here errs in trying to balance 'is not just to' with 'but also as' instead of with 'but also to'. But that grammatical lapse is not what we happen to be interested in just now. What is 'one member, one vote involvement'? The writer is trying to say: 'The case for using the one-member, one-vote system in future leadership elections is not only that it will be more democratically legitimate but also that it will encourage people to join the party.'

problem, solution, different

The word 'problem' too readily springs to our lips these days. The current drift is towards increasingly indiscriminate use of it. We need not be over-fussy about this in conversation. We know now that when the waiter says 'No problem', he means that the cook will be only too happy to do the steak exactly as requested, and when the garage foreman says it, he means that he will deal immediately with the punctured tyre or the broken exhaust pipe. Sometimes the word seems to be superfluous.

> A government research study in 1995 pinpointed insufficient iron as a problem in the underfives.

The 'problem' is the 'insufficiency of iron'. Does the word 'problem' add anything here? 'Insufficiency' cannot be present anywhere without representing a 'problem'. All that is needed is: 'A government research study in 1995 pinpointed a deficiency of iron in the underfives.'

There is a graver current misuse than that.

> The problem that faced the police was the remote site.

At first sight, that is probably not a sentence that worries us. Even the sentence 'The remote site made access difficult' may seem acceptable. Yet, strictly speaking, it is not the remote site but the 'remoteness of the site' that makes access difficult. We see immediately that it would not be right to say 'The extremely aged man made questioning difficult' when what we mean is 'The extreme age of the man made questioning difficult.' The two sentences differ sharply in meaning. Precision in that kind of statement is the sign of a logical mind.

We also need to watch the tendency to use the word 'problem' as an adjective:

> Apparently beauty salons have been using this method for years to control problem skin.

We have heard of the problem of controlling problem children in schools. Presumably that usage ('problem children') stemmed from a psychologically convenient and politically correct desire not to define the children's idiosyncrasies too blatantly. It would appear that a similar tenderness has to be employed in defining defects in personal appearance. The young woman does not want to think of her skin as in any way imperfect, but she will gladly regard it as a 'problem'.

There is no doubt of our fondness nowadays for talking, wherever possible, in terms of 'problems' and 'solutions'. The latter word is even more misused than the former. Sometimes a 'solution' is posited seemingly without reference to a problem.

> We took the scooter to Spain last winter and found it a good solution to taking a large motorcaravan off site and parking in spots where a large vehicle could be an embarrassment.

This is a striking example of allowing the pen to move faster than the brain. What the writer means is: 'We found it a good alternative to taking the large motorcaravan off site.' Such misuse is not rare. Consider this notice about an art course.

> The course questions the notion of the book, and most students have different solutions.

Here the use of 'most' and 'different' is illogical. The question arises, 'different' from what? And what about the minority of students not represented by the word 'most'? Do they share a 'non-different', that is an identical view? Better start afresh: 'The course examines what a book should be, and the students air various views.' Unfortunately this misuse of 'different' is not rare either.

> I'm a part-time nurse in Saudi Arabia where architecture and furnishings are very different.

Different from what? The implication ('different from our own') must be spelt out. When we say 'Men and women are different' and then 'Men and women are different from dumb animals' we use the word 'different' in two recognized, but 'different' ways.

convince, persuade, induce

These words should be carefully differentiated. Historically 'convince' is a powerful word. Deriving from the notion of vanquishing, it is used to convey the idea of overcoming someone so completely in argument that acknowledgement of the truth in question is made. The emphasis therefore should be on acknowledgement of some fact or theory.

> When American expatriates Sara and Gerald Murphy discovered Antibes' sleepy seaside Hôtel du Cap in 1923, they convinced the owner to keep it open for them out of season with a minimal staff.

'Convinced' here should be 'persuaded'. To 'convince' someone of some truth should be carefully distinguished from 'persuading' them to act in a certain way. Of course there is an overlap of meaning. But it is the once powerful verb 'convince' that suffers deterioration of meaning when it is misused.

> Cadbury Garden Centre, near Bristol, aimed to convince gardeners to use more exotic plants.

This should be: 'aimed to persuade' or 'aimed to induce'.

Evading and Preventing

avert, avoid, forestall, obviate, preempt, prevent

Closely related to the business of arguing in terms of cause and effect is the business of explaining how some consequence might be evaded or prevented. It will be made evident at many points in this book that bad usage often arises from failure to discriminate precisely between words which may have a slight overlap of meaning, but which nevertheless cannot be regarded as interchangeable. In discourse concerning evasion and prevention the danger is notable. Current practice seems to be to over-use the word 'avoid'. It is gradually taking over in the press and on the radio where there are other and better words to hand. When we consider the number and variety of these words, as illustrated above, we are bound to regret the excessive use of one of them.

> The driver's quick thinking avoided a major railway disaster.

This should read: 'averted a major railway disaster'. To 'avoid' something is to render it void, or of no effect. It can also mean to escape something or to have nothing to do with it. To 'avert' is to turn away. 'She averted her eyes in embarrassment', we say. Thus it means to deflect something from the course it is taking and therefore to ward off a possible development.

In the basic meaning of the verb 'avoid' the overlap with notions of preventing or averting is not sufficient to justify turning it into a verb virtually synonymous with either 'prevent' or 'avert'. Yet that is what has happened. This is not so much a question of correctness or incorrectness as of discrimination in the use of words. People who care for language will naturally not like to see subtle distinctions lost. We may 'avoid' a puddle in the road by stepping round it. We may 'avoid' paying income tax by various questionable means. But where evasion is less an issue than prevention, the word can be used very unhappily, as in the following.

> We had no criticism of the cab seats, which gave enough support to avoid fatigue.

As I read that, I get the image of cab seats narrowly escaping exhaustion. Surely 'to prevent fatigue' would be better.

> Remove each piece from the table one at a time . . . This avoids having to reconstruct the entire pattern.

Here, in instructions for practising decorative decoupage, there is an excellent chance to use a now neglected word especially appropriate where something is prevented by anticipatory action: 'This obviates having to reconstruct the entire pattern.'

A bad habit has lately developed of misusing the word 'preempt'. Although it has a special intransitive use in the game of Bridge, it properly means to acquire or appropriate beforehand. Someone might 'preempt' a deal at an auction by putting in a high offer in advance. But one does not 'preempt' someone else's announcement by getting in first with it. That is to 'anticipate' it. Nor can anyone 'preempt' the building of a motorway by organizing objections to it. That is to 'forestall' it. And again no one can 'preempt' some parallel claimant's case by accepting a low offer before that claimant's case comes up. That is to 'prejudice' it.

Exchanging and Replacing

substitute, exchange, usurp

In words for exchanging and replacing we find a carelessness that causes not just a deterioration in meaning but sometimes an almost total reversal in meaning. That happens with the words 'substitute' and 'substitution'. To 'substitute' a player for an injured player is to replace the injured one by the 'substitute'. It is incorrect to speak of an injured player being 'substituted' by a reserve. Yet we often read or hear the blunder made.

> At the moment Katie tends to have a savoury dish followed by, say, a jam tart. This could be substituted for fresh fruit, yogurt or fromage fresh . . .

This nutritionist's advice is seemingly topsy-turvy. She says she wants to replace the child's fresh fruit and yogurt diet by a savoury dish and a jam tart. What she means is: 'This could be replaced by fresh fruit, yoghurt or fromage fresh.'

> More than 20 passengers . . . rode the service on July 11, with NWT having been advised to avoid the train being substituted by a taxi, which has occurred on several occasions this year.

The writer in the *Railway Magazine* has provided us with a similar topsy-turvy misuse of the verb 'substitute' along with another unfortunate use of 'avoid'. Get rid of the redundant 'with', omit the unnecessary 'avoid' and switch the wording round: 'More than 20 passengers . . . rode the service on July 11, NWT having been advised not to substitute a taxi for the train.'

Where 'for' is used along with a verb in such constructions as 'I exchanged my old bike for a new one' it is important to remember that what you exchange is what you part with and the thing 'for' which you exchange it is what you take possession of. If readers think this an utterly unnecessary warning, let them carefully read the following. It comes from a review of a book on Mary Robinson, the former President of the Irish Republic. The review makes the point that where the Irish were once known for their devotion to religious figures, they now appear to give that devotion to secular figures. The review concludes:

> But it is not clear that the Irish have done well in exchanging secular for religious sanctity.

This error, in a quality weekly, raises one's eyebrows. The writer has got it the wrong way round. What he means is: 'But it is not clear that the Irish have done well in exchanging religious for secular sanctity.' As so often, the word 'replace' could have been used: 'in replacing religious by secular sanctity'.

Before taking leave of the word, however, we should take note of an unfortunate new development. It is a construction that works like this:

> The committee have decided to exchange a new and revised brochure with their rather old-fashioned one.

In this sentence the clear mistake was to use 'with' at all. We do not exchange a new car 'with' our old one. We may exchange the old car 'for' a new one. In any case 'exchange' is surely not the best verb to use where the issue is a matter of replacement: 'The committee have decided to replace their rather old-fashioned brochure with a new and revised one.' Oddly enough, an alternative correction would be to use the so often misused verb 'substitute': 'The committee have decided to substitute a new and revised brochure for their rather old-fashioned one.'

Another verb of replacement now misused is the verb to 'usurp'.

> The friendship ended irrevocably in 1987, when Mr Milosevic championed the cause of the Kosovo Serbs and usurped his mentor.

To 'usurp' is to seize without proper authority some position to which one is not entitled. Thus a rebel may 'usurp' a throne, but he could not 'usurp' the king. The above should read: 'championed the cause of the Kosovo Serbs and usurped his mentor's position'.

Repaying and Forbearing

reimburse, compensate, condone

A category of verbs which can easily lure to error is the kind which affects two objects in different ways. The verb works directly on the object in such sentences as 'He stole a car.' The meaning there is complete. But there are verbs which affect two objects. In 'He gave his sister a book', the verb has both a direct object ('the book') and an indirect object ('his sister'). Though 'he' truly gave the book, it cannot be said that 'he gave his sister'. But there are verbs where this double effect is more complicated. From the sentence 'He paid the retailer five pounds' it would be correct to derive both the sentence 'He paid the retailer' and the sentence 'He paid five pounds.' Because the verb 'pay' and the verb 'repay' work thus, there is a temptation to try to make other verbs of paying work similarly. Thus a minister in the House of Commons spoke of 'reimbursing the cost' of an enterprise. One hears this error repeated on the radio. The announcer tells us that the National Health Service is to recoup the cost of treating road accident victims from insurance companies. There is determination to 'track down the money and reimburse it to the Health Service'. But money cannot be 'reimbursed'. To 'reimburse' is to repay someone, not to repay a sum. Thus the words 'it to' should be omitted in the above: 'track down the money and reimburse the Health Service'.

A comparably faulty use of the verb to 'compensate' occurs when it is treated as though it worked like the verb to 'pay'. We may 'pay someone five pounds' because we can either 'pay someone' or 'pay five pounds', but we cannot 'compensate someone five pounds' because, though we can 'compensate someone' we cannot 'compensate five pounds'.

> They are now working out how much he should be compensated.

Thus that statement on Radio 4 will not serve. Add the word 'by': 'They are now working out by how much he should be compensated.'

We can 'compensate' a person but not a sum of money. Conversely, however, we can 'condone' an offence but not the person who committed it. We hear on the radio:

> A lot of parents condone their truant children.

To condone is to forgive or overlook an offence, not a person. Thus this should be: 'A lot of parents condone their children's truancy.'

Approving and Disapproving

creative, dogmatic, pathetic

Words of strong approval or strong disapproval acquire emotive force which sometimes gets out of hand. That is to say, speakers or writers latch on to them for giving vent to likes or dislikes with a rather loose awareness of their exact meaning. An instance is provided by the words 'creative' and 'creativity'. The precise connotation of such words requires us to use them of acts which produce something where nothing of the kind existed before. One thinks of the acts of creation recorded in the Book of Genesis. And so one feels a certain verbal discomfiture when one reads in a travel article of a Spanish township, 'It was here that the study of medicine and surgery was created.' Why not just 'began'? When one thinks of the kind of context in which the word 'creative' is properly at home, what comes most readily to mind is perhaps the towering genius of a Shakespeare or a Beethoven. But the word so conveniently arouses feelings of wonder that it gets bandied about in relation to all kinds of activities calling for our approval where, strictly speaking, true creation is not at issue. There are courses in 'Creative Cookery' and 'Creative Advertising', not to mention less publicized activities in 'Creative Accountancy'. We perhaps ought not to be too solemn about such usage. We naturally smile when we read 'Owing to the creativity of the weather this year, her garden has been subject to some confusion.' But there are plenty of misuses. Advertisements of vacant posts in various spheres, business or professional, would seem, by the wording of their demands for 'creativity' in their applicants, to be expecting some as yet unrecognized Botticelli or some mute inglorious Milton to emerge from suburbia and take the bait.

We have looked at the decay of a word through its positive connotation; let us look at the decay of a word through its negative connotation. The adjective 'dogmatic' takes its meaning from the noun 'dogma' used of a system of authoritative doctrines, especially religious doctrines. To assert such doctrines with due authority is to be 'dogmatic'. Now such assertiveness, especially in a liberal age, will be described as 'bigotry' by those who reject the doctrines. Gradually the word 'dogmatic' acquires overtones more and more pejorative. Thus, although even a recent dictionary defines the word 'dogmatic' objectively as 'forcibly asserted' or (of a person) 'prone to forcible assertion', it is scarcely possible now to use the word without a condemnatory implication.

> Today many teachers realize that there is little point in imposing dogmatic dress or disciplinary codes.

Here is a case in point. A 'code' is a conventionalized set of rules. The adjective 'dogmatic' therefore adds nothing to the strict connotation of the word, but the pejorative emotive resonance conveys that such codes are to be disliked.

A more remarkable degeneration of meaning has occurred in our use of the word 'pathetic', the adjective deriving from the noun 'pathos'.

Like the word 'pathetical' in Shakespeare, it was applied to persons or things which evoked or expressed genuine sympathy. In his *Life of Samuel Johnson* Boswell quotes a poetic tribute paid by Johnson on the death of his old friend, Robert Levett. Boswell declares that Johnson had such an affectionate regard for Levett 'that he honoured his memory with the following pathetic verses'. Thus at that time one might have praised an actress's sympathetic and moving performance in a tragedy by declaring it 'pathetic'. If that were said today, it would be more likely to mean that the acting was 'pitiably' bad.

derisory, derisive, abusive, nauseous

Sad to say, there are cases of misuse of words which we find sanctioned by new dictionaries. Where there are adjectives which define human attitudes we generally distinguish between the attitude and the object at which it is directed. That is to say, a man may be described as being 'desirous' of something and the object of his desire as 'desirable'. Similarly a person may be described as 'contemptuous' and, if the object of the contempt merits the attitude, we say it is 'contemptible'. If I developed a bad habit of mixing up these two words and describing a thing as 'contemptuous' when I meant that it was 'contemptible', the pedants would rightly be unwilling to give me their support. But in fact that is exactly what has happened in connection with the verb to 'deride'. By all reasonable linguistic tradition, a person who derides is being 'derisory' or 'derisive' and the object of the derision is 'derisible'. My *Shorter Oxford English Dictionary* (1933 edition, reprinted with corrections 1947) presents all this clearly. Yet I find a new dictionary accepting the assumption that what is to be derided is 'derisory'.

Adjectives such as 'derisive' and 'decisive' are descriptive in the first place of human attitudes. So is the adjective 'abusive'. An 'abusive speech' is a speech full of abuse. Yet a speaker on BBC Radio 4, reporting on child-abuse, declared that 'people have been making their abusive claims for years'. Clearly a claim that there has been abuse cannot be called an 'abusive claim', any more than a protest against indecency could be called an 'indecent protest'.

A word misused in the same way as 'derisory' is the word 'nauseous'. What is 'nauseous' is nauseating. It causes nausea; it is repulsive and distasteful. Indeed the word has the connotative strength of 'loathsome'. Yet journalists regularly misuse the word.

> The first signs that Cardinal Hume was ill appeared when he began feeling nauseous at mealtimes a few weeks ago.

Thus *The Times* tells us that the Cardinal felt loathsome. He did not. He felt 'nauseated'. He was affected by nausea.

Use of Fashionable Abstractions

concept, value

There are some abstract nouns found once in rigorous philosophical usage that are now so inappropriately exploited that they have become almost unusable. The word 'concept' has the same root as 'conceit' and means an idea or notion, something that the mind has 'conceived'. Yet just as the word 'idea' has been weakened in conversational usage ('the very idea!'), so now the word 'concept' has lost its anchorage in the realm of thought. Here is a statement about a new block of open-plan offices with café and shops:

> This concept of management on the move has been made possible by the design of Waterside.

Now the 'concept' of the change, that is the idea for the change, existed before anything was done about it. The 'concept' would have been exactly what it was, had nothing been done about it. It was the 'realization' of the concept that was made possible by the design of the building: 'The concept of management on the move has been realized in the design of Waterside.'

The word having been thus weakened, it becomes a way of muffling exact thought. Thus we get someone explaining the pains of having to sack employees.

> To tell them they're now on the scrap heap – I found that as a concept very difficult.

Again what the speaker meant was surely that the realization of the concept would be difficult. Merely to think about sacking people hurts no one. To correct the sentence, simply omit 'as a concept'.

What has happened to the word now is that it has achieved a life of its own as a kind of adjective. The AA tells us that 'special concept cars of the 21st century' will be an attraction at a show. And *The Times* captions an illustration 'Concept cars on show at the NEC, Birmingham'. So 'concept' now carries associations of the latest thing in design. Indeed we are reminded of what happened to the word 'designer' a few decades ago. Taken over as an adjective to describe an item of clothing, flaunting the designer's label, it came to mean 'trendy' in a desirable sense.

The word 'value' is a word with deep resonances for those who worry about moral or metaphysical issues. Consider how it is now abused.

> Modern, in that it uses environmentally friendly materials, the Monaco [kitchen] still had traditional construction values.

The kitchen 'still had traditional construction values'. Does that mean anything other than that it was 'well made'? The truth is that the word 'value' is often used, especially by advertisers, so as to be conveniently evasive of what particular benefits are supposed to accrue to the responsive readers. The word 'value' becomes an all-purpose way of praising without having to specify too clearly what you are praising.

> Epitomizing the Volkswagen approach to motorhome base vehicles, the L. T. shares the values Volkswagen have been building into leisure vehicles for decades.

SOME VERBAL DISTORTIONS

Reversals of Meaning

There is an odd, and fortunately rare, kind of misuse which causes not so much a deterioration in meaning as an almost total reversal in meaning. As we have seen, words for substituting and exchanging provide notorious examples of this.

deceptively, availability

Another glaring example is provided by the word 'deceptively' as used by estate agents. They will advertise a house as being 'deceptively spacious', intending to mean that it is really much more spacious than it appears to be at first sight. If a man is described as 'deceptively considerate', it is implied that though he appears to be considerate, that appearance is deceptive. On this reading a 'deceptively spacious' house would be one which appeared to be spacious, but in fact was not so. One wonders whether the word 'deceptively' can be rescued in contexts like these. For instance we read:

> Giles Turner held the lead on Mavis Davis, before Geoff Glazzard dislodged him with a deceptively fast round on his first ride, Hello Oscar.

Are we really to believe that Hello Oscar appeared to be running fast but that this was a *trompe l'œil* and he was really taking his time? Clearly the construction must be changed. One can hardly substitute 'dislodged him with a deceptively leisurely round'. It would not be very neat to substitute 'dislodged him with a round much faster than it seemed', but that is probably the best we can do.

A comparable kind of misuse threatens the word 'availability'. It too is in danger of suffering reversal of meaning.

> A real concern of AA members is the high cost of petrol, and its availability as rural petrol stations struggle to stay open.

Clearly the availability of petrol can never be a concern. It is the lack of petrol or the possible unavailability of petrol that is or might be a matter of concern. 'A real concern of AA members is the high cost of petrol, and the doubt whether it will continue to be available as rural petrol stations struggle to stay open.'

help, improve

There is sometimes near-reversal of meaning in the use of words for improving, curing or helping. Here are two instances from magazines on the subject of restoring hair. The first is a caption:

> Hair-raising electrichogenesis, a process to help baldness, being launched at Manor House Hospital in North London.

The question arises whether helping baldness is the same thing as helping the man who is bald. Clearly the need is to get rid of baldness, which sounds as though it ought to be the opposite of 'helping' it. The passage should read: 'a process to help to cure baldness'. The second example seems to represent the same error:

> However, increasing intake of iron itself and vitamin C to aid iron absorption often fails to improve hair loss . . .

Again the question is whether to improve hair loss is the same thing as to improve the hair. A 'loss' is not something that needs to be 'improved', but to be repaired. So the sentence should end: 'often fails to repair the loss of hair'.

Adjectives That Cannot be Qualified

Dissipation of meaning has its worst effects when the connotation of a once powerful word is virtually forgotten. There are adjectives which cannot be qualified. That is another way of saying that, if something is the very 'best', there cannot be anything 'more best'. The same is true of the word 'equal'. In *Animal Farm* George Orwell mocked totalitarian communist propaganda when the pigs amended the slogan 'All animals are equal' by adding the illogical form, 'but some are more equal than others.'

ideal

Here is a case in point. An 'ideal' concept or article is one which cannot be improved upon.

> There could be no more ideal Christmas gift than a flight on Concorde.

The 'ideal' Christmas gift is the perfect or 'best' conceivable Christmas gift, and therefore the concept of a 'more ideal' one is inadmissible.

minimal

> They feel there is everything to gain from keeping a start-up service on the go, however minimal.

Just as the 'minimum' is the least possible amount, so the word 'minimal' describes the smallest possible quantity. Thus there can be no degrees of minimality, and the words 'however minimal' do not make sense. If 'minimal' is kept, 'however' must go, and vice versa: 'They feel there is everything to gain from keeping a start-up service on the go, however small.'

normal

A 'norm' is an average level qualitatively or quantitatively. Just as a certain level of achievement or behaviour cannot be described as 'more average' than another, so it cannot be described as 'more normal' than another. What the weather forecasters mean when they mistakenly promise us 'more normal' temperatures tomorrow is that the temperatures tomorrow will be 'nearer to the average' (or the 'norm') for the time of year.

perfect

> I find it hard to imagine a more perfect view.

If the speaker could imagine a 'more perfect' view, then the view in question would not be 'perfect'. What is 'perfect' cannot be improved upon.

true

A statement is either true or false. If John is six feet tall, the statement 'John is five feet eleven' is not 'truer' than the statement 'John is five feet six.' Both statements are false.

> Would it not be truer to admit that we can never guess at the workings of the divine mind?

This kind of rhetorical flourish, whatever it follows, is totally illogical. 'Truer' could be replaced by 'true', but the introduction of the word is unnecessary: 'Must we not admit that we can never guess at the workings of the divine mind?'

unique

If something is 'unique' it is absolutely the only one of its kind. Therefore one cannot speak of anything being 'more unique' than other things, nor of something being 'very unique'. The word 'unique' is properly applied to a thing of which only one exists, yet the number of 'unique' opportunities now offered by the business world seems to be limitless.

WORDS DAMAGED BY MISUSE AND OVER-USE

As in so many departments of life, fashion in language has a deleterious effect on usage, cheapening terms by misuse and then by over-use in too many different contexts. The most obvious kind of misuse is that which results from sheer error in understanding. One or two people make mistakes and others follow suit. We have shown how the words 'substitute' and 'substitution' have been confused with the words 'replace' and 'replacement', and now they are so widely misused that one is likely to be accused of pedantry if one draws attention to the error.

In many cases over-use cheapens words without damaging them to that extent. There is a gradual process of change in which can be traced the drift from the orthodox connotation. This chapter is much concerned with words which manifest that drift. We are considering the questions: What are the spoilt words of today, the words damaged by being misunderstood, and the words whose meaning is dissipated in lax over-use? It would take a very long list to contain them all. But we have already considered several in this chapter and we can pick out a few more of the most glaring examples. Over-use is not, of course, an arithmetically calculable matter. If you work in a restaurant, you and your colleagues may use the word 'table' thousands of times a year without affecting the meaning of the word in the slightest. Here we are concerned with the kind of over-use which weakens and distorts meaning.

access

We accept that, largely perhaps through the influence of the computer world, the noun 'access' has taken new life as a verb.

> It is part of our policy to present visual art to people who might not normally visit a gallery by accessing through other artforms.

My dictionary classifies 'access' as a transitive verb that requires an object. One 'accesses' a source of information on the internet. But in the sentence here we do not know what is being accessed nor who is accessing. The grammar suggests that 'our policy' is to help people 'by accessing' through other artforms. But in the back of the mind one guesses that it is the people who are being helped who will be able to 'access' something unspecified.

address

There are contexts where this is the exact word needed. Used of putting the appropriate directions on an envelope or of speaking formally to an audience, it is not replaceable. But the word is now being used where better words are available.

> At last the editor has addressed an issue which is of vital importance to all of us.

Thus people speak of addressing 'issues', 'situations', 'problems', and the like where they might better use verbs such as 'deal with', 'tackle', 'attend to', 'cope with' or even 'study'. I have just heard a BBC Radio 4 comment on a report about the treatment of cancer by the National

Health Service. The report found that the wealthy do better in this respect than the poor. The announcer spoke of the report as 'a catalogue of injustices that will have to be addressed'. The word 'addressed' is not happily used here of dealing with a 'catalogue'. There are mail-order firms that regularly address catalogues to potential customers. The usage has to be handled with care because there are contexts where it might easily lead to ambiguity.

> While the voluntary code of practice has been welcomed by park officials and rangers, Maryl Carr feels that it does not adequately address the increasing number of participants or their impact on other mountain users.

To speak of not adequately 'addressing' participants inevitably suggests a public 'address' from a platform. The mistake here needs to be analysed. To address a problem is one thing, and to address a crowd of participants is another thing. What the writer means is that the 'problem' of the increasing number of participants has to be 'addressed'. If the verb to 'address' is used, there can be no way of avoiding some such word as 'problem'.

alternate / alternative

Basically the verb 'alternate' defines movement this way and that way, as of a pendulum. Thus day 'alternates' with night. The word can be used only of such balanced couples.

> This may be more so now that the Game Fair alternates between only four central sites . . .

If there are more than two variants, as here, then the word 'alternate' will not do. One must write: 'now that the location of the Game Fair varies between only four central sites'.

The word 'alternative' is even more frequently abused. 'Alternatives' are two mutually exclusive possibilities. When we choose between two possibilities, say going to the theatre or staying at home, we choose between two 'alternatives'. There can never be more than two alternatives. If a third possibility is presented to us, then the three possibilities become 'options'. More often than not the word 'alternative' is now being used as though it meant 'option'. This development has led to usages such as the following:

> ContiFlug is a relatively small airline. It offers a highly cost-effective alternative for commuter travel to Berlin.

The question arises: alternative to what? If there were only one other means of commuter travel to Berlin, the word might be appropriate. But often now, especially in advertising, the word is used too vaguely of a possibility which the advertiser wishes to recommend.

> The purpose of the advertising campaign is to present self-catering holidays as an attractive and economic alternative.

Clearly what we are really being offered here is again an 'option'. But the most satisfactory correction would be to use neither 'alternative' nor 'option': 'The purpose of the advertising campaign is to present self-catering holidays as attractive and economic.' After all, a self-catering holiday might be an attractive alternative to staying at home, but it would not be an economic alternative to staying at home.

There are usages which seem to remove from the word even the notion of an option.

> I wanted to create an alternative trading model.

There the word simply means 'fresh' or 'new'. And now we have to allow too for the fact that, in recent decades, novel movements which questioned the status quo and prevailing climates of opinion began to define their innovative life-styles as 'alternative', and the word has stuck.

answer

Shortly before she died Gertrude Stein is said to have muttered 'What's the answer?' and shortly afterwards to have added 'What's the question?' The partnership of the two nouns is such that to use the word 'answer' when there is no notion of a question, or even a problem in the background, is lax. Yet that is what happens.

> The real answer is periodically to have a thorough clean . . .

The recommendation that it may be a good idea to clean vehicles ought to be able to be made without turning it into an 'answer'.

approach

We know well enough when this word is exactly the right one, whether used of coming nearer to a physical position or making advances towards influencing someone. Too often neither notion is involved.

> Running a mobile snack-bar falls into two distinct approaches. You must decide whether you want to sell at the roadside or in a market.

The notion of falling into two 'approaches' when running a mobile snack-bar suggests a Road Traffic Accident. What the writer means is: 'There are two possible sites for a mobile snack-bar.'

> My actual manner of painting in gouache is not that different from my approach to oils.

If one wants to say that the manner or method used for one medium is similar to that used for another medium, why drag in the word 'approach'?

area

The use of the word 'area' has been adopted in place of a wide range of possible options.

> The way peer pressure stimulates in children the demand for ever more unsuitable footwear is another area of concern.

One can think of many a word which would have saved the writer from this over-used word 'area'. The simplest correction would be to omit 'area of': 'demand for ever more unsuitable footwear is another concern'. But possible words such as 'matter', 'issue' and 'topic' also suggest themselves. Elsewhere we hear that 'Truancy is an area that must be looked into', where there would be no loss in substituting 'Truancy also must be looked into.'

> The committee will be responsible for areas such as funding, excursions and new members.

There is gross incongruity in labelling 'excursions' as one area and 'new members' as another. Again it would be better to substitute 'matters' for 'areas'.

aspect

One of the situations in which the writer ought to pause and scratch the head is well illustrated here, where the writer is recommending the varied delights of exploring an area of waterways:

> For instance, canals, industrial history, wildlife, landscape, cycling or walking the towpaths, or many other aspects may appeal to you.

Canals, industrial history, wildlife, landscape, cycling and walking together represent a mixed bag. How many of them can properly be called 'aspects'? Probably none of them, so the expression 'many other aspects' is totally out of place. The first four of the items listed are really cited as topics of interest for possible study. The other two items, cycling and walking, are activities. The six items cannot be classed together as 'aspects'. The distinction between them must be made: 'For instance, the study of canals, industrial history, wildlife or landscape may appeal to you, or activities such as cycling or walking the towpaths.'

ballot

A 'ballot' is an instance of the practice of electing a representative by voting. We speak of the 'ballot paper' on which voters register their vote and the 'ballot box' into which the papers are consigned. Voters 'cast their votes'. They do not 'cast their ballots', a fact which ought to be conveyed to the news writers of the BBC.

> The Israelis are expected to cast their ballot early in the spring.

This should be either: 'The Israelis are expected to cast their votes' or: 'The Israelis are expected to hold their ballot.'

challenge, challenging

The words 'challenge' and 'challenging' have lost whatever overtones they once had of knightly encounters in the lists, meetings with pistols at dawn, or any other such desperate situations. Over-use of the word in business has emptied the word 'challenging' of resonance.

> We provide a challenging, unique environment where those with ability can realize their ambitions.

The same applies to the word 'challenge'. Over-use has rendered it null and void.

> PowerGen has continued to move ahead to new challenges during the year.

This, of course, is tantamount to saying nothing at all except that the firm still exists.

component

Feeling for the right word to apply to a bunch of supposedly related items, the mind may throw up such words as 'aspects', 'elements', 'features', 'attributes' and 'factors'. It is worthwhile to pause before plumping for one. The following is a piece of evolutionary theorizing on BBC Radio 4:

> We got to having a higher intelligence because shorter people had to be cleverer, they had to be faster on their feet, they had to adapt in different ways, and that may be one of the components in our progress.

The word 'component' (officially defined as 'a constituent part of something more complex') has strong technical and mechanical overtones, and is out of place in this human context. Why not: 'and that may have contributed to our progress'?

compromise

A 'compromise' is a settlement between two parties in a dispute, by which they meet each other half way. In wider use it can therefore indicate a half-way meeting point between two opposing interests.

> We chose a 40 ft boat because it seemed a sensible compromise between the amount of living space aboard and running costs.

A boat cannot be a 'compromise' between living space and expenditure. A modest outlay might represent a compromise between heavy spending and sharp economy. A 40 ft boat might represent a compromise between an 80 ft boat and a 10 ft boat. There must be the relationship between the two elements of the 'compromise' that allows of a meeting point on the same plane. What the writer meant was: 'We chose a 40 ft boat, adjusting our wish for living space aboard by calculating the running cost.'

core

Used for the central part of something, this word carries colourful overtones of what you find in the middle of an apple. Over-use in the business world is now reducing its connotation to the same diluted level as that of words like 'central', 'important' or even 'essential'. Where an employee might once have been allotted his 'main task', he is now given his 'core remit'.

credible / credibility

These two words, like the words 'creed' and 'credulous', have to do with belief. A man who is 'credulous' is too ready to believe what he hears, accepts things on inadequate evidence, and is easily taken in. What is 'credible' is worthy of belief. The word has suffered lately from over-use in contexts where it is little more than a term of general approval, roughly equivalent to 'effective' or 'convincing'.

> On European integration I don't find his attitude credible.

This is the equivalent of saying 'I don't agree with his attitude to European integration.' The same looseness affects the word 'credibility'.

> The double lining is a guarantee of the jacket's credibility in wet weather.

Here 'credibility' presumably means 'reliability'.

decimate

This word derives from Latin. The Latin verb was used of the practice of Roman generals to punish by killing every tenth man in a given force. There are two current misuses of the word. The one occurs when use of the verb implies that a body of people has been all but wiped out. In that case it is as though the meaning of the verb is that a body of troops or a section of some population has been reduced to a tenth of its original size, instead of to nine-tenths. The other misuse occurs when the word 'decimate' is seemingly confused with some other word such as 'devastate', as when a judge tells a criminal that he has 'decimated the lives of two whole families'.

diagnose

An interesting case of changing usage is provided by the verb to 'diagnose'. The verb strictly means to identify something, most usually a physical condition. Thus the doctor may examine a patient and diagnose whooping cough. It is the condition that is diagnosed, not the patient. Yet over the past few years usage has veered confusingly. 'You should be properly diagnosed by your doctor' should be either: 'You should be properly examined by your doctor', or: 'Your condition should be properly diagnosed by your doctor.' It is now common to speak of someone having been 'diagnosed with epilepsy' when, strictly speaking, 'epilepsy has been diagnosed'.

emerge

The verb 'emerge' carries its own clear meaning, but it is now being over-used as a means of avoiding the verb to 'occur' or to 'happen'.

> The most amazing escape from the Nairobi carnage emerged yesterday when an Israeli team rescued a mother and her son from an upper floor in the 22-storey building.

No doubt the mother and her son 'emerged' from the building, but to describe the escape as emerging from the carnage is just careless usage.

equate / equation

Popularization of the word 'equation' has diluted its meaning. It is used as an alternative not just to 'problem', but to 'situation'. 'I've nothing new to add to the equation' apparently just means 'I've nothing to say on the subject.' Correspondingly the verb to 'equate' is in fashion.

> But sensual and sexy equate to two different things for me.

This simply means: 'are two different things'.

factor

Properly used of an element that contributes to some result, the word 'factor' suffers from the same loose treatment as 'aspect'.

> But the exact make-up of his [Schröder's] government was unclear last night because of the complicating factor of small parties which might not gain the 5 per cent needed for parliamentary representation.

Here the word 'factor' is a dead counter and the word 'complicating' not needed if the argument is simply presented: 'But the exact make-up of his Government was unclear last night because the small parties might not gain the 5 per cent needed for parliamentary representation.'

focus

The 'focus' in Latin is the hearth around which people gather. The word has been usefully adopted in the mathematical and scientific worlds. Now that the business world has discovered its usefulness, that usefulness is being destroyed.

> Nigel Woods, accounts director for the UK's fastest growing motivations group, MotivForce, says travel is often a more focused way of rewarding staff.

In what sense is the present of a holiday package 'more focused' than the present of a cheque or of private health care, or of any other of the perks that companies distribute? 'Focus' is a nice-sounding word with the air of some intellectual meat about it, of some clarity and resonance. But what the writer means is that 'travel is often a good way of rewarding staff'.

impact

When a word has some dramatic thrust it is especially destructive to use it so as to deprive it of colour or force. Here the word 'impact' is used in a piece of advice about prettifying the home:

> To add impact, choose flowers that make a statement.

'Impact' is a powerful word, used of fatal crashes at high speed on the motorway, or of dramatic effects produced by some spectacle of rare impressiveness. The writer of the above, however, reduces the word to the level of any old piece of worn-out currency; then, to make things worse, trundles out the most hackneyed of current non-sayings, 'flowers that make a statement'.

instigate

My dictionary definition of this verb is 'to bring about, as by incitement' and 'to urge on to some violent or unadvisable action'. The notion of stirring things up into a state of excitement attaches to the verb, which has been much used of fermenting rebellion. The word is now used increasingly as though it meant no more than 'initiate' or 'start'.

> His grandfather instigated the first public transport system in the city.

Here 'initiated' or 'started' would be better.

> He joined the society soon after going up to Cambridge, instigated by a former school friend.

Here 'encouraged' would be the right word.

materialize

Something which 'materializes' takes on material form. Therefore the verb is used of things which become fact, which actually take place. Thus the word has been increasingly used of plans which 'come off', as we say. The usage is not favoured by the pedants. The modern tendency to use the verb as an alternative to the verbs to 'happen' or to 'occur' is regarded as lax and imprecise. As one looks at instances of its use one can see why. Here is a sentence from the controversy about student loans.

> Nor is there much evidence that the least affluent will be adversely affected. This claim was made when student loans were first introduced nearly a decade ago: it did not materialize in practice.

The trouble here is that a 'claim' is not something that might 'materialize'. A 'claim' of this kind may prove true or false, but if it is made about the future it is probably better called a 'forecast': 'This was forecast when student loans were first introduced nearly a decade ago: it did not happen.'

optimistic

A descriptive term increasingly misused is the word 'optimistic'.

> The truth [about cancer] is far more optimistic: cancer is largely a preventable disease.

An 'optimistic' person is one who expects the best. The philosophical doctrine of 'optimism' holds that good will ultimately triumph over evil. 'Truth' can be neither optimistic nor pessimistic. It appears that the writer means 'The truth is far more encouraging', that is, productive of optimism rather than 'optimistic'.

option

This word is being misused in the same way as 'alternative'.

> If you are one of the growing number of owners who are trying to give their pets the healthier option . . .

What this means is: 'If you are one of the growing number of owners who want to keep their pets healthy . . .' Use of the word 'option' should be restricted to contexts in which there are at least two possible courses of action from which one may be chosen. One cannot speak of the 'healthier option' in a context where no other option is mentioned.

potential

What is 'potential' is possible but not yet actual, latent but not yet realized.

> We need to look at the present situation, where potential nannies need no qualifications for training.

'Potential nannies' is not a satisfactory usage. In a sense every girl is a 'potential nanny', just as she is a potential mother, wife, or wage-earner. 'Would-be nannies' is the simplest expression for aspirants to nanny-hood.

pragmatic

A 'pragmatic' attitude is an attitude adopted rather for its practical consequences than on any basis of principle or theory. Thus, in loose use, it refers to practical, everyday business.

> But in recent years the Princess has become the pragmatic and acceptable face of royalty at a time when other, younger members of the Royal Family have behaved in a manner which not only saddens the Queen, but also sullies the reputation of the monarchy itself.

The contrast between the Princess Royal's conduct and that of other members of the Royal Family might reasonably bring the word 'acceptable' into play, but the concept of the pragmatic as opposed to the theoretical is scarcely relevant. A better wording would be: 'the Princess has become the fitting and acceptable face of royalty'.

priority

The list of words already 'spoilt' or in the process of being 'spoilt' must surely include this one (not to mention 'prioritize'). It is now thrown about far too freely. Here is a piece of advice to parents wondering whether to send their children to holiday camps.

> Your main priority is whether or not your child is going to be happy away from home.

Do we really need a 'priority' to be mentioned? What is lost if we write: 'You must first decide whether or not your child is going to be happy away from home'?

properly

This is one of those words which we readily throw about in conversation: 'You haven't cleaned the car properly', 'He doesn't brush his hair properly.' The lax usage jars on the printed page.

> Old enamelware is now quite hard to find, but if hunted down properly can still be found at car boot sales.

Here the sense of appropriateness which the word should convey is absent. There is no issue of 'propriety' here. The word could be replaced by 'carefully' or 'keenly', or, better still, could be omitted.

prospective

We find a boarding school advising 'prospective parents' to get in touch with the school secretary. But a 'prospective' parent is either a pregnant woman or the father of her child. The word is out of place here. The message is meant, not for prospective parents, but for prospective customers.

proverbial

There is a point in the decay of a word's meaning at which the question arises whether the word is worth using at all. Does it add anything?

> She was the warmest, sweetest person you could ever meet, the proverbial prostitute with the heart of gold.

Now although there is no well-known 'proverb' about a prostitute, we recognize that the word here serves the purpose of conjuring up a certain stereotype exploited in literature. But what is the result when the word 'proverbial' is dragged further from any anchorage?

> You could have heard the proverbial pin drop as Kilbaha entered the arena for the jump-off.

It requires no great mastery of the English language to be familiar with the expression 'You could hear a pin drop.' Not to be able to use it without annotating it as though attention needed to be drawn to its hallowed position in our linguistic tradition is surely pretentious. It is like talking of 'the thin end of the proverbial wedge' or 'barking up the proverbial tree'.

scenario

The 'scenario' is basically the plot of a stage play or film. The first person to use the word outside its theatrical context showed some imagination to inspired effect. The usage became fashionable. Over-use has now diluted its significance. It is done to death.

> Jane revels in major contracts, and starting from scratch is her ideal scenario.

The word gets applied to any sequence of events. We even hear 'Getting up late in the morning is his ideal scenario.' Thus the original connotation is dissipated.

sector

'Sector' meaning a part or subdivision has a geometrical basis. It has been much used in the expressions 'public sector' and 'private sector', but it is best not applied to groups of human beings. There is nothing to be gained from saying (rather ungrammatically) 'There is a sector of the police force who are racist' instead of 'Some policemen are racist.' The word is equally unhappily used in the following:

> This scheme represents a new era in reproductive medicine and helps certain sectors who before couldn't get treatment.

Why not: '. . . and helps certain people who before couldn't get treatment'?

spectrum

In the case of words such as 'concept' we have seen how a technical term may be taken over, quite usefully, for more general use, and then may suffer a gradual loss of definable meaning. This has begun to happen with the word 'spectrum'. Strictly it means the band of colours into which a prism resolves a beam of light. The image is useful, but we are beginning to hear the word applied more and more widely when people want to sum up a range of attitudes. Speaking for social workers, someone says 'Yet we deal with a spectrum of emotional issues in the course of our work', where 'spectrum' would be better replaced by 'range' or 'variety'.

theme

The word 'theme' is not perhaps a vivid word, but it is rich in association with accounts of symphonic movements in music and metaphorical sequences in poetry.

> But humiliation was the theme of Yeltsin's position in those days.

If we want to say that Yeltsin was being humiliated, do we need to drag in the word 'theme' at all?

unnecessary

Here again is a forceful word which ought not to be employed so as to weaken its connotation.

> Sight Savers International desperately needs your help to wipe out this cruel and unnecessary disease.

This illustrates the increasing tendency to misuse the word 'unnecessary'. The question of 'necessity' or its absence simply does not arise. What the writer means is: 'Sight Savers International desperately needs your help to wipe out this cruel and avoidable disease.'

vandalism

This word is chosen as representative of abstract nouns ending in '-ism'. If one considers, say, the verb to 'colonize', it is matched by two distinct nouns, 'colonialism' and 'colonization'. 'Colonialism' is the abstract word for the theory and practice of colonizing, but any single act of colonizing itself represents 'colonization'. It would be a mistake to confuse the two words.

> His head chef at l'Oranger, the restaurant, has been arrested after the alleged theft of £1,500 and the vandalism of the restaurant, the night after he was sacked.

Here that mistake is made with the word 'vandalism'. To vandalize a building is to commit an act of 'vandalism', but the process of vandalizing a building is 'vandalization'. Here the sentence could read: 'has been arrested after the alleged theft of £1,500 and the vandalization of the restaurant', or: 'and the vandalizing of the restaurant'. Better still would be: 'has been arrested for allegedly stealing £1,500 and vandalizing the restaurant'.

virtually

'Virtually' means 'in effect' as opposed to 'in fact'. We might say 'She was only a recently elected member of the committee but she was virtually in charge of everything.' But increasingly the word is being weakened.

> It was virtually sixty years ago that Edith Smith took the photograph.

There is no contrast here between what happened in effect and what happened in fact. To use 'virtually' to mean 'almost' or 'nearly' is bad enough. But here it means neither. What is meant is: 'It was about sixty years ago that Edith Smith took the photograph.'

CHAPTER 2

The Right Words and the Wrong Words

Choosing the wrong word sometimes results from getting confused between two words which are very similar in sound or spelling. The mistake is even more likely to occur if the two words are also close in meaning. The extreme form of confusion between two words similar in sound is the 'malapropism', so called after the character Mrs Malaprop in Sheridan's play *The Rivals*. Mrs Malaprop declares that she would have no wish for a daughter of hers to be a 'progeny' of learning, when she clearly means 'prodigy'. She considers her niece Lydia to be by no means 'illegible' for a certain match, but she finds her 'as headstrong as an allegory on the banks of the Nile'. There is perhaps little need now to warn readers against confusing an 'allegory' with an 'alligator' or using 'illegible' instead of 'ineligible', but I have quite recently seen 'prodigy' misused where the word should have been 'protégée'. Of the many pairs of words which lend themselves to this confusion, observation suggests that the following deserve attention.

abjure / adjure

To 'abjure' is to renounce, often used of formal recantations. 'This rough magic / I here abjure' says Shakespeare's Prospero, when he renounces the practice of magic at the end of *The Tempest*. To 'adjure' is formally to command, earnestly to bind or appeal to ('His friends earnestly adjured him to take care of his health').

abrogate / arrogate

To 'abrogate' is to cancel, to repeal, officially to revoke. When Holofernes in *Love's Labour's Lost* seems to be about to tell a *risqué* tale. Sir Nathaniel warns him to 'abrogate scurrility'. The verb to 'arrogate', derived from a Latin verb meaning to adopt as a child, came to mean to assume to oneself rights to which one is not entitled. In *Paradise Regained* Milton attacks false philosophers who 'arrogate' all glory to themselves and none to

God. Thus an 'arrogant' person is one who unwarrantably lays claim to dignities, qualities or knowledge.

accede / exceed

To 'accede' is in the first place to enter upon an office ('He acceded to the throne'), and in the second to give assent to ('She acceded to my request for admittance'). The verb 'to exceed' means to be greater than, to surpass ('The total sum collected exceeded their wildest hopes').

accessary / accessory

Practice has now run these two words together. Historically 'accessary' (connected with the word 'access') is the word for someone who aids and abets in an offence, whether before or after the event. An 'accessory' (connected with the words 'accede' and 'accession') is an adjunct. Since the spelling 'accessory' has now for some time been accepted in place of 'accessary', a useful distinction has been lost.

activate / actuate

To 'activate' is to render active, used mainly of scientific processes, but sometimes used non-technically of launching a plan of action. To 'actuate' is also to set something going, but is used more generally to mean motivate ('Her proposal was actuated by the most generous intentions').

adduce / deduce

To 'adduce' an argument or a proposition is to bring it forward for consideration as evidence ('He adduced a series of instances to corroborate his case'). To 'deduce' is to derive a conclusion logically from some proposition or piece of evidence ('From the evidence before him he deduced that it was a case of murder').

adverse / averse

'Adverse' means hostile. We speak of 'adverse circumstances' when those circumstances are unfavourable to what we want to do. 'Averse' means personally disinclined. A nervous man may describe himself as 'averse to speaking in public'.

affect / effect

To 'affect' is to influence ('Coming across the work of Tolstoy affected his own ambitions as a writer') or to disturb ('Her son's distress affected her deeply'). To 'effect' is to bring about ('The teaching of Tolstoy effected a revolution in his thinking').

allusive / elusive

The verb to 'allude' means to refer to something indirectly or just to mention it. An 'allusion' therefore is a passing reference ('In the whole speech there was only the slightest allusion to his own desperate state of health'). The verb to 'elude' is to escape something or avoid it, very often something which ought not to be evaded ('For seven years he managed to elude the police'). The balancing noun 'elusion' is now obsolete. The adjective 'allusive' means rich in allusions and is often used of literary style. One might apply it to the prose of Joyce's *Ulysses*. The adjective 'elusive' refers to what easily escapes attention or is difficult to get hold of. It might be applied to the narrative content of Joyce's *Finnegans Wake*.

ambiguous / ambivalent

The element 'ambi', based on the Latin word for 'both', occurs for instance in 'ambidextrous', meaning equally skilled with both hands. Something which is 'ambiguous' is open to more than one interpretation, and the word is used primarily of statements, but also of actions. The word 'ambivalent' is not a synonymous alternative to 'ambiguous', as some writers seem to think. An attitude which is 'ambivalent' involves two different and perhaps conflicting emotions, not interpretations. ('There was ambivalence in her attitude to the man who had both aided and injured her.')

amend / emend

To 'amend' is to improve, make better. 'God amend us, God amend!' says Berowne in Shakespeare's *Love's Labour's Lost*. In the House of Commons efforts are made to 'amend' bills being put before members when they think an 'amendment' advisable. The verb to 'emend' is used in a more specialized way of correcting errors or making textual improvements in manuscripts and printed material. The correction is an 'emendation'.

amoral / immoral

The prefixes 'a-' and 'im-' cancel out the meaning of the word 'moral' in two different ways. What is 'immoral' transgresses moral laws and the word is used generally of unethical and corrupt behaviour. What is 'amoral' is totally outside the realm of the moral; behaviour or beliefs which accept no such measure of behaviour as the 'moral' and the 'immoral'. The prefix 'a-' signifies negation or privation just as 'in'- and 'un-' do. It is used nowadays in such words as 'asocial' and 'asymmetrical' as well as in the technical musical terms 'atonal' and 'atonality', of the absence of key in some twentieth-century compositions.

appraise / apprise

To 'appraise' is to assess the value of something, to make an 'appraisal' of it. To 'apprise' is to inform. Thus 'The authorities could not act before they were appraised of the break-in' should be: '. . . before they were apprised of the break-in'.

assume / presume

To 'assume' is to take something for granted ('As he had got engaged to the girl, we assumed that he would marry her'). It is also used of taking things up other than mentally ('He assumed the role of guardian'). Similarly there is an impersonal use ('The situation began to assume a threatening character'). In its most common use, 'presume' may be substituted for 'assume' ('Dr Livingstone, I presume'). Often, however, to 'presume' is arrogantly to take up a position to which one is not entitled. That is the case in Pope's celebrated couplet:

> Know then thyself, presume not God to scan,
> The proper study of mankind is man.

In legal usage an accused person is 'presumed' innocent until proved guilty.

authoritarian / authoritative

The difference between these two words, both concerned with the exercise of authority, is that 'authoritarian' generally implies some exercise of authority which is undesirable, while 'authoritative' carries no such pejorative overtone. An 'authoritarian' government or management lays the law down from above without democratic consultation, and an 'authoritarian' personal manner is similarly inflexible. An 'authoritative' statement or action is one which carries the weight of due authority, such as for instance an announcement by the Prime Minister in Parliament.

baleful / baneful

Both words now have a faintly archaic flavour. 'Bale' is evil, both in the sense of malignancy and in the sense of torment. 'Rome and her rats are at the point of battle' says Menenius Agrippa at the beginning of Shakespeare's *Coriolanus*, and adds 'The one side must have bale', meaning 'One or the other is going to come a cropper.' 'Bane' is death and destruction. Thus the two words 'baleful' and 'baneful' overlap in that they threaten misery. 'Baleful' became a literary word for sorrowful and miserable, and we still hear the expression 'baleful news'. 'Bane' means 'poison' in the word 'ratsbane'. Milton left us a memorable expression when he told how riches grow in hell, which naturally supplies the ideal environment for the 'precious bane'.

bathos / pathos

As the word 'pathetic' properly refers to what arouses sympathy or pity, so the word 'pathos' is the power of arousing feelings of sympathy, pity or sorrow. It is used of works of literature and of oratory as well as of personal situations. Burns wrote:

> To make a happy fireside clime
> To weans and wife,
> That's the true pathos and sublime
> Of human life.

The word 'bathos' is used of any sudden switch from what is exalted and dignified to what is pedestrian and trivial. It is also used of attempts at pathos which are overdone or fail to come off.

beneficence / benevolence

There is a subtle distinction between these two words. Where 'beneficence' is generosity in action, 'benevolence' is generosity of spirit. Thus it is an act of 'beneficence' for a benefactor to endow a new hospital, but the action stems from the benefactor's 'benevolence'.

biannual / biennial

As 'annual' means occurring once a year, so 'biannual' means occurring twice a year. But a 'biennial' event is one that occurs every two years.

carousal / carousel

As to 'carouse' is to drink freely, so a 'carousal' is a drunken feast. (In pronunciation the stress is on the second syllable.) A 'carousel', originally a knightly tournament with racing horses, came to be used of a merry-go-round. Hence it is used for the revolving luggage conveyor at an airport and also for the circular tray into which slides are slotted and produced one by one for a projector.

classic / classical

A 'classic' is a work of art of the highest excellence which has stood the test of time. The word is used for something created which is of the first rank and must be regarded as definitive. Hence comes the less strict connotation of the adjective 'classic' exemplified in such statements as 'It was a classic case of parental negligence', where the word means little more than 'typical'. The word 'classical' was applied to the civilization of ancient Greece and Rome and to later forms of art and architecture that preserved the same tradition of formality and restraint. In this respect contrasts between 'classical' and 'romantic' styles were drawn. More recently the word 'classical' has come to be used of music belonging to serious traditional culture as opposed to ephemeral 'popular' music.

complacent / complaisant

To be 'complacent' is to be over-easily satisfied with things, and especially with one's self and with one's own achievements. It is to be unmoved by matters which really should cause concern, and thus the word is much used in criticism of political opponents. Conversationally 'complacent' means smug. The bachelor essayist Charles Lamb found nothing more distasteful than the 'complacency and satisfaction which beam in the countenances of new-married couples'. To be 'complaisant' is to be agreeably obliging, accommodating one's self readily to the requests and needs of others. In Buckingham's burlesque play *The Rehearsal* (1672), which satirizes contemporary drama, a Mr Smith avers that it's 'very complaisant to be of another man's opinion before knowing what it is'.

complement / compliment

These two words are often confused, both as verbs and as nouns. A 'compliment' is an appreciative or respectful tribute paid to someone. A 'complement' is basically a person or thing which completes something. We speak of a 'full complement' of staff or crew. The word is most commonly used of a person or thing which nicely balances or partners another. Thus in grammatical usage the word 'policeman' in the sentence 'My husband is a policeman' balances the subject 'My husband' and is therefore its 'complement'. 'Compliment' is the more frequently misused of the two words. We find new cutlery advertised as the 'perfect compliment' to a new china dinner service, where the word should be 'complement'. The parallel adjective 'complimentary' is similarly misused.

comprise / consist

The point to remember about this tricky couple of verbs is that 'consist' is intransitive. It cannot be followed by an object. It is most commonly followed by 'of': 'The company consisted of old-age pensioners.' (The rarer use of the words 'consist in' is exemplified in 'His filial devotion consists in visiting his mother once a year.') But to 'comprise' is a transitive verb. It takes an object ('The company comprised people of all ages'). What it amounts to is that 'to consist of' means 'to comprise'. To 'comprise', meaning to be made up of ('The choir comprised fifteen men and fifteen women'), covers the whole number (unlike the verb 'include').

> He will accept a company cheque from anywhere in the world as long as the shareholders are comprised principally of individuals from whom personal donations can be solicited.

This *Times* leader misuses the verb. (One should not say 'The members are comprised of' instead of 'comprise'.) Moreover, 'principally' cancels out the proper meaning of 'comprise', which covers the whole, not a part. The sentence should read: 'as long as the shareholders are composed principally of individuals'.

connote / denote

Both words are used in defining what words or signs mean. The word 'connote' is the more comprehensive of the two. If someone says 'She is a real lady' the expression 'real lady' implies notions of charm and grace associated with the aristocracy. The 'connotation' of the word includes all such implications. What a word 'denotes' is exactly what it literally stands for. But, used of signs other than words, 'denote' now has wider reference ('The fellow's sly smile may denote a degree of untrustworthiness').

continually / continuously

A matter that continually affects me does so repeatedly, but not unbrokenly. I might complain if my work were 'continually' interrupted by telephone calls. What happens 'continuously' is not something that recurs but something that is ceaseless ('She went to bed and slept continuously for ten hours').

converse / inverse

The word 'converse' is used of something which is the opposite of something already referred to. 'She is certainly not helping to support her mother; indeed the converse is probably the case.' This would mean that far from supporting her mother, it is likely that her mother is supporting her. In such a case, 'The converse is true' is the equivalent of 'The boot is on the other leg.' But the word 'converse' does not always bring in the notion of contradiction. It may introduce a reversal rather than a contradiction. 'She is of great assistance to her mother, and of course the converse is true' would mean that just as she helps her mother, so too her mother helps her. The word 'inverse' overlaps in meaning with 'converse' but is primarily used of what is turned upside down or reversed in order.

We hear winners listed in 'inverse order' when a judge announces the results of a race, reserving the name of the first to the last.

council / counsel

A 'council' is a body of people gathered together for consultation or administration. The members of the council ('councillors') are appointed or elected to direct the affairs of a given society or a given area of the country. 'Counsel' is advice or guidance, and hence the word is used too for the barrister who undertakes to advise clients and to pursue legal cases for them. Outside the legal profession a person giving advice is called a 'counsellor'. The verb to 'counsel', meaning to give advice or comfort, is used in the fields of psychology and social work. The expression 'to keep one's own counsel' means to be noticeably reticent over matters public or private when perhaps some opinion or revelation is being sought.

defective / deficient

What is 'defective' has a defect, and a 'defect' is a fault, a shortcoming. The word is much used of objects or materials that have not been manufactured without flaws, and of flawed ideas and schemes. A thing that is 'deficient' lacks something necessary to its completeness. It has an inadequacy. A socially clumsy person may be said to be 'deficient' in tact.

definite / definitive

Something which is clearly defined is said to be 'definite'. The word implies sureness and precision. 'We must have a definite answer' is a call for an end to vagueness or prevarication. The words 'a' and 'an' are called 'indefinite' articles because, unlike the 'definite' article 'the', they do not point to a specific subject. The word 'definitive' means conclusive and final. It is used of statements which put an end to doubt or controversy.

defuse / diffuse

To 'defuse' a situation is to remove the tension from it. The connection is obvious between this general meaning and the particular process of making a bomb safe by removing its 'fuse'. To 'diffuse' is to pour out, to scatter or to spread out in all directions. Thus the adjective 'diffuse' is used of ideas that lack clear focus and conciseness. The word 'diffuser' has a technical usage in relation to scattering light to reduce glare, and to dispersing sound waves in a radio.

delusion / illusion

A 'delusion' is a mistaken notion or belief ('She suffered from the delusion that her family were all against her'). An 'illusion' is a false or misleading appearance or perception ('Whether he had actually seen a ghost or whether what he saw was an illusion he could never decide').

dependant / dependent

A 'dependant' is someone who depends for their living on another. 'Dependant' is thus a noun. 'Dependent' is the matching adjective. A 'dependant' is 'dependent' on someone else for a living.

> Year-round travel insurance is provided without an additional cost to any cardholder, his or her spouse and dependant children.

This should read: 'dependent children'. Correspondingly we find an advertisement for 'Eurocamp Independant Holidays', which should be 'Independent Holidays'. Confusingly, the noun 'dependant' does not have a matching noun 'independant'. So a parliamentary candidate is called an 'Independent' and the newspaper is called '*The Independent*'.

deprecate / depreciate

To 'deprecate' something is to express earnest disapproval of it ('We strongly deprecated the movement's decision to resort to a public demonstration'). To 'depreciate' is to belittle or to reduce the value of something by criticism or ridicule. The verb is also used intransitively. As to 'appreciate' is to rise in value, so to 'depreciate' is to fall in value.

discreet / discrete

'Discreet' means careful and tactful in behaviour, and is used especially of being able to be trusted with confidences. The corresponding noun is 'discretion'. The Book of Common Prayer gave us the expression 'years of discretion' as representing the age at which the growing person can begin to exercise sober judgement. 'Discrete' (related by contrast to the word 'concrete') is used of separate parts that cannot be assembled together. It is quite erroneous for advertisers who seek sexual partnerships through the columns of *Private Eye* to propose 'discrete' contacts. Under such arrangements they would never meet.

disinterested / uninterested

The word 'disinterested' is more often used incorrectly than correctly. It does not mean 'uninterested'. 'Uninterested' negates 'interested' in the most common use of the word ('I am not interested/uninterested in ball games'). The word 'interest' has a special connotation in the sentence 'Smith is personally interested in the sale of the property', which conveys that Smith has a financial 'interest' in the matter, and may benefit or fail to benefit from the transaction. That is the usage which the word 'disinterested' negates. To be 'disinterested' in any matter is to be in no position either to benefit or to be disadvantaged by whatever transpires. 'Disinterest' is impartiality.

> We're told that growing children need a healthy diet, but how can you put this into practice when you're faced with a disinterested toddler?

Here the word should be 'uninterested'.

dispense with / dispose of

Basically, to 'dispense' is to distribute, and a 'dispensation' is an act of distributing. Its connection with the issuing of acts of papal pardoning in the Middle Ages is the root of the modern usage in which to 'dispense' is to exempt from some rule or obligation and therefore to do away with something and to manage without it. To 'dispose' something was basically to arrange it suitably, to settle it. ('My Author and Disposer' Milton's Eve calls Adam in a moment of wifely compliance.) To 'dispose of' a matter was to deal with it finally and thus to get rid of it. But whereas to 'dispense with' implies an attitude of removing what is superfluous or redundant ('After a successful operation for cataract, he was able to dispense with his glasses'), to 'dispose of' carries no such overtones ('He disposed of his country house and bought a town house').

The development in use of the corresponding nouns, 'dispensation' and 'disposition', is noteworthy. Whereas the noun 'disposition' is now chiefly used of a person's temperament or frame of mind (the arrangement of personal idiosyncrasies), the noun 'dispensation' tends to be used of the public system of administration (the ordering of its regulations). In T. S. Eliot's *Journey of the Magi* the three kings, having witnessed the newborn Jesus, return to their kingdoms 'no longer at ease here, in the old dispensation'.

equable / equitable

'Equable' means unvarying and uniform. A generally calm and placid person may be described as 'of an equable temperament'. 'Equitable' means fair and just. Where 'equable' relates to the word 'equality', 'equitable' relates to the word 'equity'.

erupt / irrupt

To 'erupt' is to break or burst out as a volcano does from time to time. (On the appearance of the Ghost in *Hamlet* Horatio foresees 'some strange eruption to our state'.) To 'irrupt' is suddenly and forcibly to break in, as an invading army might after besieging a stronghold.

exclude / preclude

To 'exclude' is the opposite of to 'include'. It is to keep out, to prevent from entering a place, or from taking part in an activity or celebration. The dictionary definition of to 'preclude' is 'to make impossible, especially beforehand'. It is used of disbarments made necessary by other factors ('Smith's parlous state of health precludes him from taking part').

> A consultative paper sent out to members [from Tory headquarters] excludes a Prime Minister Hague restoring the hereditary principle to the Lords.

The reporter used the wrong verb here: 'precludes restoration of the hereditary principle to the Lords by a Prime Minister Hague'.

exhausting / exhaustive

The verb to 'exhaust' means to draw off, to drain of resources, and therefore to empty and to weary. The word 'exhausting' is thus generally used to mean tiring, but we speak of 'exhausting' all possibilities in trying to find something lost. The word 'exhaustive' is a favourite word to use of investigations or books which thoroughly and comprehensively finish the task they were intended to deal with ('This book is an exhaustive account of the French Revolution').

expedient / expeditious

To 'expedite' is to push quickly forward some action or project, clearing away any obstacles. The word 'expeditious' is used with emphasis on the speed of such action ('At this crisis the demand for more troops called for an expeditious response'). The word 'expedient' is used with emphasis on the appropriateness of the action ('As his former wife remained on the same staff, he found it expedient to seek a new post elsewhere'). The emphasis on convenience produces an implicit contrast with action that is inconvenient but is dictated by principle and propriety. Thus politicians get accused of being motivated by 'expediency' rather than by principle.

explicit / implicit

What is 'explicit' is clearly and precisely expressed, leaving no room for doubt ('There was an explicit requirement that employees should wear formal dress'). What is 'implicit' is not directly stated in so many words but implied. The notice 'Thank you for not smoking' in a restaurant is an 'implicit' request that customers should not smoke. That request is 'implicit' in the notice.

fallacious / fallible

Something which is 'fallacious' contains a fallacy, an inaccuracy or a deception. The forbidden apple which Adam and Eve eat in Milton's *Paradise Lost* is described as the 'fallacious' fruit. To say something which is 'fallacious' is not necessarily to lie, because the speaker may not know that what is said is false; 'falsehood' is assumed to be dishonest, where a 'fallacy' may merely be a mistake. The word 'fallible' means liable to be deceived or to be erroneous. In Shakespeare's *Measure for Measure* the Duke advises Claudio, who faces a death-sentence, not to comfort himself 'with hopes that are fallible'.

fatal / fateful

A 'fatal' event or decision is one which leads to disastrous consequences. A 'fatal' accident or a 'fatal' disease is one which causes death. (Lady Macbeth tells how the hoarse raven 'croaks the fatal entrance of Duncan' into the castle where he will be murdered.) The word 'fateful' is used of events or decisions which have momentous consequences, but which are not necessarily unfortunate. A person's decision to drive to a certain meeting might be described as 'fateful' if an accident en route proved 'fatal'. But similarly a woman's decision to seek work in a given firm might be described as 'fateful' if she there met her future husband.

febrile / frenetic

It is helpful to remember how these two words are related to others. 'Febrile' is basically a medical term, the adjective formed from 'fever'. Thus it means 'feverish' and appropriately describes a person in a state of restlessness and discomposure. The word 'frenetic' is related to the words 'frantic' and 'frenzy'. So its associations are with madness rather than with physical illness. It will be seen that while 'febrile' implies a rather enfeebled restlessness, 'frenetic' implies frantic activity.

ferment / foment

To 'ferment' is to cause fermentation and therefore to stir something up into an agitated condition. The word is often used of stirring up trouble. An agitator may be said to 'ferment' rebellion. To 'foment' is originally to bathe in warm healing water, hence to cherish, to encourage or to promote. Since it is sometimes used of promoting or encouraging the growth or development of what may be undesirable ('The failure of his application fomented his frustration') it may come near to 'ferment' in meaning.

fewer / less

'Fewer' refers to number, whereas 'less' refers to bulk or amount. One rarely finds 'fewer' used where the word should be 'less'. But the converse error is still very common.

> If public transport were better, there would be far less people going about in cars.

There the word should be 'fewer'. 'Less people' would be people of smaller stature. It would be correct to say 'If public transport were better, there would be far less use of cars.'

> However, it is sad, to many of us who remember it, that the passing of time has caused less and less converted lifeboats and pontoons to be seen being boated by those less concerned with what their boat looked like, but more where they could take it.

The first two uses of 'less' are wrong: 'the passing of time has caused fewer and fewer converted lifeboats to be seen'.

fictional / fictitious

Both words derive from the word 'fiction', used to classify imaginative works of literature, more especially in prose. Thus Jane Eyre is a 'fictional' character, not a person from real life. The expression 'fact or fiction' highlights the contrast between what is true and what is invented. So the word 'fictitious' carries the connotation not only of the invented, but also of the false as opposed to the genuine ('He carried on a correspondence with his mistress from a fictitious address').

flammable / inflammable

These two words both mean susceptible to being inflamed or easily set on fire. Confusion can arise because in so many cases adding the prefix 'in-' to an adjective turns it into a negative. Thus the positive 'soluble' becomes the negative 'insoluble'. But the prefix 'in-' serves the same positive purpose in 'inflame' as it does in 'inspire'.

flaunt / flout

These two words are confused in spite of the fact that their meanings are totally unrelated. To 'flaunt' something is to display it proudly and ostentatiously. Thus a rich man may be said to 'flaunt' his wealth, a glamorous actress may be said to 'flaunt' her charms. To 'flout' is to reject scornfully and arrogantly some authority, some regulation, or some code which one ought officially to accept and observe ('He flouted the firm's rules by smoking in the office').

gourmand / gourmet

Both words refer to a person who is devoted to eating and drinking. But whereas 'gourmand' is used pejoratively of a gluttonous person who may shovel food away without much discrimination, 'gourmet' is used of a connoisseur with a cultivated and sophisticated taste for food and wine.

heritage / inheritance

Both words have to do with what is inherited. A man's 'inheritance' is what is handed on to him from his ancestors in the way of money, possessions, and such things as titles or family prerogatives. The word 'heritage' is used more generally for what is handed down from generation to generation, not only in the way of personal possessions, but also in the way of institutions and public properties, culture and knowledge.

honorary / honourable

Both words are obviously connected with the word 'honour'. What is 'honourable' is worthy of honour. What is 'honorary' is bestowed as an honour. Thus a university degree awarded as an honour and not as the result of any examination is an 'honorary' degree, and a post held without payment is an 'honorary' post. Confusion can arise because the abbreviation 'hon.' is widely used in more than one context. In parliamentary reference to the 'Hon.' Member for Bedford the abbreviation stands for 'honourable', whereas in a society's reference to the 'hon.' secretary the abbreviation stands for 'honorary'.

imaginary / imaginative

What is 'imaginary' is a product of the imagination in the sense that it has no real existence ('He is a hypochondriac whose ailments are largely imaginary'). What is 'imaginative' is the product of the imagination working creatively in the arts or in original thinking.

immanent / imminent

The word 'immanent' is used in philosophy to define what dwells or operates within. Thus God has been sometimes defined as 'immanent' within the universe rather than overlooking it. The word 'imminent' basically refers to something that overhangs as a lofty mountain may overhang a valley. From this sense of 'overhanging' it derives its most common meaning today of something immediately, and often threateningly, impending ('Little did we know that the explosion was imminent').

immunity / impunity

There is a slight overlap of meaning between these two words. The word 'immunity' is used medically of the body's ability to resist disease and more generally of freedom from legal obligations and from official restraints ('In return for agreeing to assist the authorities, the former criminal was granted immunity from prosecution'). 'Impunity' is exemption from charge or penalty and thus now describes a state of safety ('He ridiculed the authorities with impunity').

imply / infer

To 'imply' something is to convey it by what is said, perhaps indirectly. If a father informs his unemployed son that there is work to be had in a nearby firm, he is probably 'implying' that the son should go and apply for a job there. In fact the word 'imply' is rarely misused. What goes wrong generally is that the word 'infer' is used as though it meant the same as 'imply'. 'By every thing she said, she inferred that I was lazy' should be: 'she implied that I was lazy'. In modern usage to 'infer' is not to convey a message but to deduce one ('From his sickly appearance and lack of appetite I inferred that he was ill').

inapt / inept

A thing which is 'apt' is highly suitable to its purpose. Thus what is 'inapt' is inappropriate. The word is also used to mean unskilful, that is, lacking in aptitude. 'Inept' is originally the same word spelt differently but we tend to apply it to a degree of inappropriateness and lack of skill that implies clumsiness or stupidity ('It was inapt of him to miss his mother's funeral, and inept to imagine that no one would notice').

informant / informer

The history of these two words is curious. In present-day usage, an 'informant' is simply a person who conveys information, while an 'informer' is someone who lays information against another, bringing to light offences against the law. In the eighteenth century, however, the word 'informant' was used in this latter sense, and the word 'informer' could be used to mean one who animates and inspires. Thus in Pope we find 'Nature! informer of the human heart'.

ingenious / ingenuous

An 'ingenious' person has skill and inventiveness, and the products of his cleverness are also 'ingenious'. The word 'ingenuous' once meant straightforward and candid but now indicates (especially when qualified as 'over-ingenuous') not mere lack of duplicity but rather over-simplicity, naivety and even gullibility.

junction / juncture

A 'junction' is the point at which two things join, especially used of the place where a road or a railway line divides into two. The word 'juncture' is now generally used for a point in time at which the convergence of events creates a significant moment, perhaps a moment of crisis ('In the autumn he lost his job, and at this juncture his wife chose to leave him').

loathe / loath (loth)

To be 'loath' or 'loth' to do something is to be reluctant, unwilling to do it ('I was loth to part with my collection of stamps'). The verb to 'loathe' means to detest. Because the spelling 'loath', for reluctant, is now more often used than the spelling 'loth', confusion with the verb 'loathe' occurs.

luxuriant / luxurious

Both words are related to the word 'luxury'. The word 'luxuriant' is used to describe things (such as houses, artefacts, gardens, works of art) that are richly ornate and profusely decorative. The word 'luxurious' overlaps in meaning, but conveys more the sense of what indulges human appetite for ease and comfort, and for all that delights the senses ('In retirement he was able to live a luxurious life in luxuriant surroundings').

militate / mitigate

Here the similarity in sound between the two verbs causes confusion in spite of the totally different meanings they convey. To 'militate' is to combat or oppose ('Our genteel upbringing militated against the call to go and work down the mines'). In fact the word is rarely misused. The verb to 'mitigate' means to soften or soothe ('His daughter's decision to come and live with him somewhat mitigated his grief at the loss of his wife'), but it gets used mistakenly in the place of 'militate'.

momentary / momentous

A moment is a short space of time and the word 'momentary' means brief, lasting for only a moment. The word 'moment' has another use in expressions such as 'a matter of great moment'. It is this use that is reflected in the word 'momentous', which means 'of great moment' or very important.

nationalize / naturalize

A business or an organization is 'nationalized' when it is taken under public ownership and becomes the property of the state. The word is not used of human beings who change their nationality. If someone of foreign birth seeks to become a citizen of their adopted country, the official process is known as becoming 'naturalized'.

naught / nought

Strictly speaking, where 'aught' means anything, 'naught' means nothing ('I tell you naught for your comfort' says the visionary voice to King Alfred in Chesterton's *Ballad of the White Horse*). 'Nought' is the digit which, oddly enough, we pronounce 'Oh' when making a telephone call. The spelling 'nought' is now used as a variant of 'naught'.

obsolete / obsolescent

Increasingly 'obsolescent' is being used where the word should be 'obsolete'. What is 'obsolete' is out of date, no longer in use or no longer fashionable. What is 'obsolescent' is becoming obsolete, gradually perhaps going out of date and ceasing to be of use.

official / officious

The adjective 'official' relates to an office and in particular to what issues authoritatively from it ('As an MP's secretary, she has an official permit to enter the House'). One may be called to attend an 'official' meeting or invited to an 'official' dinner. The word 'officious' has a pejorative connotation. It is applied to self-important people who are unnecessarily free with attention or advice.

ostensible / ostentatious

Here are two more related adjectives, like 'official' and 'officious', with vastly different overtones. What is 'ostensible' is apparent, plain to see.

Sometimes the word is used to distinguish what is seemingly apparent on the surface from what lies hidden beneath ('The ostensible purpose of the journey was to visit his aunt, but he had far more sinister motives'). The word 'ostentatious' implies showiness that is pretentiously extravagant ('He never concealed his wealth: indeed he was ostentatious enough to run two Rolls-Royces, each with its own chauffeur').

perspicacious / perspicuous

The word 'perspicacious' (along with the noun 'perspicacity') is related to such words as 'perspective' and used to mean 'clear-sighted', but is now applied only to mental clear-sightedness and means penetrating or sharply perceptive. The word 'perspicuous', related to the word 'conspicuous', means transparently clear, and therefore, applied to people's thought or utterance, lucid and easily understood.

practical / practicable

The word 'practical' often offsets the word 'theoretical' and means related to actual experience and the world of daily action. A 'practical' person will quickly respond to an emergency by doing what common sense would recommend. The word 'practicable' means strictly able to be put into practice, and is therefore used to express a strong recommendation for any plan or scheme that is as yet at the theoretical stage.

precipitate / precipitous

In non-technical usage the verb to 'precipitate' is to bring something about too soon, over-hastily ('The quarrel in public precipitated a breakdown in their relationship'). The adjective 'precipitate' thus means overhasty or rash. The verb also means to hurl down from a height. 'Precipitous' means steep. The connection of both words with the word 'precipice' is what makes for confusion.

prerequisite / perquisite

These two words have nothing in common except a number of identical letters. A 'prerequisite' is something required in advance, often used of conditions required by an employer ('A prerequisite of the appointment was that I should move into the area'). The word 'perquisite' (abbreviated to 'perk') is now used chiefly for benefits from employment additional to the salary, such as a waiter's tips or an executive's company car.

prescribe / proscribe

To 'proscribe' is officially to outlaw or prohibit some conduct or person. Words including the syllables 'scribe' or 'script' (from the Latin) are to do with writing. To outlaw a person was to publish his name publicly in writing, to 'proscribe' it. To 'prescribe' is to lay down authoritatively some regulation or, in medicine, some treatment or potion. Thus the doctor 'prescribes' medicaments for us and we take our 'prescription' to the pharmacist. There is a danger of misusing the words as 'diagnose' is now misused:

> I have been prescribed with a variety of medicines.

The word 'with' must go. Just as doctors diagnose illnesses and not patients, so too they prescribe medicines and not patients.

presumptuous / presumptive

The word 'presumptuous' is related to that usage of 'presume' which implies that someone is taking more for granted than they have the right to do ('It was highly presumptuous of him to gatecrash that very exclusive party'). The word 'presumptive' is related to the usage of 'presume' which is disinfected of all such overtones, and simply means highly probable. The 'heir presumptive' to the throne is the one who will succeed provided that no stronger claimant comes on the scene. In the United Kingdom if the monarch had a daughter as first-born child, she would be the 'heir presumptive' unless or until a brother was born. The 'heir apparent' is the heir who will definitely succeed, provided that death does not intervene.

prevaricate / procrastinate

To 'prevaricate', deriving from a Latin verb meaning to walk crookedly, is to deviate from the proper course and hence to be deceptive or evasive in action or speech. To 'procrastinate' is to postpone action, to put it off to another day. 'Procrastination is the thief of time' said the almost forgotten eighteenth-century poet Edward Young in his *Night Thoughts*.

principal / principle

People continue to be tripped up by the similarity of these two words. The adjective 'principal' means first in importance ('The resignation of the Chairman is the principal business of the meeting'). Thus we use the noun 'principal' of the person in charge of an institution. A 'principle' is a fundamental law or a basic proposition from which other deductions follow.

prone to / susceptible to

The word 'prone', basically meaning bending forward or lying prostrate, flat on the face, came to mean having a natural inclination to do something. We stress the words 'to do'. A naughty child might be said to be 'prone' to telling lies. It would be less satisfactory to say that someone is 'prone to attacks of bronchitis'. That is where the word 'susceptible' is better. For where 'prone' means having an inclination to 'do' something, 'susceptible' means having an inclination to be responsive to something. Yet we read:

> My own limitations, of energy, time, or approach, make me always susceptible to behaving badly.

Bad behaviour does not come upon us from outside like the flu germ. It is something we do, not something we suffer: 'My own limitations make me always prone to behaving badly.'

recourse / resort

If you 'resort' to something you turn to it in need, and what you turn to is your 'resort'. Thus Polonius tells Ophelia to lock herself away from Hamlet's 'resort'. The use of the word for a holiday destination was a natural development. Whereas 'resort' is both a noun ('That is our last resort') and a verb ('All else having failed, we had to resort to the use of force'), the word 'recourse' is a noun only. What a person resorts to is in fact his recourse. 'He resorted to force' and 'He had recourse to force' are two ways of saying the same thing.

remission / remittance

Both words derive from the verb 'remit'. 'Remission' means forgiveness (the Bible speaks of the 'remission of sins') or release from some obligation or penalty. It is applied to the reduction of a term of imprisonment ('a remission of three years from the life sentence') and to a temporary period of abatement from a life-threatening disease. A different kind of obligation is finished off by a 'remittance', a payment that settles a debt.

reversal / reversion

'Reversal' means the act of reversing, physically going back on one's tracks, or coming up against something which stops one in one's desired progress ('The failure of her second novel to sell brought a reversal of all her ambitions'). The word 'reversion' is used of the return to an earlier condition or attitude ('In his latest poems we detect a reversion to the style of his earliest work'). It is also used legally of the part of an estate which is restored to the original testator or his heirs after the death of some temporary grantee.

salubrious / salutary

Both words are concerned with a healthy effect. While 'salubrious', meaning conducive to health, is used chiefly of spas and other resorts where climate may benefit health, 'salutary' is used much more widely of whatever promotes health or well-being. In its looser use, it means little more than 'beneficial' ('It might be salutary at this stage of the meeting to pause for reflection').

sensibility / sensitivity

The word 'sensible' most often means showing good judgement, but is also used more technically to mean capable of being sensed or perceived. It is from the latter connotation that the word 'sensibility' derives its meaning: the capacity to respond to emotional needs or aesthetic qualities. An art critic needs to be a person of cultivated 'sensibility'. The word 'sensitivity' is used generally of ready personal responsiveness. It is usually a tribute to call a person 'sensitive', but there is another usage where the word implies over-ready responsiveness which is 'touchy', the responsiveness of someone who is quick to take offence.

sensual / sensuous

Both words are concerned with the appeal to the senses or the responsiveness of the senses to what is physically attractive, but 'sensual' is pejorative; it is used of excessive indulgence in what appeals to the physical appetites. The word 'sensuous' is used of what properly appeals to the senses by its beauty and richness, especially perhaps in the aesthetic sphere, and of the sensitive human response to it. One might speak of the rich 'sensuous' appeal of a poet such as Keats or a composer such as Wagner.

stimulant / stimulus

Anything that stimulates, whether physically or mentally, is a 'stimulus' in that it encourages or goads to action or to decision. But the word 'stimulant' is mostly restricted to use for drugs or other consumables, such as alcohol, coffee or tea, which at least temporarily revitalize the body or raise the spirits.

substantial / substantive

These two words, both obviously connected with the word 'substance', overlap somewhat in meaning, but the overlap scarcely justifies the recent tendency to use only 'substantive' where 'substantial' would be equally or more appropriate. The word 'substantive' was the technical name of a noun. As an adjective it stresses therefore the independent and essential basis of whatever is referred to. The word 'substantial' has been more used to refer to the magnitude, the importance, the solidity of a thing. It also distinguishes what is actual and soundly based ('Substantial evidence was produced against him').

testament / testimony

A 'testament' is a will. Because it testifies to the intentions of the testator, being indeed the expression of his 'will', the word has come to be used more generally of what can stand as a proof or attestation. It is at this point that the meaning of 'testament' overlaps with the meaning of 'testimony', which is most commonly used in law for the evidence of witnesses. It has become evident that people are using 'testament' where once they would have been inclined to use 'testimony':

> The tyre gouges on the roundabout bore testament to the frequency of accidents.

This is a case in point. The gouges really bear 'testimony', that is, witness to a fact as in a court of law.

titillate / titivate

'Titillate' derives from a Latin verb meaning to 'tickle'. Hence its present meaning, to excite pleasure by some delightful gratification. It is used of comparatively trivial delights. One would not speak of being 'titillated' by a Beethoven symphony; one might of being 'titillated' by a delicious trifle or a nice new hat. 'Titivate' is a nineteenth-century word developed out of 'tidivate', that is to make tidy. It is used of the final touches to hair, to make-up or to dress, made just before appearing in company.

tortuous / torturous

I have just heard on the radio a reference to the experience of a man who was kidnapped. There was emphasis on what he endured in 'several tortuous months' of imprisonment. Clearly the person who wrote the report thought that the word 'tortuous' was connected with the word 'torture'. But it isn't. The word the newswriter wanted was 'torturous', the adjective derived from 'torture'. The word 'tortuous' derives from the word 'tort'. It refers to what is twisted, winding or crooked, the reverse of direct and straightforward. Thus one might speak of someone having to make a 'tortuous' journey by some difficult and circuitous route. Coincidentally I read in the newspaper that it was inevitable that 'Danny Wilson's torturous season in charge of Sheffield Wednesday would take another debilitating twist.' Plainly the word here should be 'tortuous'.

tragedy / travesty

A 'travesty' is an unworthy mockery of something, farcical in its extravagance. Yet we read this about a shrine to D. H. Lawrence in New Mexico, which is suffering from neglect.

> It's going to be lost to future generations, and that will be a travesty.

This appears to be one of those blunders which result from confusing two words that are similar in sound. Presumably the writer meant: 'and that will be a tragedy'.

trustful / trustworthy

It seems surprising that anyone could confuse these words. Adjectives that end in '-ful', such as 'truthful' and 'fearful', convey the meaning 'full of truth' and 'full of fear'. Just so 'trustful' means 'full of trust'. By contrast, adjectives which end in '-worthy', such as 'praiseworthy' and 'blameworthy', mean 'deserving of praise' and 'deserving of blame'. Nevertheless, in a BBC Radio 4 discussion about the quality of treatment provided by the Health Service, we hear an educated voice declaring:

> I, as a patient, want to feel absolutely trustworthy about any one who attends to me.

She means that she wants to be able to be 'trustful', and she wants those who attend to her to be 'absolutely trustworthy'.

CHAPTER 3

Words at Work

COMBINING WORD WITH WORD

Preserving Consistency

The 'right word' does not exist in isolation. What may seem to be the right word in the first half of the sentence may have to be questioned when we see what follows it. The exact combining of words is what guarantees clarity and precision. It is no use getting what seems to be the right word if you then attach to it something that is not precisely appropriate.

> Delay, even for a month, could be too late.

The sentence is a case in point. Delay can make some action or event 'too late'. But the delay in itself cannot be too late. It is whatever is delayed by delay that may be 'too late'. The delay is 'too long'. Similarly the sound beginning of the following sentence is thoroughly spoiled by the words at the end:

> It might be damaging to Mr Clinton to provoke a crisis which he might then lose.

When a 'crisis' arrives for a statesman, there may be grave dangers, whether political or physical. The person who faces a crisis may 'survive' it successfully or go under. But a 'crisis' is not a kind of competitive event which one might either 'win' or 'lose'. This straightforward collision of meanings between the subject of the sentence and what follows it is surprisingly common. Here is a sentence from a piece about the building of new railways in the nineteenth century.

> Parliamentary powers were passed in 1866.

'Powers' were not 'passed'. The writer means either that 'powers were taken' to do this or that, or that 'legislation was passed'.

It is perhaps when we are being conversational in our style that it is easiest to lose exact consistency of meaning.

> There are a few simple tips that if used with care should help your little problem quite nicely.

A 'tip', when it is not a gratuity given to a waiter or waitress, is a useful piece of advice. We do not, however, speak of 'using' such pieces of advice, but of 'following' them. And the desirable thing is not to 'help' a problem, but to solve it or get rid of it. Since the tone of the whole is conversational, we need not quibble about 'quite nicely', though it is not the most precise expression for the meaning required. We should correct to: 'There are a few simple tips that, if carefully followed, will help you in your little difficulty.' And if one is seeking a gem of thoughtlessness in this connection perhaps the following will do:

> Even today weather forecasting is difficult to predict.

That is the equivalent of saying 'Even today weather forecasting is difficult to forecast.' Nobody could possibly be interested in having forecasting predicted instead of the weather.

Simple, familiar words that are frequently on our lips may make an ill-assorted anarchic concoction if they are allowed to slide out unchecked.

> There is a clear funding gap which, if not resolved, will stunt future development of small businesses in London.

The way to deal with a 'gap' is to bridge it, not to 'resolve' it. And how can a 'gap', whether 'resolved' or not, 'stunt' future development of small businesses? A better sentence would be: 'There is a shortage of cash which, if not made up, will impede future development of small businesses in London.'

The word 'gap' has a metaphorical element here. And where metaphors are used, it is crucial not to mix them too glaringly.

> Throughout Central Europe the loss of monopoly on power reduced overnight the individual communist parties to an insignificant fraction in a blossoming political landscape.

The good writer would never speak of a 'fraction' in a 'blossoming landscape', any more than he would speak of a bunch of lilies in a quadratic equation.

Utterance at the political level too readily overstretches the meaning of words to the point where connotation collides with connotation.

> One of the most basic elements of US concern for any freed hostage is his or her privacy. Yesterday Mr Ronnegut violated that policy.

To begin with, a 'concern' is not a 'policy'. Secondly, a 'policy' is not something that can be 'violated'. A 'principle' might be 'violated' and a 'policy' might be 'abandoned'. Then again, the use of the words 'basic elements' is unnecessary. We may write: 'One of the basic US concerns for any freed hostage is his or her privacy. Yesterday Mr Ronnegut ignored that concern.'

Preserving Coherence

The kind of verbal inconsistency we are investigating can lead to partial or total loss of coherence. Indeed it is possible to cancel out the meaning of a word by careless choice of a succeeding word or words. For instance, something which is 'inescapable' obviously cannot be avoided. It may be said that death is an 'inescapable' consequence of swallowing cyanide. Writing of a natural disaster, a journalist says:

> The inescapable conclusion is probably that most of the missing are dead.

Here the force of the word 'inescapable' is destroyed by the succeeding word 'probably'. Clearly, if the conclusion is a matter of probability only, then it is not 'inescapable'. In any case, the writer has sufficiently hedged his bets by use of the word 'most'. One of the two words should go, either 'inescapable' or 'probably'.

It is perhaps easiest to lose coherence when sentences are clogged with words. Nevertheless economy with words can sometimes have the same effect. Here is a sentence from an article on the nocturnal threat to cattle farms in Africa from hyenas.

> Often only a part of the victim was eaten and when found next morning had to be shot.

The sentence tells us that part of the animal was eaten, found next morning, and shot. But it was not the part that was eaten that was shot. It was the remaining uneaten part. Economy with words is the trouble here. What is needed is: 'Often only a part of the victim was eaten, and when the animal was found next morning it had to be shot.'

A similar miserliness with words leads to trouble in the following sentence. It is part of a plea for keeping sewage and other contamination away from our lakes.

> If we don't, we may have to forgo our favourite lakeside walks with kingfishers, dragonflies and water lilies.

We may take our country walks with our friend or with our dog, but we don't take them with kingfishers and water lilies. Some words must be inserted: 'our favourite lakeside walks and the glimpses of kingfishers, dragonflies and water lilies'. That is the kind of error produced by over-hasty writing. Journalists often work under pressure and their prose sometimes bears the mark of hasty composition. In the attempt to be concise and not to waste words they may transfer on to paper the freedoms which are proper only to conversation.

> She set about a rigorous training programme culminating in a 20-mile sponsored canoe from Lancaster to Preston.

This will not do in print. A training programme cannot culminate in a canoe. Nor, strictly speaking, is the canoe 'sponsored'. It was the ride in the canoe that was twenty miles long and was sponsored. That is a fairly crude example of the effects of over-compression. At a subtler level the error is not so easy to spot.

> Shareholders have angrily denounced the company's speedy receivership over the weekend.

The word 'receivership' means 'the condition of being administered by a receiver'. This is not in itself a condition that can be either speedy or tardy. What the writer means (and what the reader understands in spite of the illogicality) is that: 'Shareholders have angrily denounced the company's speedy recourse to receivership.' It was the decision that was over-hasty in the shareholders' eyes.

The risk of combining words together incoherently is especially strong with over-used words. The more a word is used, the weaker and vaguer its connotation becomes. The word 'problem' was cited in this connection in Chapter 1. Here is a sentence about dealing with antelopes in Kenya:

> Controlling these problems does not come under the heading of sport.

The 'problems' concern the business of 'controlling' antelopes and, in a very crudely conversational sense, the antelopes may 'be' problems. But however one looks at it, the difference is that antelopes have to be 'controlled' and that problems have to be 'solved', and you can no more 'control' a 'problem' than you can 'solve' an 'antelope'.

Another much used word, 'issue', also tends to such vagueness that precision gets lost in its use. Here is an observation on football tactics by a commentator:

> The issue of diving and over-reacting, basically cheating, needs to be quickly eradicated, probably using video technology.

There is more than one 'issue' here. To use the word 'basically' as the equivalent of 'in other words' is characteristic of what is now a general loose treatment of the word. But more serious is the claim that an 'issue' should be 'eradicated'. It is not the 'issue' which the writer really wants to be rid of, but the 'practice' of diving and over-reacting.

Preserving Congruity in a Sequence

Loss of consistency and coherence occurs in improperly controlled accumulations of items. Track is lost of a crucial word because what follows it wanders away from accurate preservation of its meaning. Here is some publicity material from a major bank:

> This means that our income on retirement is likely to be based on pensions from a number of different sources. Each of these must be tracked down, calculated and taken into account for someone to build up an accurate picture of the kind of retirement they will enjoy.

The writer's first sentence focuses on the 'sources' of pensions. 'Each of these must be tracked down' makes sense, because 'these' means the 'sources' of the pensions. But to continue by saying that 'each of these' must be 'calculated' is totally incongruous. One does not 'calculate' a 'source'. A different subject is required for the verb 'calculate' and what follows. The mistake arises because the writer has used the word 'these' and then forgotten exactly what it refers to. Better avoid it: 'Each source must be tracked down, the pensions calculated and taken into account.'

Just as use of a pronoun such as 'this' or 'these' can bring about a lapse of congruity in word usage, a long parenthesis can produce the same danger.

> The moves towards allowing more of us to take control of our working environment – whether that means working for ourselves from home full-time or working for an employer from home two days a week – are coming true at last.

The long parenthesis causes the writer to forget what the subject of the sentence was. 'Moves' may lead to action. 'Moves towards' something may eventually get there. But 'moves' cannot be said to be 'coming true'. It would be better to get rid of the word 'moves': 'Plans towards allowing more of us to take control of our working environment . . . are being realized at last.'

It should be noted that it is when a sentence gets somewhat clogged with words (as by the introduction of the parenthesis in the sentence above) that the logical sequence from subject ('The moves') through verb ('are coming') to what follows ('true') may be defective.

> His combination of talent, daring, intelligence and dedication amounts to the most impressive sportsman of our time.

Here, for instance, the accumulation of the four words ('talent, daring, intelligence and dedication') clogs progress sufficiently for the sequence from subject ('His combination') through verb ('amounts to') to what follows ('the most impressive sportsman') to be upset. The writer would not have been tempted to write 'His combination amounts to the sportsman', but when divested of the verbal clogging around it, that is the basic construction used. A simple change of verb would correct the error: 'His combination of talent, daring, intelligence and dedication mark him as the most impressive sportsman of our time.'

Avoiding Just the Wrong Word

If you fasten on just the wrong word, you put consistency and coherence at risk. Consider the following advertisement for insurance in a magazine for people with equestrian interests:

> A unique choice of cover for all the flexibility you need – from family ponies to competition horses.

It is less than exact to convey that the need for satisfactory insurance for a variety of activities or possessions can be summed up as a 'need for flexibility'. But then seemingly to define 'flexibility' as a category of beings ranging from family ponies to competition horses makes matters worse. What should be offered is: 'cover for whatever you need it for, from family ponies to competition horses'.

Where a metaphor is involved it is all too easy to attach the wrong word to it. An image which has lately become popular is that of a 'raft'. A 'raft' is a platform which floats and can usefully carry a load of items carefully arranged together. Hence we hear that the government is producing a 'raft of proposals' on this matter or that. That is a useful expression, if handled properly.

> The government has unveiled a raft of proposals.

Here it is mishandled. The writer has opted for the wrong initial verb, and the imagery breaks down. It might be appropriate to 'launch' a raft, but the picture of someone 'unveiling' a raft will not do.

There are words which can be used in different senses in different contexts. Exploiting double meanings can be a source of humour or, in poetry, of profundity. One might flippantly say 'The baby was delivered at eight o'clock in the morning, at the same time as the newspaper in fact.' There is always a risk for the writer in using any word which has the sort of double usages that are exploited there in the verb 'deliver'. For it is possible to call up the 'wrong' meaning unintentionally.

> A glass of wine and an introductory lecture will precede a special guided tour of the exhibition by gallery staff.

The verb 'precede' means to take place before in time. It also means to go before in movement. The glass of wine and the lecture 'precede' the guided tour in time. But the concept of people walking through the gallery on a guided tour is apt to bring the other meaning of 'precede' to mind, so that one pictures a procession headed by a glass of wine.

Even the shortest words can be used to exploit this kind of ambiguity. The word 'in' is made to do double duty in Dickens's celebrated account of the agitated Miss Bolo in *Pickwick Papers*, who 'went straight home, in a flood of tears and a Sedan chair'.

The writer has to take care not to allow an unintended ambiguity to intrude through lack of watchfulness.

> A summerhouse is a treat. People buy them as a self-indulgent present for their garden.

I assume that what the writer means here is that people give themselves a present by purchasing a summerhouse 'for' the garden ('People buy them for their garden as a self-indulgent present'). But the sentence fails to allow for the divergence in the usage of 'for' in 'He bought a wheelbarrow for the garden' and 'He bought a present for his wife.' By using the word 'present' the writer has unintentionally brought to mind the second usage, which makes it sound as though people buy presents for their gardens.

Confusion Between Word and Fact

In a variety of ways word may be confused with fact, form with substance.

> The catalogue is packed with everything you need to keep your dog safe while in the car – for example harnesses for all sizes . . .

It may sound pedantic, but it has to be pointed out that the catalogue is not packed with harnesses or with any other bits of apparatus to keep a dog safe. The catalogue is packed only with 'information' about such items, in print, and perhaps in pictures too. There is no escape from including the necessary clarification: 'The catalogue is packed with details of everything you need . . .'

This mistake occurs at many different levels of literacy from the crude to the subtle.

> These walks are written by over twenty different authors.

That is an example of the mistake at a rather crude level. The sentence is from a review of a book giving routes for walks. It is not the walks that are 'written' but accounts of the walks. If the word 'written' is to be kept, then the missing verbal link must be supplied ('Accounts of these walks are written by over twenty different authors'). But of course it may be better to get rid of the verb 'written': 'These walks are described by over twenty different authors.' The mistake occurs quite often in accounts of books or other publications. There is confusion between speaking about the publication as a whole and speaking about the contents contained within it.

> In a survey of 100 wetland Sites of Special Scientific Interest a majority are beginning to suffer from eutrophication.

This is like saying of a history book 'The funeral of King Edward VII takes place in chapter seven.' The wetland sites are not suffering from eutrophication in the survey any more than King Edward VII is interred in the history book. The survey and the developments it reports are two different matters. All that is needed to correct this error is the insertion of a simple parenthetical expression such as 'we learn that' or 'it is revealed that' after the word 'Interest'. But even that need could have been obviated if the writer had not begun the sentence with the word 'In': 'A survey of 100 wetland Sites of Special Scientific Interest reveals that a majority are beginning to suffer from eutrophication.'

It is not only in accounts of books and in official reports that we find this error. The word 'news' is misused in similar fashion on the radio. We hear from the commercial world that a certain rather questionable financial deal, involving huge profits for the fat cats, has just been agreed. Then we are told that 'The Shadow Chancellor has condemned the news.' Clearly it is not the publicization of the facts ('the news') that angered the politician, but the facts recorded. After another such announcement of a possible scandal, the BBC reporter tells us 'The news is part of a continuing investigation' – which it plainly is not. The investigation is one thing, the news of the scandal another thing.

Confusion between statement and fact, between words and what they convey, lies behind many such errors. In the extreme case we read this on the subject of stag-hunting:

> Words such as biodiversity and Agenda 21 Local Plans are the way forward.

No one is likely to defend this as a justifiable verbal short cut. If the writer means that 'biodiversity' should be encouraged, then he should talk about it and not about the 'word'. Clearly to recommend certain 'words' as a 'way forward' is not going to get anyone very far.

Keeping Connotation Intact

A peculiar form of misusing a single word occurs sometimes when a word is made to do duty in two different ways in the same sentence. The error can turn up in accounts of football matches.

Wolverhampton's victory thrilled him, for it was his native city.

The victory was scored by a team of footballers. 'Wolverhampton', meaning that team, cannot in the same sentence mean the place. It is like saying 'Wolverhampton is a magnificent team with a fine town hall in the middle.' There is no escape from repeating the word: 'Wolverhampton's victory thrilled him, for Wolverhampton was his native city.' The error is not rare in the world of sport.

Mr Scoular travelled to England every week to watch Liverpool, where he was a season-ticket holder.

The word 'where' gives the word 'Liverpool' a double usage which it cannot have. For the place 'where' Mr Scoular was a ticket-holder was not the same thing as the band of players he came to watch. 'Mr Scoular, a season-ticket holder, travelled to England every week to watch Liverpool.'

The same error can occur in speaking about the past. A confusion arises between the record and the reality.

Even this building has a most fascinating history which is well worth reading.

The 'history' of what the building has been through is one thing and what you can read is another thing. It would be correct, but rather awkward to say: 'Even this building has a most fascinating history, which is well worth reading about.' Perhaps it should rather be: 'which is well worth knowing'. Not very different in category is the slip in the following recommendation for certain wines.

Currently the range consists of three wines . . . , each of which has a recipe on the back that you can peel off and keep.

We may overlook the fact that it is the bottle and not the 'wine' which has a recipe 'on the back'. This, of course, represents a shift in meaning of the word 'wine'. More interesting is the shift in meaning of the word 'recipe'. First it is a real 'recipe' with advice about use of the wine. But a moment later it has become a piece of paper that you can 'peel off' the bottle. 'Currently the range consists of three wines . . . , and each bottle has a recipe on the back label which you can peel off and keep.'

These transitions in meaning, however, are less stark than the following:

> She immediately passes the information on to the social services, who leave at once to find the boy.

Now it may be argued that the person who received the information did indeed leave at once. But 'the social services' to whom the communication is sent is surely an organization with a substantial staff. They do not all 'leave at once'. If 'who' is to be kept, then 'leave' must be changed: 'who send someone at once to find the boy'.

PERSONAL AND IMPERSONAL

A peculiar kind of inappropriateness can be found when words and images that should be personal in their connotation are used in contexts where the impersonal is required. We use of living creatures words and expressions inappropriate if applied to inanimate or abstract objects. We must not be too solemnly pedantic about this. Poets often rely upon fanciful applications of the personal idiom to the impersonal world. Shakespeare tells the winter wind that it is 'not so unkind/As man's ingratitude'. The poet Thomas Nashe tells how, in spring, 'the daisies kiss our feet', and Wordsworth declares that 'Earth fills her lap with pleasures of her own.' We do not protest that the wind can be neither kind nor unkind, that daisies have no mouths to kiss with, and that the earth lacks the kind of build which would grant it a lap.

Can 'plain English' prose, utilized for day-to-day communication, allow such liberties? There are indeed contexts in which the mixture causes us to smile rather than to criticize. We indulge weather forecasters as they personalize aspects of the climate. When the forecaster tells us that the 'rain will be reluctant to move away', or when she says that 'temperatures will struggle to get up to 15' we probably feel that she has as much right to this exercise of the 'pathetic fallacy' as the poet has. Our long struggles with weather encourage us to endow it with a will. We tend to nod in approval in mid-winter when the forecaster announces that 'there is a bit too much weather about today'. We may jib at the extension of the linguistic liberties, however, when the forecaster predicts 'more organized bands of rain'.

Temperatures may be allowed to 'struggle' and rain to be 'reluctant', but in colder prose argument is marred when such liberties are taken.

Personal Verbs Misused

Here is a sentence from an article complaining of the decline of grouse on moorland and the problem of dealing with harriers:

> Other methods – translocation, disturbance prior to breeding, and removal of eggs – have all stumbled on the legal fence.

The metaphor of stumbling at a fence can be appropriately applied to any human experience of frustration. But 'stumbling' is essentially something that living beings do. To attribute the capacity to 'stumble' to a series of 'methods' of tackling a problem will not do. The sentence would more appropriately read: 'Other methods – translocation, disturbance prior to breeding, and removal of eggs – have all been rejected on legal grounds.' There is a comparable misapplication of personal vocabulary in this sentence from my morning paper:

> The Derby has become an occasion racked with self-doubt.

Neither a horse race nor an 'occasion' of any kind can suffer self-doubt. It is the people involved who may suffer so.

Some verbs are so frequently on our lips in a personal context that they slip too readily out when the context is decisively impersonal. A legal spokesman, speaking on BBC Radio 4 of defects in the prosecution service, argues the need for 'a system that can enjoy public confidence'. So accustomed are we to the expression 'enjoy public confidence' that it slips out here irrespectively of the fact that enjoyment is a human experience that no 'system' could feel. There is no advantage in not saying: 'a system that the public can trust'. There is a similar liberty taken in the following:

> A rise in interest rates will exert further pressure on the Bank of England to consider an emergency cut in interest rates.

My dictionary gives the meaning of 'exert' as 'to apply (oneself) vigorously, make a strenuous effort'. The bracketed 'oneself' indicates the propriety of using the verb for personal effort. A 'rise in interest rates' cannot make a strenuous effort. It is a pity to weaken the verb 'exert' by making it the equivalent of the more colourless verb 'put', which would be better used in the sentence we are looking at. The same issue arises with the verb 'achieve' in the following.

> The paper used with gouache is significant; different types achieve different qualities.

Paper is not capable of 'achieving' anything. The meaning is that different types of paper enable the artist to achieve different qualities.

A rather subtler question arises from a statement made on Radio 4:

> Cannabis should be allowed to be prescribed.

This is like saying 'Meat should be allowed to be eaten'. If one says 'It should be legal to prescribe cannabis', one is urging that doctors should be 'allowed' to do something, but this does not empower cannabis in any way. Although we are used to notices saying 'Smoking is not allowed', it is clearly better to avoid the converse instruction 'Cigarettes should be allowed to be smoked' as a variant of 'People may smoke.'

The issue arises again with the verb to 'enable'. It is better reserved for the personal field. 'The grant enabled us to finance the foreign tour' represents the personal usage. 'The whole discussion is about enabling a framework to be in place' represents the far less satisfactory, impersonal usage. Strictly speaking, a framework cannot be 'enabled' to 'be' anything. As material things such as cannabis ought not to be said to be 'allowed' privileges, so material things such as frameworks ought not to be said to be rendered capable of doing anything.

Before leaving this topic, we should note that there is one verb properly reserved for the activity of living beings which has long been used idiomatically of inanimate beings in certain contexts. It is the verb to 'see'. We use the word widely of actual vision and also of registering by the mind ('See what I mean?'). I doubt whether any pedants are shocked when someone writes 'The year 1945 saw the defeat of Germany' even though years are not gifted with either vision or mental understanding. But the acceptance of such an idiom does not justify extending its use into other and very different contexts. Here is an account of some horse trials.

> Twenty-four started over Keith Bristow's track . . . and some tricky related distances saw only five reach the jump-off.

The notion of 'related distances' witnessing or registering this or that number of successful riders strains the idiom too far. The same may be said of the following account of repairs to railway trucks.

> Despite experiments with aluminium doors, a programme of repairs to OBA open wagons sees the original wooden dropside doors replaced in kind.

Again there is no advantage in using the verb to 'see'. No verb other than 'replaced' is required: 'in a programme of repairs to OBA open wagons the original wooden dropside doors are replaced in kind'.

Like other metaphors, the verb to 'see', meaning to register, ought not to be used in a context where metaphors might collide. A newspaper headline about a speech made by an opposition spokesman in Serbia reads 'Dissenting voice seen as proof of split in Belgrade'. Since voices are heard and not seen, this particular use of the verb to 'see' ought to be avoided.

Personal Terms Used Inappropriately

We suffer advertisers to take certain freedoms in this matter of using a personal vocabulary where it is strictly inapplicable.

> Sensitive skin needs treating with respect and understanding.

The advertiser purposely takes the regularly partnered words, 'respect' and 'understanding', out of their normal psychological milieu. Both respect and understanding are desirable human qualities most often directed towards other human beings. Here the advertiser treats them as proper attitudes to be taken up towards one's skin. The point made is valid enough, but we should observe that the more the two words 'respect' and 'understanding' are thus used, thus 'depersonalized' as it were, the more the resonances of human warmth and appreciation are dissipated.

Of course a writer has a perfect right consciously to mix the personal and the impersonal to comic effect, such as in:

> What self-respecting garden would be without a few bold clumps of Cornflower Blue Ball?

Just as one should be wary of attributing actions and processes proper to human beings to the inanimate, so one must be wary of describing the inanimate in inappropriate personal terms. The attempt to personalize the impersonal, even when consciously made, can easily fail to come off.

> A well-designed playground in a park or school can be a child's paradise, particularly if the ground is forgiving.

Presumably this means: 'particularly if the ground is soft to fall on'. Whatever allowances one makes for metaphorical experiment, the attempt to endow the earth with the capacity to forgive surely misses fire. There is a similar, if less stark, failure in the following sentence:

> Some private companies provide safe, well-organized camps during the holidays, of which Camp Beaumont is probably the most experienced.

The writer was trying not to waste words here, but the camp must not be said to be 'experienced'. Either persons must be involved: 'of which Camp Beaumont is probably in the most experienced hands' or the word 'experienced' must go: 'of which Camp Beaumont is probably the best run'.

We have in English a number of adjectives which can be used either personally or impersonally. The questions 'Are you comfortable in that chair?' and 'Is that a comfortable chair?' amount to the same thing. Either a human being or a chair can be said to be 'comfortable'. An 'innocent' child may be playing an 'innocent' game, and a 'naughty' child may be up to 'naughty' tricks. A 'wicked' man does 'wicked' deeds and a 'brave' man does 'brave deeds'. There is an old illustrated Yorkshire joke about a young hiker climbing over a gate into a field in which there is a bull. A farmer approaches and the young man addresses him: 'I say, farmer, is that bull safe?' The reply is 'A damn sight safer than you are.' This double application of the word 'safe' to the man's situation and to the threat from the animal is perfectly acceptable. We ask ourselves 'Is it safe?' or 'Am I safe?' in many a situation. But we cannot extend this freedom of duplicated reference to any word we choose. A journalist tells us of the discovery of something vitally important to the food industry:

> . . . a plant that provides sugars that can make non-fattening and guilt-free sweets and cakes.

To speak of sweets and cakes as 'guilt-free' is to make an unacceptable transfer of qualification from consumer to commodity. We may feel 'guilty' about eating too many chocolates, but the chocolates do not share the guilt.

What applies to personal descriptions applies too to personal definitions. In a statement about proposed legal reforms a spokesman on the radio committed himself to this:

> We have put into process measures that will be witnesses to our intention to put things right.

Imaginatively to describe, say, objects in a room in which a murder had been committed as 'witnesses' to the crime would be appropriate because of the emotional quality of the situation. But to define vague 'measures' thus is verbally insensitive. It would be better to write: 'We have put into process measures that will prove our intention to put things right.'

We turn to an example of the imprecision now affecting use of the word 'role'. It is not so long ago that respectable publishers spelt it 'rôle', as though it had not yet settled down fully in the English language. Now it is on everyone's lips. Correct usage requires one to limit it in application to human beings. They are the beings who can play 'roles' whether on the stage or in real life. Licence may be allowed to such expressions as 'the role of management today' because 'management' consists of human beings. But this, from a railway magazine, surely abuses the word:

> The managing director and general manager will continue to run the railways' daily role.

One may 'assume' a role, but scarcely 'run' one. And to apply to the machinery of the railway a word which should be rich in associations of theatrical performances by world-famous actors is woefully insensitive. But what we are concerned with is the sad tendency to use the word 'role' as though it meant 'function' and then, as here, as though it meant 'operation'. There is also use of the word as an adjective, especially in the expression 'role model'. Here again, provided that the words refer to some human being, the usage is unobjectionable. But there is the danger that it will be used simply to mean 'example'. That has happened in the following comment on the Politically Correct decision to reprint photographs of the great Victorian railway engineer Isambard Brunel and to blot out the cigar he habitually smoked.

> They think the cigar is an inappropriate role model for the young.

Brunel may be less useful as a 'role model' if he is represented with a cigar in his mouth, but to apply the expression to the cigar will not do.

Favourite Personal Expressions Misapplied

It is all too easy to slip into use of some much used expression which is distinctly personal in a quite inappropriate impersonal context.

> Either end of the outside edge of the top berth is usually higher than the mattress in the hope of stopping its occupants from falling out when they turn over.

Human beings can take action 'in the hope' of achieving certain results. Indeed someone might design a berth in a certain way, as described here, 'in the hope' of preventing occupants from falling out. But we must not say that the 'berth' takes this or that form 'in the hope' of preventing occupants from falling out. We need mention of a person, directly or indirectly, to justify reference to 'hope'. The direct mention of a person would satisfy the purist: 'The designer made either end of the top berth higher than the mattress in the hope of preventing its occupants from falling out.' The less dogmatic stylist might be satisfied with the implicit reference to a human agent which use of the passive voice involves: 'Either end of the outside edge is usually made higher than the mattress in the hope of preventing its occupants from falling out.' Here one understands that, if something 'is made', a person is involved in the making.

Here is a rather more subtle confusion of the same kind:

> The course, she believes, has made the Bar more accessible to those from less privileged backgrounds, 'and that can only be good news for the depth and diversity of the legal system'.

What the writer means here is: 'that can only serve to improve the depth and diversity of the legal system'. And it is insensitive to equate the expression 'to bring good news to' with the expression 'to benefit' or 'to improve'. Only human beings can be sensitive to 'good news'. Good news cannot excite any response in the depth and diversity of a system. Nor can a system experience 'hope'.

> The railway is pinning its hopes that any outstanding work on *Ditcheat Manor* will be completed in time.

The sensitive reader jibs at the notion of a railway 'pinning its hopes' anywhere, but the attribution of human characteristics to railway systems attracts railway enthusiasts. Perhaps generations brought up on *Thomas the Tank Engine* are imbued with enthusiasm for an anthropomorphic railway.

> That month also saw the demise of *Caerphilly Castle*, which with 1,910,730 miles under its running plate, was withdrawn to be exhibited at the Science Museum, Kensington.

The writer here takes the familiar expression from the personal field ('A promising young writer, he had two successful novels under his belt'), and applies it to the engine, changing 'belt' to 'running plate'. The joke is taken. By contrast we finally cite an instance where flippancy fails.

> Every five years or so, London Fashion Week is supposedly about to meet its Maker.

The words about going to meet one's Maker have been a traditional euphemism for dying. Applied to anything other than human beings, they represent a failed flippancy in rather bad taste.

READY-MADE USAGES

Established Combinations

There are established combinations of words which come naturally to mind because they are so apt and useful. To speak of someone having a 'steady hand' or an 'infectious smile' can often enough be appropriate. To describe someone's hardships as a 'crippling burden' and an addition to them as a 'terrible blow' is to reach for very well-used expressions. That a combination of words is stereotyped does not prevent it from being genuinely usable. Some of the most useful and forceful such combinations have a metaphorical content. We speak of someone having received a 'bloody nose' when he has merely been rebuffed. There is only a metaphorical iciness about being in a 'cold sweat', having 'cold feet' or giving someone the 'cold shoulder'. And we move further still from literalness when we say things are 'in apple-pie order' or when we describe a grandiose creation as a 'white elephant'. The origin of the former is disputed, but the latter expression apparently dates back to a Siamese king who presented expensive white elephants to out-of-favour courtiers who couldn't afford to keep them.

But combinations establish themselves which lack spark or freshness and which are done to death by over-use. Habit then prevents the quick speaker or quick writer from using the dominant word in the combination without the other. We hear that someone is 'totally committed' to a project or 'thoroughly tired' of some involvement. Words such as 'totally' and 'thoroughly' (which the grammarians call 'intensifiers') increase the force of what is said, but so vaguely and colourlessly as to be little more than the equivalent of underlining or italicizing the words they accompany. Similarly we say something is 'completely useless' or someone is 'utterly stupid' and the words 'completely' and 'utterly', although they are in themselves meaningful words when properly used, in that context just exercise that function of intensifying the words 'useless' and 'stupid' without any connotative clarity.

When over-use leads to an automatic coupling of such words, then meaningful words are diluted of content, and are turned into colourless intensifiers. 'He's hopelessly inefficient', we say, and the word 'hopelessly' means no more than 'very' or 'thoroughly' would have meant. This does not just apply to adverbs such as 'utterly' and 'thoroughly' and 'hopelessly'. Adjectives too can be so over-used in certain combinations that they are deprived of content, and function only to lay emphasis on the words they are partnered with. When we read that some advertiser is offering us a 'unique opportunity' we understand that the opportunity is supposed to be a considerable one, but the word 'unique' does not convey anything clearer than that. Over-use has emasculated it.

The careful writer will always be on guard against falling back on words which serve only as counters for enhancing the importance of the words they accompany. Not every opportunity is a 'golden opportunity', not every failure a 'dismal failure'. Indeed it is even possible to 'beat a retreat' that is not 'hasty'.

There are, however, a couple of now much-used combinations which deserve attention. I have just heard a comment on a sportsman who surprised by suddenly achieving success after a string of mediocre performances. The commentator said he was 'shaking off his wooden-spoon reputation'. The image of the 'wooden spoon' is in popular use just now. In the early twentieth century the person who achieved the worst result in such organized competitive activities as whist drives would be presented with the 'booby prize'. The use of the word 'booby' for a silly person was clearly well established in the eighteenth century when

Fielding made his Lady Booby the absurd would-be seductress of innocent Joseph Andrews. The image of the 'wooden spoon', now more commonly used, has a curious history. The associations of insensitivity and comparative worthlessness which the word 'wooden' carries date well back. In Shakespeare's *Henry VI Part 1* the Earl of Suffolk writes off the king as 'a wooden thing'. It became the custom at Cambridge University to present a wooden spoon to the student who obtained the lowest marks in the Mathematical Tripos. From this derives the image now popular with journalists.

Imaginative inventiveness is revealed sometimes in adding to the stock of such expressions. Consider the expression 'golden handshake'. The two words 'golden' and 'handshake' are rich in associations which offset each other powerfully in the partnership. 'Golden' endows a concept with preciousness. The word 'handshake', used of a parting, can convey a deep pathos. In Shakespeare's *Troilus and Cressida* there is a fine image of how the parting handshake differs from the welcoming embrace.

> For time is like a fashionable host
> That slightly shakes his parting guest by the hand,
> And with his arms outstretched as he would fly,
> Grasps in the comer.

Put together the image of the golden gift and the limp parting handshake, and there is something which sums up a world of emotional complexities that victims of involuntary and half-voluntary redundancies experience.

The effectiveness of the expression 'golden handshake' has inspired further verbal partnerships. When an employing board is induced to give a new top manager a package of pecuniary benefits, the manager is said to have received a 'golden hello'. Similarly, a person may be appointed to a post in management or in the professions and granted pecuniary benefits (such as removal and resettlement costs) which must be repaid if the appointee stays less than two or three years in the post. The employee is then said to be held in 'golden handcuffs'. Moreover, I see now that a person employed at the top level of a major business who is given a lump sum and required to leave his lucrative post for a much more modest one is described as being brought down to earth in a 'golden parachute'. Journalists seeking an expression to convey an even rarer and more valuable gesture to a departing director have now spoken of a 'platinum handshake'.

Familiar Metaphorical Expressions

A living language is rich in well-used phrases and expressions that have stood the test of time. We are always ready to fall back on them when they seem to meet our need. Using old biblical images, we may call a hypocrite a 'whited sepulchre' or a favourite child 'the apple of my eye'. We speak of something occurring 'at the drop of a hat' and of someone being 'at the end of their tether'. On occasions we feel that there is no equally expressive alternative to speaking of 'a pig in a poke' or 'a pain in the neck'. We have a stock of long-established metaphorical sayings to hand which we readily resort to. How we should miss the metaphor 'He has hit the nail on the head'! And that use of the verb 'hit' reminds us how fruitful certain basic verbs have been in supplying us with multifarious expressions. When someone gave us the expression 'hit the bottle', we gained a vivid way of saying something for which no crisp and neat alternative could be found. One could only match it in meaning by qualifying the verb to 'drink' ('heavily', 'continually', 'addictively') or by having recourse to terms like 'alcoholic' or 'dipsomaniac'. And how richly different from 'hitting the bottle' is 'hitting the roof', 'hitting the headlines', 'hitting the hay' or 'hitting the jackpot'.

We have other verbs which have supplied such expressions. The verb to 'drive' gives us 'drive a hard bargain', 'drive a coach and horses through', 'drive a point home' and 'drive a nail into someone's coffin'. The word 'run', as verb and noun, gives us 'run the gauntlet', 'run rings round', 'run the show' and 'the run of the house'. The best such metaphorical expressions have a colourfulness and a vividness which seem to make them indispensable. Where should we turn for an alternative when we want to say that someone is 'barking up the wrong tree'? This particular experience is typical in the way it encapsulates human experience. For it derives from hunting with dogs. The dog chases its prey but fails to identify the tree up which the animal has escaped. The saying is one of many associated with dogs, such as 'I have a bone to pick with you.' There the hostile struggle caused by giving one bone to two dogs to share is in the back of the mind. 'His bark is worse than his bite' is an apt description of someone who is superficially threatening or hostile but is unlikely to harm anyone in practice. When we want to criticize someone for playing a double game and trying to protect his own interests by keeping in with two opposing parties, we say 'He's trying to run with the hare and hunt with the hounds.'

Our stock of such sayings is rich in reference to animals. We advise someone who hesitates to grapple decisively with a problem to 'take the bull by the horns'. We talk about having 'backed the wrong horse' when we have made a costly misjudgement. Indeed horses seem to appear frequently in imagery about the limitations of the human lot. When all our best efforts fail to produce the desired effect on someone, we say 'You can take a horse to water, but you cannot make it drink.' We refer to effort wasted on a failing project that is beyond recovery as 'flogging a dead horse'. On the other hand, when someone is seemingly questioning or hesitant as some real benefit is offered, we tell him 'not to look a gift horse in the mouth'.

To understand the full meaning of that last example, we need to know that the expert judges the age of a horse by examining its teeth. Many of the most used traditional expressions of this kind are self-evident in meaning and indeed self-explanatory. We do not yet need to inquire how the expression 'I take off my hat to him' comes to mean I am full of respect for him. But even this seemingly most obvious expression will perhaps be less easy to understand as headgear disappears and fashions of courtesy change. Other sayings were self-evident in meaning at an earlier stage in history but might need to be explained to the youth of tomorrow. The origin of the expression 'to strike while the iron is hot', for acting at exactly the most propitious moment, was more immediately evident to the villager who passed the blacksmith's shop every day than it is to us now. Even the advice 'You must make hay while the sun shines' presupposes a knowledge of the farming year. But these sayings are not so far removed from our daily life as, for instance, the saying 'He has more than one string to his bow', which derives from the fact that the prudent archer would go into battle with a spare string. And when we talk of 'taking someone down a peg', meaning to dislodge them from their pretentiously assumed superiority, we are using imagery derived from the raising and lowering of flags on ships. There is a naval background too behind the expression 'show a leg', meaning 'bestir yourself'. It derives from the morning call to sailors to jump out of their hammocks.

Not all such sayings can be received as feelingly as they once could. When there is talk of some breadwinner 'bringing home the bacon' or of someone who has narrowly escaped disaster 'saving his bacon' we get the full force of it only by recalling how important once was the bacon preserved in the house for the family's food through the winter. Eating is in the background too in that most useful way of expressing doubt about the literal truth of what someone has said: 'You must take it with a pinch of salt.' The implication is that the thing cannot stand on its own without qualification. The degrees of obviousness in such sayings vary greatly. To 'save one's face', meaning to protect one's reputation, may be obvious enough, as is the expression for a rebuff, 'to shut the door in someone's face', but to 'face the music', meaning to face up to the dire consequences of one's mistakes, is not at all obvious. It has been suggested that the basis of the saying was the fact that an officer in the army who was guilty of some offence had to face the drums when the charges were formally put to him. We have no such explanation for the seemingly illogical saying 'He'll laugh on the other side of his face', meaning 'His rejoicing will be turned to disappointment.'

It will be noticed that many traditional sayings testify to the wisdom acquired through experience. They warn us against rash optimism ('One swallow does not make a summer'), against being deceived by outward appearances ('All that glisters is not gold'), against overvaluing seeming promise ('All her swans are geese'), against wanting too much of life ('She thinks she can have her cake and eat it'), and against thinking we can escape the consequences of our own mistakes ('He has made his bed and he must lie on it'). When we shrug our shoulders over some failed enterprise we quote (or misquote) Robert Burns:

> The best laid schemes [not 'plans'] o' mice an' men
> Gang aft a-gley.

So familiar is the quotation that it is only necessary to mention 'mice and men' together to make the point.

It is because of the homely wisdom and the moral guidance enshrined in such sayings that literary figures (and after-dinner speech-makers) can have fun in turning them upside down. G. K. Chesterton insisted that 'If a thing is worth doing, it's worth doing badly.' And, for one person, sad experience turned the comforting saying 'As one door closes, another opens' into 'As one door closes, another shuts.'

Misuse of Metaphorical Expressions

What concerns us especially here is the proper use of common expressions. Unfortunately, vivid sayings can have their force dissipated by over-use. Moreover, sometimes over-use leads to misuse by people who hear them and fail fully to understand them. Let us consider some such cases.

begging the question

Here is one striking case where a familiar expression is being widely misunderstood. We hear a speaker saying 'That begs the question whether first past the post is a fair electoral system' as though it meant 'That raises the question whether first past the post is a fair electoral system.' But strictly to 'beg the question' in controversy is to assume in argument a conclusion which is in fact at issue in the controversy. From this, by a natural development, derives the accepted practice of using to 'beg the question' to mean to evade the issue. The current habit of treating to 'beg the question' as meaning to 'raise the question' is thus inexcusable.

breathing down the neck

When an athlete is closely pursued in a race so that the nearest rival seems to be challenging most strongly, we say that the challenger is 'breathing down the neck' of the one in front. The expression is useful quite outside the sports field. A candidate in a parliamentary election whose voting figures seem to be threatening his rival's position could be said to be 'breathing down his neck'. Using another metaphor from athletics, the challenger could be said to be close on his rival's heels. It is as well to keep such images clearly sorted in one's mind. On the eve of elections in Northern Ireland we heard a BBC Radio 4 spokesman declare of one candidate 'He's breathing heavily down Mr Trimble's heels.'

the end of the road

Here is a saying which needs to keep its connection with human beings. The image of people 'reaching the end of the road' is a telling one. But what can we make of the following?

> Water gardens are still popular, but I think they have reached the end of the road.

The notion of gardens in progress along a road is absurd. The difference between good writers and bad is that good writers think about what they are saying, word by word, and image by image.

entering a minefield

We find similar liberties taken with the expression 'to enter a minefield'.

> A divorce court faced with assessing the potential pension of a healthy man of 38, and then calculating how much of it his divorcing wife is entitled to, is entering a minefield.

The phrase is used here with a proper sense of its meaning. But one must question whether it is proper to speak of a 'divorce court' as entering a minefield. Surely the phrase is one that should be used only of a person or perhaps a vehicle. The reader will not easily picture the assembled personnel of a court aboard a tank or even a bus. Nevertheless, the above usage is far less unsatisfactory than the following:

> Once you start organizing walking expeditions for other people, you find that your bright idea can turn into a minefield of snarling legislative traps.

Here one is unhappy with the notion of the 'bright idea' turning into a minefield rather than leading one into a minefield. And what is buried in this minefield? Not explosives seemingly, but traps which 'snarl'. Users of motorways know all about the inconvenience of being 'snarled up'. But the threat of being locked into an entanglement simply does not fit with the 'minefield' image of being blown up by hidden explosives.

flash in the pan

The old flintlock had a flashpan to hold the gunpowder. It was hit by a hammer when the trigger of the gun was pulled. The act of firing was a failure if there was a flash in the pan but no other result. Hence the use of this metaphor to describe the promising first display of seeming brilliance by someone who in fact produced nothing afterwards to justify the promise. We read in a piece on flat racing:

> Will they prove to be champions this year? Or just a couple of flashes in a notoriously volatile pan?

Again we see the need to have full understanding of the imagery we use. The word 'volatile' has come to mean changeable. Unless one accepts an insensitive connotation of the word as meaning 'unreliable', it could scarcely be applied to anything so solid as a flashpan.

a running sore

In an article about the possibility of holding referendums on the subject of hunting, we read:

> Anything which did reach the statute book as a result would be a recipe for a 'running sore' with no final resolution.

It may be that the writer thought the quotation marks justified the freedom taken with the image of the running sore. But to speak of a 'recipe' for a sore introduces the smell of the kitchen into the pharmacy, and to suggest by use of the word 'resolution' that a sore should be 'resolved' rather than healed is equally incongruous.

stepping into the breach

The word 'breach', familiar to us in its legal usage ('breach of promise') was used of a gap in fortifications through which a besieging enemy might make an entry. Thus Shakespeare's Henry V calls his men 'Once more unto the breach' outside the walls of Harfleur. The more general use of the phrase now is of taking over from a missing or injured person in an emergency:

> Emma Gibson . . . fell heavily on her feet. The subsequent injury to her knee kept her from riding her impressive heavyweight hunter Shelford Rupert. Fortunately, her friend Sam Fisher, who has not ridden him before, stepped into the breech, and went on to win.

Stepping into the 'breech' is rather a matter of getting dressed than of taking over in an emergency, for 'breech', like the more common form 'breeches', is a word for trousers.

striking a chord

Where a familiar expression has a metaphorical content, it is important not to use it in such a way that incongruous metaphors collide.

> When companies blame the pound they know they are striking a politically sensitive chord on the back of which it is easier to push through measures that would otherwise seem draconian.

To speak of pushing through a measure 'on the back of' some forceful but not necessarily wholly relevant argument is an effective way of making the point desired. But the effect is destroyed, indeed swamped in humour, by the reader's need to picture first the 'striking' of a sensitive 'chord'. The struggle to conceive of something pushed through on the 'back' of this chord dissolves in farce.

thin end of the wedge

It is not a good idea to mutilate colourful idiomatic expressions. A 'wedge' is something solid shaped like a letter 'V', which can easily be inserted into a narrow space at the thin end. We speak of 'the thin end of the wedge' to define something seemingly slight which, if pushed further, will turn into something unwanted or threatening. It is one of those expressions which perfectly fits the case where the only alternative would be a clumsy circumlocution. Such expressions are valuable, and should not be lightly exploited.

> This is the end of the wedge for our town and the problem needs to be stamped on.

Unless the wedge is introduced from the thin end, we may point out, the threat that it represents would decrease rather than increase. We can't have the idiomatic wedge divested of its thin end. Moreover, though subversive movements perhaps need to be 'stamped on', problems do not call for that treatment.

watch like a hawk

One danger is that such established images as this one may float from the mouth so automatically that the demands of grammar, and even of common sense, are ignored. We readily say that some close observer watches like a hawk, but on BBC Radio 4 an eminent public figure declared:

> Prescribing practice should be watched like a hawk.

To speak of being watched like a hawk seems to put the leg into the wrong boot.

the winning hand

Here is another expression which is best kept for reference to human beings. To speak of someone having 'the winning hand' in some testing situation makes a point forcefully. We think of card games. We know that a player may recognize that he has in his hands a selection of cards likely to bring him victory. The image is useful because while the favoured player recognizes his good luck, the other players cannot see what he has in his hand. But we hear this from a speaker explaining why he chose to accept a certain post:

> The attractions of the job had the winning hand.

This is to waste a useful image in a context where half its meaning is lost. It is no more appropriate than to explain one's choice on the menu by saying 'The attractions of the profiterole had the winning hand.'

Some Other Overdone Expressions

We have looked at a handful of established metaphorical expressions which readily come to mind when we are speaking or writing. It is now worth adding a few usages which have no metaphorical content but which are often misapplied.

no exception

An error of misuse which regularly occurs in the press and on the radio is represented by statements ending with the expression 'no exception'. The proper use of these words requires some generalization to be made ('Englishmen like their roast beef on Sundays, and John Smith is no exception'). Too often there is no appropriate generalization to which the expression may be appended.

> Cricket statisticians are oft-times a breed apart and Anandji Dossa is no exception.

Here there is no generalization to which an 'exception' could be made. The statement is that cricket statisticians are 'oft-times' a breed apart. This implies that they are not in all cases a breed apart. Therefore the question of an individual statistician being an 'exception' cannot arise. If the writer had said 'All cricket statisticians are a breed apart' then it would have been reasonable to point out that Dossa was no exception to this generalization. Yet one can find worse misuses of the exception than that one. Here is an advertisement:

> You rely on your horse's ability to respond to your commands. But your horse relies on you too, and your insurance is no exception.

One has to ask 'no exception to what?' The writer seems to assume that a generalization has been propounded on the subject of reliance to which not insuring a horse would be an exception. It is only by a process of imaginative detection that one deduces the existence of this fragile connection in the writer's mind.

in the event that

An increasingly used construction that is generally better avoided is introduced by the expression 'in the event that'. It is a rather clumsy way of avoiding simple constructions.

> In the event of a breakdown or accident in the UK or Europe, help is just a phone call away.

Since firms are not usually shy of using the second person, one wonders why this did not begin 'If you have a breakdown or accident in the UK or Europe'. A similar question arises over this advertisement for an insurance company.

> New Disposal cover to help you with the costs in the event that your horse may lose its life.

In this case the writer is committed to use of the second person, openly referring to 'your' horse. So why not: 'New Disposal cover to help you with your costs, should your horse lose its life'?

least of all

It is odd that this particular expression gets used when its opposite is required.

> Turks and Cypriots will find it difficult to agree about anything on that divided island, least of all about the current anniversary.

What the speaker meant was that the Turks and Cypriots will find it especially difficult to agree about the anniversary. If the opening of the sentence is kept ('Turks and Cypriots will find it difficult to agree') then what follows must be: 'most of all about the current anniversary'. That sounds a little clumsy. The better correction would be: 'Turks and

Cypriots will not readily agree about anything on that divided island, least of all about the current anniversary.'

few and far between

One danger to be avoided is that of falling back on a familiar expression when in fact it merely wastes words.

> The number of vacancies there are is rather few and far between.

That is a comment on the employment situation made on the radio. 'Few and far between' is a telling expression where it is appropriately used, say of habitations in a largely unpopulated area. But here it slips from the speaker's tongue to fill time. In fact 'There are few vacancies' would say all that the speaker said, reducing the number of words from twelve to four, indeed saving two-thirds of them.

in terms of

This expression means 'as represented by' and is properly used in such statements as 'In terms of public influence he counted for nothing.' It is now being used indiscriminately.

> They have no use for civil servants in terms of getting things done.

Here 'in terms of' simply means 'for'.

> In terms of the current controversy I have nothing to add.

Here 'in terms of' simply means 'about'.

CHAPTER 4

The Make-up of the English Vocabulary

THE HISTORICAL BACKGROUND

It is time to pause in our exploration of some of the vagaries of current English usage. For one cannot give close attention to choosing the right words without becoming aware of what a remarkably rich vocabulary English has. In order to understand why that is so, and also in order to understand what kind of variety it is that English has, it is necessary to look briefly at the historical development of the language.

Roman Britain

The Britons inhabiting our country, who faced the first Roman invasions by Julius Caesar in 55 BC and then the actual conquest undertaken by the Emperor Claudius some ten years later, were Celts. The Romanization of the country, of which we still see so many reminders in our roads and in the scattered relics of houses, baths and temples, had its effect on the language spoken here. Many people must have used Latin. Natives who prospered and took advantage of Roman civilization in the form of centrally heated country houses no doubt had to use Latin from time to time. But whereas Latin replaced the Celtic language in Gaul, its use in England seems to have been limited to a small section of the population.

The Romans withdrew, the last troops finally leaving round about AD 410. There followed the invasion of Britain by tribes from Denmark and the Low Countries. These were Teutonic tribes defined by early historians as Jutes, Angles and Saxons. The Anglo-Saxons, as they came to be called, no doubt settled down with the Celts comfortably enough in certain areas. But elsewhere the Celts fiercely resisted the invaders and were gradually driven west to settle in Wales and Cornwall. Roman towns were destroyed and abandoned. A different kind of social order developed. The organization of life in tribes under various leaders gradually produced separate kingdoms, such as Northumbria, Mercia, Essex and Wessex. The relationship between the Anglo-Saxons and the Celts was such that very few words from Celtic were taken over into Anglo-Saxon. (If we want to find Celtic elements in our vocabulary, we must look chiefly to place names.) But, even before the Teutonic invaders came to England, their own languages had already been enriched by words from the language of the conquering Romans. And that enrichment continued after they settled here.

The Old English Period

We speak of the years between about 450 and 1150 as the Old English period and the years between about 1150 and 1500 as the Middle English period. Old English, or Anglo-Saxon, was an inflected language. That is to say, nouns changed their endings according to their grammatical function in a sentence, as they do in German or Latin. In modern English we distinguish between 'The dog bit the man' and 'The man bit the dog' by word order alone. The biter comes before the verb and the bitten comes after. In inflected languages the distinction is made by a change in the form of the noun in question. Modern English retains just enough of the old inflexions in its pronouns for the principle to be easily understood. The differences in meaning between 'I gave her a book' and 'She gave me a book' are registered by the changes from 'I' to 'me' and from 'her' to 'she' as well as by the word order.

Inflexions, it appears, tend to disappear if the educated classes do not watch over them. We can see it happening in our own day as the distinction between 'who' and 'whom' is gradually being lost. Our dialects in particular tend to play fast and loose with inflexions. In Hampshire I once heard three workmen emptying a lorry of sand, and two of them were chaffing the third. 'Oh George, 'e don't get on with the girls. 'E don't like they, and they don't like 'e.' There we see the distinction between 'he' and 'him' being lost and the distinction between 'they' and 'them'.

The Old English period was a period of cultural development. The conversion of the country to Christianity began with the coming of St Augustine in 597. Some scholars claim that by the time Charlemagne called Alcuin from York to run his Palace School in 782, England had become the intellectual centre of Europe. Be that as it may, the crucial event in determining the future character of the English language was the Norman Conquest in 1066. From that point our country had a ruling class who spoke French. Not unnaturally natives found it useful to learn the language of their superiors. English became the language of the less educated and socially inferior people. It is worth recalling that our words for animals who were looked after by peasants, such as 'ox', 'cow', 'sheep', 'pig' and 'hog', are Anglo-Saxon, while when the animals reach the table to be eaten by the better off, the meat is defined in French as 'beef', 'mutton' and 'pork'.

The Middle English Period

It was in the thirteenth century that English reasserted itself. Although French was still much used in the upper classes and in business and administrative circles, its preservation became increasingly a matter of social convention, no longer a natural inheritance of the mother tongue. For English was adopted more and more in general use among all classes. By the beginning of the fourteenth century English was understood by all. And here we must note that the English which had been in the care of the uneducated peasantry since the Norman Conquest had been freed from the pedantic oversight of the educated classes. Consequently it had largely lost its inflexions. The English of Chaucer may look strange to us at first sight, but, by comparison with it, the English of the Anglo-Saxons is a foreign language. To master it we are required to sit down and learn how to inflect (or to 'decline') the nouns, adjectives and pronouns, and how to conjugate the verbs. It is salutary for linguistic scholars and protectors of the purity of our language to recall that it made such progess when it was freed for a century or so from the control of the educated.

If the changes in our grammar consequent on the Norman Conquest were so beneficial, the changes in our vocabulary were equally so. We have seen how the Norman-French occupation left us with two words where we might have had only one in the case of 'cow' and 'beef', 'pig' and 'pork'. This enrichment of vocabulary, sometimes by duplication, sometimes as straight additions, came about in many areas. Words poured in, words to do with government (realm, sovereign, adjourn, alliance), words to do with nobility (duchess, countess, marquis, baron, squire), words to do with the Church (religion, theology, sacrament, communion), words to do with law (assize, plea, plaintiff, defendant). So too did words to do with the army and the navy, with food and fashions and social life, with art, medicine and learning. It is true that many native words were lost, but the new borrowings more than compensated, numerically speaking.

French is one of the European languages directly descending from Latin. When the words which came directly into English from Latin in the various periods of our history are added to the words which came indirectly into English from Latin through French, the double ancestry of modern English becomes evident. A basically Teutonic language which shares much of its vocabulary with German has acquired an immense vocabulary from Latin which it shares with French. Whether we ought to rejoice in Harold's defeat at the Battle of Hastings becomes a question hard to answer. Because of it the English language has become the richest in Europe, a language which can act as a bridge between the Teutonic races and the Latins.

OUR DUAL VOCABULARY

Homeliness and Sophistication

It is not surprising that so often our words from Latin carry a flavour of sophistication which our Anglo-Saxon vocabulary lacks. It is not surprising that our Anglo-Saxon vocabulary has an earthiness and a homeliness that our Latin vocabulary lacks. It is not surprising that when we want to be very friendly we use our Anglo-Saxon vocabulary, and when we want to be formal and dignified we use our Latin vocabulary. 'Can you call at our house next Tuesday' we say to a close friend. But when the formal occasion arises it's 'Mr and Mrs George Smith request the pleasure of your company at the wedding of their daughter Mary to . . .' The words 'request', 'pleasure', 'company' all derive from French and ultimately have Latin roots.

Certainly there is fascination in the dual vocabulary we enjoy. Philologists have contrasted the warm word 'darling' with the less touching word 'favourite', the homely word 'deep' with the dignified word 'profound', the intimate word 'lonely' with the resonant word 'solitary'. Such duplication does not always produce synonyms. Indeed the tendency was for duplicated terms which began as synonyms to drift apart in meaning. That is what happened with 'darling' and 'favourite'. And this drifting apart often produced subtle differentiations of meaning. Even where the meanings remained for dictionary purposes identical, the duplication allowed of subtle distinctions resonating in the overtones of the words. 'Sorrow' is an Anglo-Saxon word, 'misery' a Latin word. They have drifted apart in their emotive baggage. 'Hearty' and 'cordial' give us synonyms which strike the ear with very different resonance. 'We greeted him heartily' rings different mental bells from 'We saluted him cordially.' No one would suggest that there is much difference in meaning between the verb 'begin' and the word 'commence'. Even so we use the two words in different contexts.

It is risky to generalize about this drifting apart of native and parallel Latin words. Where, say, the word 'grasp' is a forceful word in its concrete sense ('He grasped the pole and hurled it in the air') and the parallel Latin words 'comprehend' and 'apprehend' are likely to be associated with getting hold of things with the mind rather than with the body, nevertheless we readily speak of 'grasping' new ideas and we used to refer regularly to the business of 'apprehending' criminals. Usage does not stand still in this respect. We now use the word 'heavy' chiefly in reference to physical weight. We use the word 'weighty' of both physical items and arguments. The Latin equivalent, 'ponderous', tends to be used only in a metaphorical sense of over-solemn personages. Yet I have just read a notice issued by the Midland Railway in 1875:

> This bridge is insufficient to carry weights beyond the ordinary traffic of the district, and the owners and persons in charge of Locomotive Traction Engines and other ponderous carriages are warned against passing over the bridge.

A century or so later that use of the adjective 'ponderous' can only be said to seem too ponderous.

Otto Jesperson pointed out that our native vocabulary seems to have been short of adjectives, with the result that we tend to shift from native nouns to foreign adjectives. He cites the noun 'mouth' and the adjective 'oral', the noun 'nose' and the adjective 'nasal', the noun 'eye' and the adjective 'ocular', the noun 'son' and the adjective 'filial'. The adjectives here have no native equivalents, unless we count the adjective 'nosey' (and what a homely, unsophisticated word that is). In cases where there has been recourse to foreign adjectives despite the existence of parallel native ones, the two words tend to drift apart in meaning. Thus 'timely' is not an exact synonym for 'temporal', and 'earthy', 'earthly' and 'earthen' differ each from each as well as from 'terrestrial'.

What most of us first think of when reference is made to the Latin half of our vocabulary is that mass of words which have at best a sophisticated, at worst an artificial flavour: words like 'speculate', 'cogitate', and 'meditate', which contrast with words like 'think', 'weigh' and 'brood'. We must not oversimplify this issue. 'She was always showing off' says what 'She continually conducted herself ostentatiously' says. But in practice we do not find ourselves asking whether we should use this word or that, 'drive' or 'impel', 'showy' or 'ostentatious'. A kind of instinct for what is appropriate operates.

Choosing the best word is not always a matter of choosing the native Anglo-Saxon word instead of the Latin borrowing. Our minds enter different linguistic worlds according to where we are, whom we are talking to, and what the occasion is. There is a time to say 'I told him to shut up' and a time to say 'I requested him to keep silent.' And however great the overlap between seeming synonyms, ingrained habits prevent us often from treating them as always interchangeable. We may speak interchangeably either of 'burying' someone or of 'interring' them, but we should never exclaim of someone, 'Oh, she's always got her head interred in a book!'

It should go without saying that it is the Latin part of our vocabulary that can trip us up most easily. All those words that end in '-ation', how easy it is to get one wrong. We are amused when someone is shown up picking the wrong one. We laugh aloud when *Private Eye* records how a speaker on the radio said 'The script evolved after three years of gesticulation', when he should have said 'after three years of gestation'. It is not just the slip-up that is funny, but the image produced of radio programme-makers devoting themselves for three years to 'gesticulation'.

Monosyllables and Polysyllables

Very often the difference between the homely and the more sophisticated word can be measured in length. We tend to use shorter words (not always native Anglo-Saxon ones, of course) in the home than in public. When differences or tensions in relationships within the family or between close friends arise and are at issue, words such as 'vex' and 'fret', 'nag' and 'pester', 'badger' and 'taunt' come to our minds. But when the affairs of societies and institutions, political parties and public figures are involved, then words such as 'aggravate' and 'exacerbate', 'irritate' and 'exasperate', 'reproach' and 'discountenance' are more likely to be used. The first six words together contain eight syllables, the other six words together contain twenty syllables.

But the longer word is not always the more artificial and less vivid one. The Anglo-Saxon practice of forming abstract nouns by adding such endings as '-ship' and '-hood' has left us with some sturdy and vivid longer words such as 'friendship', 'fellowship' and 'courtship', 'motherhood', 'sisterhood' and 'brotherhood'. Here again, in the context of the family, there is a discrepancy in emotive power between the words 'fatherly' and 'fatherhood' on the one hand, and the Latinate 'paternal' and 'paternity' on the other, between 'brotherly' and 'brotherhood' on the one hand, and the Latinate 'fraternal' and 'fraternity' on the other.

The number of syllables in the words we use also affects the sturdiness of our utterance. A series of monosyllables can give a strikingly urgent and dramatic flavour to utterance. John Donne begins a celebrated poem with a line of ten monosyllables:

> For God's sake, hold your tongue and let me love!

William Cowper manages two full lines of verse in monosyllabic words and there are sixteen of them:

> Lord, we are few but Thou art near,
> Nor short thine arm nor deaf thine ear.

In Shakespeare the proportion of polysyllables to monosyllables is often quite low. The line 'To be or not to be, that is the question' contains one two-syllable word to nine monosyllables. The lines 'Friends, Romans, Countrymen, lend me your ears / I come to bury Caesar, not to praise him' contain one three-syllable word, three two-syllable words and twelve monosyllables.

Uninhibited use of polysyllabic words does not necessarily produce nervelessness or spinelessness. No writer used our Latinate vocabulary more freely than Dr Johnson, but it is done with such care for exactness of meaning and for rhetorical balance that it pleases the ear at the same time that it stimulates the mind. Here he is defending Shakespeare against the charge that he ignored the old classical unities (of time, place and action) in the construction of his plays.

> He that, without diminution of any other excellence, shall preserve all the unities unbroken, deserves the like applause with the architect, who shall display all the orders of architecture in a citadel, without any deduction from its strength; but the principal beauty of a citadel is to exclude the enemy; and the greatest graces of a play, are to copy nature and instruct life.

To be able to use freely phrases like 'diminution of any other excellence' without sounding pedantic or pretentious indicates Johnson's mastery of the polysyllabic vocabulary. Such is the shaping of the prose that to replace 'without any deduction' by 'without taking away from' would not strengthen the passage. Similarly, to replace 'to exclude the enemy' by 'to keep the enemy out' would upset the balance. Such possible changes would merely introduce an alien aural element and disrupt the flowing rhythm.

There is a place for heavily Latinate diction. Johnsonese might sound incongruously artificial at the breakfast table among the family. It might sound very appropriate in a eulogy on a world figure from the lips of a distinguished diplomat at a state funeral.

FOREIGN WORDS AND PHRASES

French Words: Pronunciation

We have seen that our language has taken in words from Latin and French throughout its history. Yet we find in current English a number of words and phrases from these languages which retain their foreignness. In the case of words from the French accents are preserved in spite of the fact that English has no accents. Moreover, among the educated classes at least, the French pronunciation is preserved, or something like it. When French words were introduced in the past there was often a considerable space of time before the pronunciation got anglicized. We know that when the word 'oblige' came in from French in the sixteenth century, it was pronounced 'obleege', and indeed that pronunciation survived right up to the nineteenth century. In this connection it is interesting that we keep the French pronunciation in our use of the expression 'noblesse oblige' (literally 'nobility obliges'), which we quote, often ironically, in reference to the honourable and generous conduct which is expected of the aristocracy.

Anglicization, in respect of French accents, is happening all the time, if very slowly. Where 'rôle', which came in in the seventeenth century, has lost its accent during the last few decades, 'cliché', which came in last century, still keeps its accent. The word 'cortège' we sometimes see nowadays without its accent. Yet 'tête-à-tête' (a confidential conversation, literally 'head to head'), which came in during the seventeenth century, keeps its accents. The word 'café', a nineteenth-century importation, has preserved its accent and its pronunciation hitherto.

Haute Cuisine and Haute Couture

'Café' is just one among many French words from the world of eating and drinking which have now established themselves in regular English usage. We use the French terms 'gourmet', 'gourmande' and 'bon viveur', for those who relish the delights of the table. No doubt the French preeminence in the world of what we call 'haute cuisine' ('high-class cookery') is responsible for this influence of the French language. At the restaurant we study the 'à la carte' ('according to the list') menu, from which we are free to select as we choose, and the 'table d'hôte' (literally 'the host's table') menu which contains a series of courses planned by the establishment at a quoted price. The first course may be called the 'hors d'œuvre' ('outside the work') and is supposed to consist of preparatory appetizers. If the word 'starters' seems now to be replacing 'hors d'œuvre', other French expressions at the table seem to hold their own. There are dishes such as 'pâté de foie gras' ('pâté of fat liver'), and a beefsteak cut from between the ribs is called 'entrecôte'. Our sweet dishes include a 'soufflé'. They also include a 'sorbet' and, accustomed as we are to adapting our pronunciation to suit the French, we give the word the French treatment, though in fact it comes from Turkish and is really the same word as 'sherbert'. There is a dessert called 'crème caramel', and a liqueur called 'crème de menthe' ('cream of mint').

We may add that the expression 'crème de la crème' ('cream of the cream') takes us right out of the restaurant. It stands for the very best of the best. Our inherited respect for the French as social superiors and arbiters of taste applies beyond the dining-room. Just as we speak of 'haute cuisine' so also we use the expression 'haute couture' for high-class dressmaking, another sphere of French preeminence. We used to call high society the 'haut monde' ('the high world') and the world of fashion the 'beau monde' ('the beautiful world'). We still preserve the French pronunciation of 'boudoir', 'massage' and 'coiffure'. In the wider world it is significant that when we wish to characterize an act of patronization and condescension we call it acting 'de haut en bas' ('from high to low'). The French language therefore, having the cachet or prestige of the upper class, comes in useful for veiling unmentionable items and practices in delicate terminology. When women want new underwear, they seek it in the 'lingerie' department. Their undress is their 'negligée' or their 'déshabillé'. We describe a woman's low-cut garment that exposes the bosom as 'décolleté'. When a married couple (or a pair of sexual partners) choose to live in cohabitation with a third person, the additional sexual partner of one of them, we call it a 'ménage à trois'. A comparable delicacy no doubt stands behind the now established practice of referring to hotel rooms that are fully equipped with washing and toilet facilities as 'en suite' (literally 'in sequence').

Social Niceties

Our vocabulary for the intimate and the personal is rich in French terms. We use the expression 'en famille' for someone who is at home with his family. Another French expression, 'entre nous' ('between you and me'), serves us in the sphere of confidential intimacy. We even tend to preserve the masculine and feminine spellings of 'confidant' and 'confidante' for a very special friend who can be let into all our secrets. A delicate way of speaking of a communication which amounts to a love letter is to call it a 'billet doux' (literally a 'sweet note'). Delicacy of a different kind encourages us to speak of a 'faux pas' (literally a 'false step') when someone puts their foot in it, as we say, and we call a social blunder a 'gaffe'.

Somehow in the realm of social proprieties and social indiscretions recourse to French is habitual. We hear people use the expression 'comme il faut' ('as it should be') as a delicate way of pronouncing some practice thoroughly acceptable in the best circles. We speak of damage to a person's self-respect and personal sense of propriety as something which wounds their 'amour-propre' ('self-love'). The French expression 'lèse majesté' (meaning 'wounded majesty') is used for suffering presumptuous behaviour from inferiors against their 'betters'. We describe someone who is unconventional in behaviour and commits indiscretions as an 'enfant terrible' ('terrible child'). A 'contretemps' (literally something 'against the time') is an inopportune action or an awkward situation. A 'jeu d'esprit' ('playful act of the spirit') is a light-hearted pleasantry or a display of playful cleverness. The expression is used in apologetic excuse for a prank that may have misfired. A subtle use of the word 'frisson' has established itself: it comes into play in not very earnest conversation to define a shiver of delight that is too refined and evanescent to justify the use of the cruder English word 'thrill'.

It would be difficult to account on any other grounds than those of social one-upmanship for the use of 'en passant' as an alternative to 'by the way' or 'incidentally', though in fact the usage has its origin in the technicalities of moves in the game of chess. It is also difficult to account for the survival of 'nom de plume' when the English equivalent ('pen-name') matches it perfectly, and of the word 'soubriquet' for the English 'nickname'. The same may be said of 'carte blanche' ('blank paper'): to give someone a 'free hand' or a 'blank cheque' is the English equivalent. But we can perhaps understand why there are still those who fall back (often with a shrug of the shoulders) on French expressions such as 'faute de mieux' ('for want of something better'), 'tant mieux' ('so much the better') and 'tant pis' ('so much the worse'), where the French seems slightly less clumsy than the English. We find the French 'bête noire' ('black beast') a useful way of referring to what we regard as a pet aversion. The foreignness allows one to distance oneself from the expression of personal distaste.

The French verb 'savoir' ('to know') has given us the general expression 'savoir-faire' (literally 'to know how to do') for knowingness and tact. The colloquial word 'savvy' ('He's got plenty of savvy') for shrewdness and acuteness has the same derivation. So too has the phrase 'je ne sais quoi' ('I don't know what'), which has a touch of subtlety in its connotation. When we say of a work of art or a newly furnished room 'It has a je ne sais quoi', we generally imply that it has a touch of something indefinably special. By contrast, the common English versions of the 'don't-know-what' brand are half-humorous deprecatory expressions like 'thingumabob' and 'thingumajig'. They certainly seem to belong on a different social level.

The Public Scene

In the military world the words 'aide de camp' are still used for an officer serving as a personal assistant to a senior officer. One of the dominant motivating principles behind acts of obedient self-sacrifice or heroism is the 'esprit de corps', pride in the company to which one belongs and fidelity to it. In the world of espionage and undercover work by the police we use the term 'agent provocateur' for a secret agent who is used, by disguise and deception, to provoke a suspected spy to reveal himself or a suspected criminal to commit an illegal act which confirms his guilt.

The words 'coup d'état' ('stroke of state') have long been the accepted expression for a sudden seizure of power which overturns an existing government, while a 'coup de grâce' ('blow of mercy') is the mortal blow that mercifully puts an end to the recipient's suffering. A 'laissez faire' policy is a 'let-them-get-on-with-it' policy of not interfering in other people's affairs, and therefore used of government policies that allow unrestricted freedom to commerce and industry. In the historical field we still refer to the end of the nineteenth century as the 'fin de siècle' ('end of the age'), thereby denoting a period of artistic decadence. And, suprisingly enough perhaps, we have never found an English alternative to the expression 'avant-garde' ('the vanguard') for the group of artists, composers, poets or figures in any cultural field whose work represents the latest thing in experiment and innovation. The 'pièce de résistance' is the most important and outstanding item, the one which brings a performance to a climax. We use the expression 'cause célèbre' ('celebrated case') to highlight the importance of a trial or controversy. We say someone is 'hors de combat' ('out of the fight') when they have retired from some struggle or are so placed that it is of no consequence to them. A 'trompe l'œil' ('deception of the eye') is a work of art or an artifact so realistic as to give an illusion of actuality. A 'double entendre' is a form of words which can be interpreted in two different ways, the one of them innocent, the other indecent.

Of longer French expressions, which we use because they so neatly sum up an attitude, the words 'receuiller pour mieux sauter', meaning to take a backward step in order to jump forward better, concisely hit off an attitude for which no equally brief phrase exists in English. Similarly there is a euphony about Voltaire's words 'pour encourager les autres' ('in order to encourage others'), which ensures its survival. The sentence

'Plus ça change, plus c'est la même chose' is an expressive way of saying 'The more things change, the more they remain the same.' The phrase 'Chacun à son gout' means no more than 'everyone to his taste' but is still used. People say 'Cherchez la femme' ('Look for the woman'), often not very seriously, when urging that attention be given to the possibility of a sex element or motive behind some mystery.

Latin Abbreviations

We constantly use a number of abbreviations derived from Latin. A writer may insert the word 'sic' in parenthesis. Literally it means 'thus', but we use it to draw attention to something remarkable in what has just been said, more especially perhaps when quoting another source. It may draw attention to what is anomalous or dubious in the writer's eyes. On the other hand it may draw attention to something that confirms what the writer is saying. The abbreviation 'i.e.', standing for the Latin 'id est', means 'that is to say', and is useful when clarifying a point already made by words which amount to the same thing. The abbreviation 'e.g.', standing for 'exempli gratia' ('for example's sake') and meaning 'for example', is useful when providing an illustration which exemplifies and corroborates the point made. These two abbreviations are so established that people will use them in conversation ('Did he have anything more to say - e.g. about where he was on the night in question?'). Other Latin abbreviations include 'NB' ('nota bene'), meaning 'note well', drawing special attention to what follows. Certain abbreviations have been preserved in the religious field. There are the letters 'DV' ('Deo volente'), meaning 'God willing', once much used by Christian bodies advertising future events and anxious to draw public attention to the fact that all that may be planned from day to day could take place only with divine permission. Another abbreviation much used by the Church is 'RIP' ('requiescat in pace') meaning 'rest in peace'. The same Latin noun is used in the traditional greeting 'pax vobiscum', meaning 'peace be with you'. The letters 'IHS', originally of Greek derivation, were used from the fifteenth century to stand for 'Jesus Hominum Salvator' ('Jesus, the Saviour of Men').

Some Latin words have become so firmly established that one questions whether they ought still to be distinguished as not English. The Latin word 'passim', meaning 'in many or various places', is a convenient device used especially by academic writers, when the writer wishes to indicate that a given individual or topic is referred to, not once or twice, but at many points throughout the book. I have seen this word confused in print with the Latin word 'pace', which means 'by leave of'. When a writer wishes to make a polite nod towards some known authority with whom he is disagreeing, he may insert the parenthesis, '*pace* Dr Johnson', which conveys the message, 'in spite of what Dr Johnson says to the contrary' or 'if Dr Johnson will kindly allow me to dispute his judgement'. Clearly these two expressions economize in words wonderfully.

Latin Expressions

The expression 'tabula rasa' is still in use (literally 'a clean slate' on which nothing has yet been written), though in fact the English expression a 'clean sheet' (unused writing paper) means neither more nor less. There are more useful Latinisms than that, many of a more technical kind. The Latin word 'quasi' means 'just as if' or 'just as though'. In English we have converted it into a prefix, so that a 'quasi-philosophical statement' would be a statement which passes itself off as philosophical without actually being so. One might, for instance, describe scientology as a 'quasi-religious' cult. The nearest simple English equivalent would be a 'seemingly religious' cult. The Latin expression 'a priori', meaning literally 'from the previous' is used adjectivally of a proposition that is being assumed from the beginning of an argument rather than deduced in the course of the argument. This expression came into use in England in the eighteenth century and is so well settled that the noun 'apriority' has been derived from it. Another expression used in arguing a case is 'ipso facto' (literally 'by that very fact'), which is said to introduce a point inexorably following from a point just made. The alternative form of this connecting link is 'eo facto' ('by that fact'), a slightly less forceful version. The expression 'sui generis' means 'of its own kind' and therefore sometimes 'peculiar' or even more loosely, 'unique'. It is not considered over-pedantic to use the expression 'sine qua non' (literally 'without which nothing') for an indispensable condition. The words 'status quo' are used for the existing state of affairs ('The agitators had no thought of rebellion, being anxious to preserve the status quo'). A 'quid pro quo' (literally 'something for something') is something given in exchange for some object or some advantage received ('His knighthood was a quid pro quo for his services to the party'). An interesting Latinism is preserved in the words 'pro rata' (an abbreviation of 'pro rata parte', literally 'according to what has been fixed in calculation') which means 'in proportion'. Universities award honorary degrees 'honoris causa' (literally 'for the sake of honour') in recognition of meritorious achievements.

Latinisms more likely to be used in a personal conversational context include 'mea culpa' ('my fault'), which constitutes an apology, and 'infra dig', an abbreviation of the Latin 'infra dignitatem', meaning 'beneath one's dignity' and applied to any suggestion for conduct which self-respect would not condone. And people used to be conversationally free and easy with the words 'non compos mentis' ('not master of one's mind') applied to mentally defective people. 'Inter alia' is sometimes used in place of the English 'among other matters', and likewise 'ceteris paribus' for the English 'other things being equal'. More difficult to spare would be the expression 'mutatis mutandis', a most economic way of saying something for which several words are needed in English. It is the equivalent of 'once the necessary changes have been made'.

Legal Latin

There are Latinisms much used in legal affairs which have also been taken into general usage. The expression 'de jure', which means 'according to law', is usefully balanced by the expression 'de facto', meaning 'in actual fact'. Thus a man convicted of a 'mercy killing' might be described as a 'de jure' murderer but 'de facto' innocent. The expression 'prima facie', meaning 'at first sight', is used of assumptions made before full trial of a case. Thus a 'prima facie' case must be made by police and prosecuting counsel before a person charged with a crime can be sent before an assize court. The expression 'sub judice', literally meaning 'before a judge', is applied to matters still under judicial consideration. The fact that they have yet to be officially pronounced upon limits the right of general public comment. 'Ultra vires' (literally 'beyond strength') defines something which is legally outside the power of a person or an institution to affect or control. The word 'ultra' is used also in the expression 'nec et non plus ultra', roughly the equivalent of 'so far and no further'. 'Obiter dictum' (literally 'something said on the way, while travelling') was originally an expression of opinion given by a judge which was not essential to the judgment he was making, and therefore not binding or authoritative. Hence the words 'obiter dictum' or the plural 'obiter dicta' are used of some person's incidental remark or remarks. The words 'rigor mortis' ('rigidity of death') are in common use for the state of a corpse after stiffness has set in.

Longer Latin Expressions

There are longer expressions, some of them quotations from great writers, which have been so much used that it may be necessary only to quote the first words of the saying for the rest to be understood. The words 'quot homines' will be understood to stand for 'quot homines, tot sententiae', literally 'how many men there are, so many opinions there are'. The English language does not have matching resources to make such complex comparisons so briefly. The words 'sic transit gloria mundi', meaning 'thus the glory of the world passes away', will be understood if the speaker merely says 'sic transit'. Similarly the words 'de mortuis nil nisi bonum', meaning 'only good things should be said of the dead', will be understood if only the words 'de mortuis' are said. The Latin poet Horace's famous line 'Dulce et decorum est pro patria mori', meaning 'How beautiful and honourable it is to die for one's country', comes into the same category. Wilfred Owen called one of his war poems 'Dulce et Decorum est', and in fact it is perhaps his most horrifying picture of men at the front. It includes a grim account of a soldier choking from a gas attack, whom his fellows fling on to a wagon, watching his 'white eyes writhing' in his hanging face. It was from Horace too that we gained the expression 'laudator temporis acti' ('praiser of days gone by'), used to describe someone who repeatedly compares the present unfavourably with an idealized past. Juvenal's line 'Orandus est ut sit mens sana in corpore sano', meaning 'One should pray to have a sound mind in a sound body' has left us an expression 'mens sana in corpore sano', a healthy mind in a healthy body, which has been cited as an educational ideal.

In many of the instances listed above the foreign expression has advantages of clarity and brevity as well as a peculiar neatness and forcefulness. If we take these advantages into account, we should certainly not think of condemning the introduction of foreign phrases into English prose. But over-use of such expressions, or use of them in inappropriate contexts, smacks of artifice and pedantry. There is always the risk that the writer or speaker who readily makes use of them will appear to be showing off.

ARCHAISMS

The vocabulary of a language changes over the centuries. We have seen how English has acquired new words throughout the ages. It has also of course lost words. And sometimes words are half-lost, or nearly lost. They disappear from popular general use, but turn up from time to time either in special circles with strong traditionalist leanings, or in the utterance of knowledgeable people who find them useful and, perhaps, irreplaceable. Where words stand for things once part of the environment but which have now disappeared from daily life, it is natural that they should get lost. We come across such words, say in reading Shakespeare, and when we discover that they refer to items of dress or armour long since discarded, we find the loss quite understandable. But words are also lost, not because the things they stood for have gone from the modern scene, but because they have been replaced by other words. We read Hamlet's question, 'Woo't drink up eisel?' and learn from the glossary that 'eisel' is vinegar, so the question is 'Would you drink up vinegar?' However, quite apart from nouns, which may stand for things no longer used, or for things for which we now have other names, there are words which we class as 'archaisms' for another reason. They have ceased to be used altogether, or ceased to be used much in general parlance. They sound quaint. Such is the adverb 'eke', meaning 'also' or 'moreover'. As 'eek' it was a favourite word of Chaucer. He tells how the monk's bridle would jingle in the wind 'And eek as loude as dooth the chapel belle.' It is to be distinguished from the verb which we use in saying that someone 'eked out' a living on a poor croft. It is a useful word to cite as an instance because in James Joyce's *Portrait of the Artist as a Young Man* we meet a close friend of the hero Stephen, one Cranly, whose habit of using the word 'eke' adds comically to his ironic pose of scholarly solemnity.

There are words which have not entirely disappeared from current usage yet which carry an archaic flavour. This archaic flavour is not strong enough to prevent our use of the words, but it is strong enough for us to hesitate before using them for fear of sounding affected and pretentious. Thus we may hesitate before using 'albeit' instead of 'although'.

We should think twice before using the verb 'abide'. Similarly we may hesitate before using the impersonal word 'behove'. Perhaps that is a pity. 'It behoves me to give you a grave warning' lays emphasis on the duty and responsibility of the speaker, depersonalizing the rebuke. The comparable impersonal verb 'befit' remains in use, but is subtly different from 'behove'. What is 'befitting' is appropriate. What is 'behoveful' is needed, called for. Like 'befit', the word 'beholden' remains in use while carrying a faintly archaic air. 'I am greatly beholden to you' means 'I am greatly obliged, or indebted, to you.'

A few archaisms survive in common usage because they are found in memorable quotations. We still hear the expression 'hoist with his own petard', deriving from Shakespeare. Hamlet speaks of the irony of seeing an 'enginer Hoist with his own petar', that is struck by his own machine which is meant to blow a hole in a wall with gunpowder. This quotation has only recently been rendered disposable by the equally useful phrase about 'scoring an own goal'. Another interesting survival is the use of the word 'cudgel' when we say 'I must cudgel my brains', meaning struggle to remember. A cudgel was a stick that could be used for beating people. The noun has gone but the verb lingers on in this one expression.

There is possible cause for regret over the loss of a word from general parlance only where it is not replaceable. Here we may cite the gradual disappearance of the words 'whence' and 'whither'. 'Whence' is the equivalent of 'from where' and 'whither' is the equivalent of 'to where'. We have replaced 'Whence have you come?' by 'Where have you come from?' (the change adding a word). We have replaced 'Whither are you going?' firstly by 'Where are you going to?' and then by 'Where are you going?'

The word 'where' was once used in various compounds which have mostly ceased to be used. They include 'whereat', 'whereby', 'wherefore', 'wherefrom', 'whereof', 'whereto' and 'wherewithal'. We still use the words 'whereas', 'whereupon' and 'whereabouts'. We use the word 'wherewithal' in a semi-ironic tone of voice when we are short of cash ('I haven't got the wherewithal'). But otherwise it is chiefly in legal documents that the words survive. The usefulness of some of these words is made evident by the way lawyers fall back on them when seeking the maximum clarity of definition. It is also made evident when we ask ourselves what has replaced them. 'The means whereby I live' has to become 'The means by which I live.'

What applies to the word 'where' also applies, in different degrees, to the words 'there' and 'here'. We still say 'therefore' and sometimes 'thereby', but for 'therewith' and 'thereunder' we must turn to legal and other official documents. Such documents still depend on compounds of 'here', such as 'hereafter', 'hereat', 'hereby', 'herein', 'hereon', 'hereto', 'hereunder', 'hereunto', and 'herewith'. We continue to use 'hereabouts' as well as 'whereabouts' in conversation. The intensified forms, 'wheresoever' and 'whensoever', like the forms 'whosoever' and 'whomsoever', are words which we associate now with lawyers and with past poets. When we read the poet Robert Herrick's famous lines,

> Whenas in silks my Julia goes,
> Then, then (me thinks) how sweetly flows
> The liquefaction of her clothes

we mentally accept 'whenas' and 'me thinks' as archaic poetic diction.

If we have any doubt about the value of the kind of compound here represented, we have only to study the prose of the King James Bible. When we read the words of Saint Paul in the King James Bible, 'Howbeit, whereinsoever any is bold, I am bold also', and we ask ourselves what we should now substitute for the word 'whereinsoever', we realize what a convenient word it was, and how many words it would take to replace it. For 'whereinsoever any is bold' really amounts to 'in whatever respects anyone is bold' or 'in whatever circumstances anyone is bold'. Checking up on two more recent versions, I find the words 'whereinsoever any is bold' multiplied to 'whatever anyone dares to boast of' and 'in whatever particular they enjoy such confidence'. It is perhaps a pity that we cannot rescue words so useful, but we must face facts. The discerning writer may be able to use an archaism from time to time, but clearly it is desirable to exercise restraint in that respect. People may get away with a lavish use of archaisms in the world of ceremonial officialdom. Anywhere else it will seem comic.

AMERICANISMS

That usages should have come into English from America is no more surprising than that they have come into England from France. Where words and expressions are equally well established in both the US and the UK, no problem arises. In the UK we now all say 'OK' as naturally as the Americans. We speak about 'barking up the wrong tree' or 'burying the hatchet' without picturing an American scene. The relationship between British English and American English becomes significant only when two usages do not match. We feel uncomfortable when the American says 'gotten' where we would say 'got', but the American turns out to be using a now disused English form. There was dispute among nineteenth-century English scholars about what Shakespeare meant when, in the fencing scene between Hamlet and Laertes in *Hamlet*, the Queen says of Hamlet that he is 'fat and scant of breath'. A fat Hamlet was not what readers wanted. One scholar suggested that perhaps Richard Burbage had put on weight by the time he came to play the part. The matter was cleared up only when an English scholar, walking in rural New England, was told by a farmer's wife from whom he sought a drink that he looked 'fat'. 'Sweaty' was what she meant. The seemingly provincial usage had survived among the descendants of immigrants from Warwickshire.

Thus American usage may be as historically valid as British usage where the two differ. Moreover, the American usage may be the more vivid. The Americans say 'sidewalk' where we use the Latin word 'pavement'. Resistance to American importations has often been both ignorant and irrational. There was a time when the American fondness for saying 'I guess' was ridiculed, yet Chaucer was fond of the interjection. As for American pronunciation, the American vowel sound in words such as 'path', 'bath', and 'father' is said to be closer to Elizabethan pronunciation than current English pronunciations are. I have heard intelligent people reacting in mock horror to American use of the verb to 'enjoy'. The American waitress puts down the dish on the table and says 'Enjoy!' For us the verb to 'enjoy' is a transitive verb that requires an object. We do not say 'I enjoyed' but 'I enjoyed myself'. And my latest dictionary allows of no intransitive use. But it would be a mistake to criticize the American usage as 'incorrect', for the OED cites an archaic intransitive use of the verb, meaning 'to be in a joyous state, to rejoice' from the year 1549.

All one can say of current divergences between British and American English is that they are interesting rather than culturally significant. We are amused when an American air pilot announces that 'We shall be landing at Heathrow momentarily', for to us it suggests a stay too brief to allow of safe escape from the plane. Just as the Americans use 'momentarily' to mean 'in a few moments' time', so they use 'presently' to mean 'at present' ('I'm sorry, I'm afraid the manager is presently away from the office'), where we use it to mean 'very soon'.

Sometimes new specialized usages can misfire in the US as in the UK. Failure of sensitivity to accepted meanings can be unfortunate. A recent development in US medical circles involves the word 'emergent'. Because acutely sick patients are picked up from their homes or from the street by the Emergency Services, and because they then go into hospital through the Emergency Room, the habit has arisen of calling such patients 'emergent' patients. Here is a case where innovation has failed to recognize what the word 'emergent' means and must continue to mean, that is, coming into being or making an entry. Clearly the only patient in a hospital who might justifiably be called 'emergent' would be a new-born baby. It is obvious that not all American innovations are to be encouraged. I am told by a correspondent that in programmes for the Chicago Symphony Orchestra concerts the conductor Sir George Solti used to be said to be 'concertizing' abroad.

When, during a stay in the US, my wife went into a shop and asked for a 'reel of cotton', the shopkeeper showed his amusement by asking 'Are you going fishing?' She then learned that she should have asked for a 'spool of yarn'. When she was involved in conversation with our hosts on the subject of the kitchen equipment in the apartment provided for us, she happened to use the word 'toast-rack'. The word was unknown to our hosts. Friends asked to explain it tended to make conjectures in terms of mediaeval torture. Such differences merely testify to slightly different domestic habits in our respective countries. Try to locate an 'electric fire' in any American shop and you will almost certainly fail.

In some cases, where words differ, the American word is gradually driving out the English word. That is happening as 'diaper' replaces 'nappy', as 'truck' replaces 'lorry', as 'rare' (for a beefsteak) replaces 'underdone' and 'freight train' begins to replace 'goods train'. But plenty of interesting contrasting pairs of words remain. There is 'biscuit' and 'cookie', 'boot' (of a car) and 'trunk', 'windscreen' and 'windshield', 'petrol' and 'gas', a 'wage rise' and a 'wage raise', and 'sweets' and 'candies'.

PART 2

Arranging Words Correctly

CHAPTER 5

The Use of Verbs

The key to meaningful utterance is the verb. The verb transforms the indeterminate utterance 'the plumber' into the meaningful utterance 'Call the plumber.' You can utter nouns or pronouns by the dozen without making sense. 'Potatoes, peas, cabbage, carrots.' The nouns make meaningful utterance only if a verb is added or is understood. 'Please supply me with . . .' In earlier chapters we were concerned with the choice of words. Our subject was primarily the meaning of individual words. Here, however, we are more concerned with the way in which words can properly be arranged. And since the verb is a key element in the structure of utterance, good writing is impossible without correct use of verbs. Where we go wrong in the use of verbs is something we cannot afford to ignore. If we examine current error carefully, we shall find that a few false uses of the verb corrupt current usage widely. It is our task to examine these bad habits and show how they can be avoided.

USE OF SINGULAR AND PLURAL

We say 'The bird sings sweetly' and 'The birds sing sweetly' and we do not think of the choice between the singular 'sings' and the plural 'sing' as a grammatical danger zone. Yet we may feel less confident in choosing between 'The choir is singing two madrigals' and 'The choir are singing two madrigals.'

Collective Nouns

We have raised the question of the collective noun, the noun which, like the word 'choir', refers to a group or body of objects or people. Strictly speaking, it should in most cases take a singular verb, but one finds the rule broken wherever one turns.

> Our range of tiles have many different themes to choose from.
>
> Behind the small village are a range of mountains.
>
> A range of unique water-mixable mediums have been developed.

That is but a handful of examples from the world of magazines and devoted to the one collective noun 'range' alone. In each case the verb should be singular: 'Our range of tiles has many different themes'; 'Behind the village is a range of mountains'; 'A range of mediums has been developed.'

What applies to the word 'range' applies to other collective nouns. Yet it is easy to find specimens of error. Note the bracketed corrections in the following sentences.

> An impressive array of their paintings hang [hangs] on the walls.
>
> A selection of bars, tavernas and shops are [is] within easy walking distance.
>
> A rash of television designers have [has] erupted . . .
>
> The entire fleet of Mendip Rail-operated GB Class 59s were [was] on site.
>
> Her exhibition featured a mixture of hats; a combination of transparent, woven, flexible and solid fabric structures were [was] used.

One finds the same mistake being made with a variety of words like 'combination' that gather items together. But usage sometimes presents us with problems in this respect. The following is a piece about cabinet meetings.

> In the early 1970s, there were still an average of 60 meetings a year.

Technically the singular verb 'was' would seem to be required here to go with the singular word 'average', but it would be a rash pedant who would insist on that. The safest correction would be: 'there were still, on average, 60 meetings a year'. The same applies to the following sentence:

An average of 3.3 starlings were seen in each garden.

To 'correct' this by making the verb singular ('An average . . . was seen') would not do because it was not the average that was seen but the starlings. Far better would be to change the subject of the sentence and write: 'On average 3.3 starlings were seen in each garden.'

An interesting variation occurs naturally in the use of the word 'number'. In 'There was any number of reasons for them to perform below their best' the singular verb 'was' is correct, for the issue is a list of reasons. But no one would wish to press for 'was' instead of 'were' in the sentence 'A number of people were shouting outside and clamouring for admittance', where it is the behaviour of several individuals that is being described. Similarly, while it is correct to say 'The audience was small', it is also correct to say 'The audience were screaming and waving their hands.' In the former case 'the audience' is the whole body. In the latter case 'the audience' is the gathered individuals. (To say 'The audience were small' would convey that the people were of diminutive stature.)

This freedom in mixing singular and plural is accepted in such sentences as 'This group are all paid-up members of the society', where, in spite of the singular pronoun and noun – 'this group' – the plural verb is required by what follows.

The Institutional Collective

The same distinction is regularly made in speaking of collective bodies such as the 'government' or the 'council'. Speaking of a collective decision, we say 'The government has decided to push the act through', but thinking of the body as a collection of individuals, we say 'The government are deeply divided on this issue.' Thus the following sentences need correction as indicated.

The authority plan [plans] a low-key promotion of the route.

Since then the museum have [has] funded two lots of restoration work.

The National Trust have [has] one other complete example, *Reliance*, which has been authentically restored.

The institutional collective, as used of football teams and the like, tends to take a plural verb. I hear of a match 'where Aston Villa meet Tranmere

Rovers' and I doubt whether one would often be likely to hear the equivalent of 'where Aston Villa meets Tranmere Rovers'. A rather different liberty is taken when the commentator makes this judgement:

> Seven defeats out of ten on Scottish soil tells its own story.

To make a pedantic correction here ('Seven defeats out of ten tell their own story') would be nit-picking. When a given series of events ('Seven defeats out of ten') is thus summed up as a single significant fact, the case for using the singular verb is strong. And when, moreover, the verb in question is part of a single well-worn expression ('it tells its own story'), the case is strengthened.

Attracting the Wrong Verb

Sometimes a mistake is made when the noun in question can in no sense be called 'collective'.

> Detailed analysis of the cost of rehabilitation and the potential revenue were given.

What happens here is that the writer forgets that the subject of the sentence is the singular word 'analysis' because the word has been followed by the plurality of items, 'cost of rehabilitation' and 'potential revenue'. But the subject 'analysis' is what must govern the verb: 'Detailed analysis of the cost and the revenue was given.' This blunder all too often appears in print.

> It is the abiding interest in the countryside, its landscape and wild-life, its traditions, customs and crafts, that result in constant reinterpretation . . .

By the time the six items have been listed, 'countryside, its landscape and wildlife, its traditions, customs and crafts', the writer has completely forgotten that the subject of the sentence was the word 'interest', and that it must be followed by the verb 'results'.

We may define the process that leads to this error as 'attraction' in that the nearness of the listed nouns 'attracts' a plural verb. The fatal attraction can lure journalists in the most respectable broadsheets.

> The area of interests which can be labelled 'women only' have shrivelled dramatically.

The word 'interests' exercises the fatal attraction so that the journalist writes 'The area . . . have shrunk' instead of 'has shrunk'. And just as the plural noun 'interests' lures the writer astray there, so the singular noun 'subject' lures the writer astray below.

> The tensions among naval intelligence staff inside the building known as the Citadel was the subject of a recent report.

Surely the tensions 'were' the subject of a report. Here the writer might urge that he strays where the great have strayed in that the King James Bible includes the much quoted sentence 'The wages of sin is death.'

Perhaps the attraction towards the incorrectly singular verb is at its most subtle when the verb is made to precede the subject.

> On the evidence available there does not appear to be any legal grounds for intervention.

In saying 'there does not appear', the writer fails to anticipate that what is to come is a plural noun, 'grounds'. It may seem less natural to say 'there do not appear', but that is what is needed to introduce 'any grounds'. And it is presumably out of a desire not to sound too stilted that a journalist writes:

> Also in the redheads' hall of fame is singer Belinda Carlisle and actresses Shirley Maclaine and Julia Roberts.

Over-formal as it may sound to begin 'Also in the redheads' hall of fame are . . .', that is the correct wording.

Plural Terms in Singular Units

Where the subject of a verb contains a plural noun but nevertheless represents a singular entity as a whole, the grammatical rule accords with common sense. The most obvious instance is in the case of titles. We say '*The Two Gentlemen of Verona* is one of Shakespeare's early plays.' It would be absurd to say '*The Two Gentlemen of Verona* are one of Shakespeare's early plays', making the verb plural because 'Two Gentlemen' are included in the subject that governs it. But that represents the matter very starkly. Consider the following sentence about some ancient standing stones in Cumbria.

> To the west along the valley is Long Meg and her daughters, memorial to an even more ancient presence.

Why is the singular verb 'is' correct here? Because 'Long Meg and her daughters' is the official name of the group of stones, and it is the location of that group that is being described. In a superficially similar sentence about real people the plural verb would be required ('To the west, down the road, live my friend Mrs Bean and her daughters'). We extend this freedom to have singular verbs to certain very familiarly partnered nouns. 'Bread and butter is good for you', we say, and even 'Bacon and eggs is my favourite meal.' Rhetorical tradition permits extension of this freedom to closely related pairs of nouns, as in Kipling's *Recessional* ('The tumult and the shouting dies').

The Universal Singular

The universal singular is the construction used in such statements as 'The fox is a pest', where the formally singular noun stands for the species as a whole. The usage is familiar in daily talk. 'The mini-skirt is back in fashion' we say, referring to thousands and thousands of such garments. There is a danger that quick movements from use of the universal singular to use of the normal plural will upset the grammar.

> One of the good things about a television series is the interest they generate.

Obviously this shift from 'a television series' to the words 'they generate' will not do. One must stick with the universal singular: 'One of the good things about a television series is the interest it can generate.' It may be that this particular sentence goes astray because there is no recognizable plural form of 'series', but the error is found where that problem does not arise.

> The sleeve section is also made from EXEAT and they are wool-mix lined for extra warmth.

It is easy to slip thus from the universal singular 'section' to 'they' when the garments in general are being held in mind. The safest correction here would be to stick to the plural: 'The sleeve sections are also made from EXEAT and they are wool-mix lined for extra warmth.' Perhaps the slippage in the following section is less excusable.

> Another rarity was the large mirror on the outside wall; these steam up like the ones outside.

Although we are dealing with mirrors in general in the second half of the sentence, there is no excuse for the shift from the large 'mirror' to 'these'. The singular noun must be cancelled out: 'these mirrors steam up like the ones outside'.

none / either / neither / or

These words appear to raise queries about the use of singular and plural. 'None' is basically the equivalent of 'no one'. Thus logic seems to guide us to think of it as singular. And indeed there are writers who always treat it so. But popular usage tends towards the plural. Thus Dryden, a classicist, left us the famous line, 'None but the brave deserves the fair', and we hear it misquoted as 'deserve the fair'. Schoolboys used to be made familiar with Macaulay's idealized summing-up of the probity of Roman political life in the days when Horatius kept the bridge.

> Then none was for a party,
> Then all were for the state.

That firm contrast between singular and plural for 'none' and 'all' tends to make sticklers for style uncomfortable with plural verbs after 'none'. However, from a writer as reliable as Oliver Goldsmith the *OED* quotes 'None of these however are known to us.' And the drift towards that usage today seems to be irresistible.

> None of those applicants who sent in their forms last year are required to re-apply.

It has seemingly become the mark of the pedant to prefer: 'is required to re-apply'.

The words 'either' and 'neither' match the words they refer to. Although it is obviously correct to say 'Neither Catholics nor Protestants were present at the ceremony', it is not correct to say 'Neither the bride nor the bridegroom were willing to be interviewed.' It should be: 'was willing to be interviewed'. Similarly 'Neither of us enjoy eating out' should be: 'Neither of us enjoys eating out.'

We have dealt with the permissive sportsman's 'team plural' used of football teams. It is improper, however, to extend too far the liberties granted by this collective. When we hear of two teams that 'neither side are much fancied for the title', we are bound to protest. 'Neither' is there singular. If two teams are competing, 'either' one or the other 'is' probably going to be victorious. If the match proves to be a draw, then 'neither is the winner'.

In such incorrect usages as 'Neither my father nor my mother were willing to help', the difficulty arises because the speaker or writer has just been dwelling mentally on the fact that two people failed to respond. That difficulty is not confined to the use of negatives like 'none' and 'neither'.

> For my style of working I find that top grade cartridge or hot pressed paper are best suited.

Here it is the force of the word 'or' that the writer ignores. She is mentally dwelling on the fact that two methods suit her. But 'or' separates the two items. When one says 'Paint or wall-paper is acceptable', one means that one or the other will serve. Logic demands the singular similarly in the above: 'I find that top grade cartridge or hot pressed paper is best suited.'

USE OF THE INFINITIVE

The infinitive is used after certain verbs such as to 'wish', to 'decide', to 'help' and to 'advise'. In the sentences 'I wished to leave' and 'I decided to go', the infinitives 'to leave' and 'to go' act as objects of the verbs 'wished' and 'decided'. There are also cases where the infinitive acts as subject of a verb ('To postpone decision seemed to be the best policy'). We have the occasional usage in which the infinitive is used with the verb 'to be' both as subject and as complement: 'To work is to pray'; 'To know her was to love her.'

It is important not to try to use the infinitive construction after verbs which it cannot properly follow. We say 'I allowed him to go', 'I encouraged him to go' and 'I persuaded him to go', but this cannot be a model for any verb one chooses.

> The challenge now is to prevent mass migration, by supporting people to stay on their land and cultivate, fish, or raise cattle.

We do not say 'They supported their son to try for the university', but 'They supported their son in trying for the university.' So here, if 'supporting' is kept the end of the sentence should read: 'by supporting people in staying on their land and cultivating'. However, in view of the context of the sentence, which is taken from a charitable appeal for money, it would be clear enough to write: 'by enabling people to stay on their land'.

Omission of *to*

In cases where the infinitive is properly placed, a tendency has developed of omitting the word 'to'. We find people saying 'I helped him move his house' instead of 'I helped him to move his house.' No doubt the practice of omitting 'to' is harmless enough in conversation. We ought not to get excited when someone says 'They are helping her cope with the problem', but in print that omission of 'to' can appear lax.

> The book suggests methods parents can try to help children master these basic skills.

> Parents can help their less buoyant offspring cultivate this ability.

In each of the above cases the restoration of 'to' is recommended: 'Parents can try to help their children to master these basic skills' and 'Parents can help their less buoyant offspring to cultivate this ability.' At present it is especially the case with the verb 'help' that this liberty is taken, but the thin-ended wedge is being slowly pushed further. It is a small step from 'Help her cross the road' to 'Encourage him eat his cereals.' If we too readily accept statements like 'I helped my daughter choose her engagement ring', may we soon be asked to accept 'I taught my daughter make mince pies'? For we can already read:

> A lost rail can force you bring stream-crossing skills into play.

This of course should be: 'force you to bring'. It should be added that English does have a few verbs which are properly followed by what grammarians call the 'bare' form of the infinitive (the infinitive without 'to'): 'We watched her *go*'; 'They made me *help*.'

Infinitive Misused

Misuse of the infinitive tends to occur when it stands in close relationship to a noun. We should naturally say 'He hopes to succeed in this venture', following the verb to 'hope' with the infinitive 'to succeed'. But we should equally naturally say 'We had little hope of reviving him', following the noun 'hope' with the gerund 'of reviving'. But this does not mean that infinitives cannot ever have a proper dependence on a noun. There are numerous cases of such dependence. In the sentence 'There was no doubt of his determination to leave', the infinitive 'to leave' is directly attached to the noun 'determination'. Such sentences as 'They acknowledged her promise to take part', 'We saw their willingness to participate' and 'He welcomed our readiness to cooperate' give some idea of how common this use of the infinitive is. In each of those cases the infinitive is directly attached to a noun. We say 'I have a duty to go', 'She has an obligation to be there', and 'They have a strong claim to present.' In any of these cases use of the gerund would be out of the question ('duty of going', 'obligation of being there'). But there are certain nouns which, unlike these, sometimes seemingly offer a choice to the writer. Whereas 'We saw no reason to rejoice' is acceptable usage, 'We had a hundred reasons for rejecting the proposal' is equally respectable.

The escape from use of an ill-placed infinitive cannot always be best achieved by use of a gerund. Consider the following sentence:

> Today's Airbath International is founded on thirty years of market experience, with constant research and development to improve and refine the original unique idea.

The infinitives 'to improve and refine' cannot stand thus, unhappily connected to the nouns 'research and development'. The best way to make the infinitives usable is to introduce a participle on which they can depend: 'with constant research and development designed to improve and refine the original idea'.

> The models are complete with rubber feet to prevent them from slipping or scratching the table.

Here is another sentence which requires the same treatment. Since it would be clumsy to write 'complete with rubber feet for preventing them from slipping', the participle should be inserted: 'complete with rubber feet designed to prevent them from slipping'.

Perhaps one can safely say that the use of the infinitive presents us with one of the most obvious instances of a construction which can pass in conversation where it could not in print.

> It's a sheltered spot to sit in the sun and breathe in the scent of rosemary, sage and creeping thyme.

The wild card infinitive 'to sit' can get by in conversation. On paper the sentence must become: 'It's a sheltered spot where you can sit in the sun.' And in the following sentence the infinitive 'to try' should be avoided in print.

> Rowse has produced a twelve-page booklet that contains lots of tempting dishes to try.

Correct this by anchoring the infinitive: 'contains lots of tempting dishes for you to try'. A comparable liberty is taken in the following from a concert programme.

> The two Violin Rhapsodies are rare to find in performance.

If one wanted to be technical about this usage one would call it perhaps a 'constructional transfer'. Because the idiom 'hard to find' exists, therefore on the model of that the writer describes something as 'rare to find'. It is quite illogical, for though the process of finding something may indeed be 'hard', it is not that process but the thing found that may be 'rare'.

In conversational use of the infinitive there is a curious habit of substituting 'and' for 'to', more especially with the verbs 'come' and 'try'. 'Come and see me whenever you like' we say, instead of 'Come to see me whenever you like.' In the same way we say 'Try and do your best' instead of 'Try to do your best.' Obviously there is no point in trying to disparage usages so well established. But writers should be chary of transferring them from the world of conversation to the printed page.

The Split Infinitive

One can scarcely leave the subject of the infinitive without reference to the vexed question of the split infinitive. There are linguistic issues which arouse great passion, and this is one of them. It is difficult to sympathize with those who would totally ban its use. There are times when it is tasteless. When President Nixon first faced questions about Watergate, he is reported to have told his staff 'I want you to all stonewall it.' Now clearly it would have been better to say 'I want you all to stonewall it.' But it is not difficult to assemble instances of the split infinitive which are unobjectionable.

> The steam will soften your skin, enabling you to gently remove any blackheads with tissue-covered fingers.

> You should be able to simply slot the new stud into the original mortices in these two beams.

It is difficult to see the point of replacing 'to gently remove' with 'gently to remove' and 'to simply slot' with 'simply to slot'.

THE PRESENT PARTICIPLE

We turn now to consider the first of a group of constructions which probably cause more elementary grammatical upsets than any others in our language. They involve participles and the gerund. Our first concern is with that part of the verb which ends in '-ing'. There are two such forms to be distinguished, the gerund and the present participle. That is to say, we have to distinguish the use of the word 'singing' in the sentence 'Singing is my hobby' from its use in the sentence 'I heard father singing in the bath.'

In the first instance 'singing' functions as a noun. Though it is part of a verb, it is the subject of the sentence and functions just as a real noun would in 'Music is my hobby.' That is the gerund, sometimes conveniently called the 'verbal noun'. In the second instance 'singing' functions as an adjective. Though it is part of a verb, it functions just as a real adjective would, describing 'father'. That is a participle. Of course we should tend to put the real adjective before the noun, whereas the participle often follows it.

There are various ways in which the present participle can be misused. One can say of them, as one can say of certain misuses of the gerund, that at the worst these misuses represent a crude abuse of language. But at the other end of the scale the least serious misuses sometimes merely represent the difference between good style and a touch of amateurishness.

Hanging Participles

The most common error in using the present participle is to leave it unconnected to a noun or pronoun. Thus disconnected, it is called a 'hanging' or 'dangling' or 'detached' participle.

> Reclining there in a deck chair on the lawn in the summer sunshine, the house had never looked so beautiful.

The mistake is easily made. 'Reclining' is the present participle and must agree with a noun or a pronoun. It would have been correct to write 'Reclining there on the lawn in the summer sunshine, we thought that the house had never looked so beautiful', because 'we' provides the pronoun for 'reclining' to agree with. As the sentence stands in the original, the writer declares that the house was reclining in a deck chair on the lawn.

> Listening to the Chancellor in full spate, his confidence seemed utterly disproportionate.

Exactly the same error is committed here. There is neither noun nor pronoun for the participle 'listening' to attach itself to. In strict grammatical terms, 'his confidence' is said to be listening. The participle must be properly anchored: 'Listening to the Chancellor in full spate, I found his confidence utterly disproportionate.'

being

Perhaps the worst examples of this error are to be found when the participle is formed from the verb to 'be'.

> Being mid-winter, the central heating should have been left on when we went away.

That is typical of the trouble that beginning a sentence with 'being' can lead to. The sentence tells us that the central heating was mid-winter, and that it should have been left on. The sentence should begin: 'As it was mid-winter'. At its silliest this same mistake falsely links 'being' with the reader.

> Being an Irvine Walsh book, you can guess where that rash is located, and what happens every time it gets a good scratch.

Here is a reviewer telling you that you are an Irvine Walsh book, for that is what the grammar strictly conveys. There is no escape from something like: 'As it is an Irvine Walsh book'. The truth is that the good writer will always pause before beginning a sentence with 'being', and will pause again before finishing the sentence.

Directions for Routes

We often find detached participles when writers are spelling out directions for routes, especially routes to be taken by walkers.

> Heading due east for a mile to Pen-y-bryn, there are wide views to the blue whalebacks of the Carneddau.

Here the wide views are said to be 'heading' due east. Such sentences can usually be corrected by introducing an appropriate personal pronoun to agree with the participle: 'Heading due east for a mile to Pen-y-bryn, you will have wide views to the blue whalebacks of the Carneddau.'

> Veering right at the junction of the paths, a magnificent panorama of hill and dale is opened up.

Here the magnificent panorama is said to veer right at the junction. Introduce a personal pronoun: 'Veering right at the junction of the paths, you will see a magnificent panorama of hill and dale.'

> Moving north of the border, the country turns wilder.

Here the country is said to move north. One could give the sentence the same treatment: 'you will find that the country turns wilder', but it would be just as natural to get rid of the troublesome participle: 'As you move north of the border, the country turns wilder.'

looking

This is one of the participles with which the problem repeatedly arises.

> Looking out across its central grassy space, the place is much quieter these days.
>
> Looking downwards, the sea stretches out into the distance.
>
> Looking at the plan in detail, it seems too complicated.

In each case the participle 'looking' is unanchored. In strict grammatical terms we are told that the 'place' is looking out across the space, then that the 'sea' is looking downwards, and lastly that 'it' (the plan) is looking at itself. If 'looking' is kept, then there must be a pronoun to agree with it: 'Looking out across its central grassy space, we find the place much quieter.' Similarly we could have: 'Looking downwards, we see the sea stretching out into the distance' and 'Looking at the plan in detail, we find it too complicated.' But in each case the alternative correction would be to replace the participle 'looking': 'As we look out across its central grassy space, the place is much quieter'; 'As we look downwards'; and 'When we look at the plan in detail'.

using

It is correct to say 'He removed the broken tile from the roof, using a step-ladder', because 'he' did indeed 'use' the ladder. But it is at best imprecise to say 'The broken tile was removed from the roof, using a step-ladder', because the 'broken tile' did not use the ladder. Nevertheless one can find that construction day after day in print in the press.

> Using proper firmness, most children over the age of two will sleep well.

It isn't the children who use proper firmness, as this tells us. The participle should go: 'If proper firmness is used, most children over the age of two will sleep well'.

> Using appropriate varieties, endive can be sown for much of the year.

Again endive must not be said to use varieties, as this sentence has it. And there is an excellent device for avoiding the grammatical trap. Drop the participle 'using' and substitute 'by the use of'.

Employment Advertisements

A fairly recently established version of the hanging participle can be found in advertisements for industrial posts.

> Reporting to the Deputy Managing Director and liaising with the Sales and Marketing Directors, your responsibilities will be wide ranging.

It is not the 'responsibilities' that will report to the Managing Director and liaise with Sales and Marketing Directors. The sentence can make sense only if the pronoun 'you' is introduced and the sentence ends: 'you will have wide ranging responsibilities'. The specimen illustrates a very frequent error in the business world.

> Reporting to the Northern European Marketing Manager, the key responsibility will be development and implementation of channel marketing programmes.

Again the 'key responsibility' is said to have to report to the Marketing Manager. The advertisement should read: 'Reporting to the Northern European Marketing Manager, you will have the key responsibility for development and implementation of channel marketing programmes.' The error is made so frequently that one could quickly pile up further examples.

I/me

Just as the personal pronoun 'you' is necessary in that kind of sentence, so the personal pronoun 'I' is needed in many sentences introduced by a participle.

> Writing at the end of a long hot summer, it is easy to forget that we had some cold times in the spring.

> Saying that, my personal favourites are La Prairie and Estée Lauder.

In these two sentences the personal pronoun is required to make sense of the opening participles: 'Writing at the end of a long hot summer, I find it easy to forget that we had some cold times in the spring'; 'Saying that, I personally favour La Prairie and Estée Lauder.' In matching an initial hanging participle with a personal pronoun, it is not always necessary to use the personal pronoun as subject of what follows.

> Standing in the glass-roofed, cobbled courtyard, the distinctive interior is reminiscent of Kew Gardens.

Here is a case in point. Instead of writing 'Standing in the glass-roofed, cobbled courtyard, I am reminded of Kew Gardens', it would here be technically quite correct to make sense of 'standing' by attaching it to 'me': 'Standing in the glass-roofed, cobbled courtyard, the distinctive interior reminded me of Kew Gardens.'

generally speaking

It would be wrong to leave this topic without drawing attention to various idiomatic uses of the present participle which seem to break the rules we have followed so far. For instance, we should accept the following sentences.

> Generally speaking, audiences here are poor.
>
> Strictly speaking, the fellow ought to be reprimanded.

These two expressions, 'generally speaking' and 'strictly speaking', have established themselves as detachable from the implicit pronoun ('Strictly speaking, I think the fellow ought to be reprimanded'). We have to accept that other such expressions could with popular use equally establish themselves as respectable. Is not the process happening in our hearing in the case of the participle 'looking'? Do we not hear educated people saying 'Looking at the idea objectively, it is impracticable', as though the idea were looking at itself?

THE PAST PARTICIPLE

The Passive Past Participle

There is an active and a passive form of the past participle. In 'Having heard you speak, I feel I must disagree with you' we see the active form 'having heard'. In 'Heard in silence, he soon finished his speech', we see the passive form 'heard'. Like the present participle, the past participle tends to get detached from any noun or pronoun that could make it grammatically acceptable. Errors are especially frequent in use of the passive past participle.

> Designed as part of a comprehensive series on the English counties, the author is deeply attached to his native area.

> Illustrated by beautiful colour photographs and useful sketch-maps, the reader will find delight in following in the author's footsteps.

It is curious that this particular grammatical error can often be found in book reviews. In the first sentence we never learn what it is that is 'designed' as part of a series. The wording really conveys that the 'author' is so designed. In the second sentence we never learn what it is that is 'illustrated' by photographs and sketch-maps. This time the actual wording conveys that the 'reader' is thus lavishly 'illustrated'. Participles resist being marooned. If deprived of their proper mooring, they will drift by the force of grammatical logic to an untenable attachment. If 'designed' and 'illustrated' are to be kept, then 'book' or some such word must follow somewhere: 'Designed as part of a comprehensive series on the English counties, the book reveals the author's deep attachment to his native area'; 'Illustrated by beautiful colour photographs and useful sketch-maps, the book will give delight to the reader who follows in the author's footsteps.'

There is a common version of this error which is not always easy to spot.

> Originally appointed by the monarch to oversee his affairs in the outposts of the kingdom, the Sheriff's role today is largely symbolic.

The writer begins the sentence ('Originally appointed') presumably assuming that the subject will be 'the Sheriff'. But the wording goes awry when we get to the 'Sheriff's role'. For it was not the 'role' but the Sheriff that the monarch 'originally appointed'. The Sheriff and his role must be differentiated: 'Originally appointed by the monarch to oversee his affairs in the outposts of the kingdom, the Sheriff today has a largely symbolic role.' We may call the mistaken construction here the 'possessive trap'. There is a subject involving a possessive, like 'Sheriff's role', and the writer proceeds as though the subject were really the Sheriff, and not the role.

Let us turn to a specimen of the blunder more veiled in words:

> Brought up in a family of singers and instrumentalists, his musical interests were the basis of many life-long friendships.

This wording conveys that somebody's 'musical interests' were brought up in a family of singers and instrumentalists. 'Brought up' must be attached where it belongs: 'Brought up in a family of singers and instrumentalists, he enjoyed life-long friendships on the basis of his musical interests.'

Sometimes we come across the hanging participle following a word such as 'if' or 'when'. In this usage the past participle can drift even further from any mooring.

> If confirmed, Mr Lader and his wife, Linda, are expected to continue running the annual Renaissance gatherings.

Since there is no other word for 'if confirmed' to attach itself to, this sounds as though Mr Lader and his wife will be allowed to continue their work provided that they submit to a certain religious ceremony. The best way out of this confusion is to sacrifice the participle and substitute a proper verb: 'If the appointment is confirmed'.

The same slip can occur after the word 'when'.

> The buffet had been laid out on sparkling white table-cloths. When removed, our hosts revealed that they were really trestle tables.

The strict literal sense here would surely be that the hosts made this revelation after they had 'removed'. It would also appear that the hosts identified themselves as trestle tables. Any correction would need to fill out the construction: 'When the table-cloths were removed, it was revealed that our hosts were using trestle tables.'

The Active Past Participle

The active past participle is sometimes left as isolated from grammatical mooring as the passive. The following sentence takes us into the world of caravans and the caravan site.

> The installation of a microwave oven would be a boon and at no cost, having already paid the supplement to the site fee.

Here 'having paid' hangs in total isolation. The way to bring it into the sentence grammatically is to provide it with an anchorage: 'The installation of a microwave oven would be a boon and at no cost, the owner having already paid the supplement to the site fee.'

The active past participle suffers the same mistreatment as the passive one in that it can be left in seeming attachment to the wrong noun when the writer falls into the possessive trap.

> Alan's background is in civil engineering, having worked in the coal industry for twenty years.

Here Alan's background is said to have worked twenty years in the coal industry. The necessary correction can be very simply made: 'Alan has a background in civil engineering, having worked in the coal industry for twenty years.'

Perhaps the commonest version of this error is the misuse of the phrase 'having said that'.

> The site is vast and busy; but having said that, a quiet backwater can usually be found.

Here the 'quiet backwater' is said to have uttered. For though 'Having said that, I shall accept the plan' is correct, 'Having said that, the plan will do fine' is incorrect, since the plan did not speak. The ironical thing about this error, which is made day after day on the radio, is that the correct alternative is so rarely heard. 'That being said, the plan will do fine' is the obvious correction. An even shorter one is 'That said, the plan will do fine.'

THE GERUND

The gerund is the part of the verb that is used as a noun. We use lots of gerunds in daily talk: 'Walking is good for you'; 'I love reading'; 'Too much talking tires her'; 'We have stopped going to the cinema.' These formations from the verbs to 'walk', to 'read', to 'talk' and to 'go' allow us to use the verbs as nouns, acting as subjects or objects to verbs proper.

Gerunds After Prepositions

Gerunds can follow prepositions just as nouns can. Instead of 'You will succeed only by hard practice', one might say 'You will succeed only by practising hard.' We should notice the connection in meaning here between 'practising' and 'you'. 'I hoped to improve my holidays abroad by learning French' makes sense because 'by learning' is related to the word 'I'. 'By learning French, holidays abroad can be improved' will not do because 'holidays abroad' do not learn French. This is the first common misuse of that construction, to leave it unanchored.

> By paying his own way at Loughborough, it leaves more cash in the family pot to adopt a baby girl from Guatemala.

This is the error in crude form. 'By paying' cannot be attached to 'it'. All that needs to be done is to replace 'it' by 'he'. We turn to a slightly more complex version of the misuse.

> Time-tables and advance booking forms are available by sending an s.a.e. to the headquarters.

This will not do because neither time-tables nor booking forms can send stamped addressed envelopes. (It is necessary to make the further point that these items are 'available' whether anyone sends for them or not. They are 'obtainable' only on receipt of the applications.) Perhaps the shortest correct version here would be: 'Time-tables and advance booking forms will be sent from headquarters on receipt of an s.a.e.'

> A child who dislikes walking can be a problem, but by gentle coaxing and by insisting on leaving the car at home when taking him where he especially wants to go, he will gradually respond.

Here there is no proper 'subject' to make sense of the expressions 'by gentle coaxing' and 'by insisting on leaving the car at home'. As the wording stands, the two expressions attach themselves to the subject 'he', which relates back to 'child'. The one who does the coaxing must be mentioned: 'By gentle coaxing and by insisting on leaving the car at home when taking him where he wants to go, you will gradually get him to respond.'

Such mistakes are not hard to find. Indeed it is possible to find the same error muffled up in highbrow waffle. Consider the following from a book review.

> By repeating images, and multiplying visual fragments as a kind of marginal gloss on the text, our grasp on what it is that interests Jonathan Miller about a particular example builds up in stages.

We are here told that 'our grasp' is busily repeating images and multiplying visual fragments in the process of learning something or other. Either 'by repeating images and multiplying fragments' must go, or the phrases must be detached from our unwilling grasp and placed firmly where they belong: 'By repeating images, and multiplying visual fragments . . . Jonathan Miller builds up our grasp on what it is that interests him.' But alas, at the end of the reviewer's sentence one scarcely wants to know.

Failure to relate a gerund correctly to the noun to which it applies can sometimes cause it to drift towards a noun with which it has no connection. The following words from a speaker on BBC Radio 4 show the dangers of this possibility.

> After ordering my meal, the waiter started to gossip.

In strict grammatical terms this implies that the waiter ordered the meal.

being

A special caveat is needed about the use of 'being' as a gerund. 'Being young is not always an advantage.' Such sentences as that are proper and useful, though it should be pointed out that one could equally well use an infinitive and say 'To be young is not always an advantage.'

> Being a mass market marque means spare parts are never a problem.

It would be far better here to use the participle: 'The car being a mass market model, spare parts are never a problem.'

The 'Gerciple'

There are matters of controversy in grammar, matters over which sometimes experts disagree. We approach one such now. Having acquainted ourselves with the participle, which acts like an adjective ('I found her reading') and the gerund, which acts like a noun ('She loves reading'), we must turn our attention to a form which tries to be both at the same time and fails satisfactorily to be either: 'She disliked me reading detective novels.' The word 'reading' there is a cross between a gerund (as in 'She disliked reading') and a participle (as in 'She found me reading'). Fowler called this misbegotten form the 'fused participle'. Because it tries to do the work of both gerund and participle, I have labelled it the 'gerciple'. There is logic in disallowing the construction. 'She disliked me reading detective novels' is improper because she did not dislike me at all. She disliked what I was doing. Thus it is that the correct thing to say is 'She disliked my reading detective novels.' We change the 'gerciple' into a genuine gerund, making it a verbal noun that is the object of 'disliked'.

Wherever one turns in the press today there are gerciples. But it is extremely difficult to find them in the work of good writers – not always impossible though. And have we not manufactured them ourselves? It would be a very bold writer who claimed never to have done so. For gerciples can appear at every level of impropriety from the grossly illiterate to the utterly excusable. We look first at the fondness for attaching gerciples to pronouns.

> Excuse me, I hope you don't mind me interrupting.

This should be: 'I hope you don't mind my interrupting.'

> The building remains more or less intact – thanks largely to it being listed.

This should be: 'thanks largely to its being listed'.

> The ride [in a car] is good: most bumps are swallowed without you even knowing they were there.

This should be: 'without your even knowing they were there'.

The expression 'difference between' tempts writers to illicit use of the gerciple. The following piece of parental advice illustrates the point.

> Make it clear there's a difference between you reading to him (sheer enjoyment for you both) and him learning to read (sometimes hard work).

The direct correction would simply adjust the pronouns: 'difference between your reading to him and his learning to read'.

We have corrected the sentences so far by turning the gerciples into genuine gerunds. This has meant turning 'me' into 'my', 'it' into 'its' and 'you' into 'your'. We face a different problem when the misuse involves a noun rather than a pronoun.

> If you don't mind long-term health-care becoming a means-tested service, then that's OK.

Technically this could be corrected by inserting an apostrophe: 'If you don't mind long-term health care's becoming a means-tested service'. But clearly that is intolerably awkward and clumsy. In such cases the construction must be changed: 'If you're quite happy for long-term health-care to become a means-tested service'.

It is frequently the case that clauses beginning with 'that' can rescue the writer from error in this context.

> In Britain there is a lay tradition of gifted naturalists undertaking the field work.

So here one gets rid of the gerciple 'naturalists undertaking', not by any apostrophe ('naturalists' taking') but by recourse to 'that': 'In Britain there is a lay tradition that gifted naturalists undertake the field work.'

> High tides up to 15 ft above normal were forecast, with the added risk of the hurricane stalling over the coast and dumping all its rain.

To correct by use of the possessive case is once more impracticable ('with the added risk of the hurricane's stalling'). Change the construction: 'with the added risk that the hurricane would stall over the coast and dump all its rain'.

This change is appropriate after those gerciples which tend to follow such words as 'risk', 'possibility', 'danger' and 'threat'. So 'the possibility of the whole staff being sacked' would not become 'the possibility of the whole staff's being sacked' but 'the possibility that the whole staff would be sacked'. Similarly 'the threat of all the union members coming out on strike' would become 'the threat that all the union members would come out on strike'. Thus the following comment on a stowaway cat on a flight in a Boeing 757 requires similar treatment.

> There was no danger of it being too cold for her during the flight.

Instead of correcting to 'danger of its being too cold', use 'that' again: 'There was no danger that she would be too cold during the flight.' And again here is a quotation from a letter displaying the same fault.

> Your report highlights the embarrassment which delays are already causing ministers, with the threat of the Jubilee Line not being completed in time for the public to visit the Millennium Dome.

Though 'the threat of the Jubilee Line's not being completed' would be correct, it would be clumsy. We need: 'with the threat that the Jubilee Line will not be completed'.

SOME TROUBLESOME VERB FORMS

may / might

There are few problems with the form of the tenses of English verbs. We do not find ourselves confusing the present with the past tense by accident. The difficulties that do arise involve the conditional tenses. Above all there is slackness in the use of 'may' and 'might'. The rule is that where we are speaking in the present or future tense, we use the form 'may': 'I hope I may be able to come.' And where we are speaking in the past tense, we use 'might': 'I hoped I might be able to go.' It is not difficult to find this rule broken in print.

> Some parents worried that if they complained their children may be taken into care.

> If the information about the food poisoning had been acted upon without delay, the deaths may have been prevented.

> There had been a possibility that the locomotive may have gone abroad.

In each case 'may' should be 'might'. The rule is really a very simple one. Yet a news announcer speaks thus about a woman whose daughter has died of meningitis after an unfortunate delay in finding a hospital place for her.

> Her mother believes she may not have died if she could have had the treatment she required.

Plainly, once more, this should be: 'she might not have died if she could have had the treatment she required'.

The converse error, that of using 'might' where the present tense of the main verb requires 'may', is perhaps slightly less common.

> If you continue to work hard, you might get promotion.

> Try as we might, the DETR will give us no details.

In each case 'might' should be 'may'.

Irregular Verb Forms

We have our irregular verbs (such as 'sing', 'sang', 'sung') but few of them cause us difficulties. It is interesting that we find writers today treating the verb to 'swing' as though it were exactly the same as 'sing' in this respect:

> Politically, the NUS swang decisively from the left to the pragmatic centre.
>
> The back-up teams swang into action.

Modern usage prefers 'swung'. Indeed my modern dictionary gives only 'swung' as possible. But the *OED* allows 'swang' as a rarity. We must observe that it is dangerous to assume that a verb will work exactly like a similar sounding one. 'Learnt' is an alternative to 'learned' as the past tense of to 'learn'. But there is no such alternative to the past tense of the verb to 'earn'.

> His pragmatism earnt him respect in Ulster.
>
> Her husband earnt yen in the Nippon Credit Bank in the City.

These sentences are incorrect. In each case 'earnt' should be 'earned'.

Some of our irregular verbs, however, provide us with choices in this respect. The past tense of 'weave' may be either 'weaved' or 'wove' and the perfect tense either 'I have weaved' or 'I have woven'. Other verbs too, whose irregular forms have been simplified through the years, offer us alternatives. The past tense of 'strive' should be 'strove' and the perfect tense 'I have striven'. Yet the past tense of 'thrive' may be either 'throve' or 'thrived' and the perfect tense either 'I have thriven' or 'I have thrived'.

heave / hove

The verb to 'heave' has either 'heaved' or 'hove' as the past and perfect forms. Publicity about a *Titanic* film on Channel 5 includes the sentence:

> Acting styles and accents fly in all directions, especially when the rascally Tim Curry hoves into view as a wicked steward/purser.

This is the same error as saying 'He sangs a song.' There is no English verb to 'hove'. The verb to 'heave' is used intransitively of a vessel moving. The only possible correction to the above would be: 'when the rascally Tim Curry heaves into view'.

lead / led

Such words as 'hove' are not often on our lips. It is ironic that the main area of current error in the forms of verbs is to be found in one or two of our most commonly used verbs. The verb to 'lead' has the past tense 'led'. But because there is a noun 'lead' (the metal) which is pronounced exactly the same as 'led', the wrong spelling turns up for 'led' with remarkable frequency.

> My work with adults had lead us into many ventures.
>
> The workshop will be lead by Caroline E. Darl and Denise Allen.

In each case 'lead' should be 'led'.

lay / lie

Overriding all other seeming difficulties with verb forms is the persisting confusion between the verbs to 'lay' and to 'lie'.

> The harassed parent only wants to lay drowsing in the sun.
>
> It's as good a place as any to lay for a couple of weeks in the sun.
>
> I just couldn't lay about the house eating cake.

In each case 'lay' should be 'lie'. 'Lay' is a transitive verb. It takes an object. A hen 'lays' an egg. A waitress 'lays' the table. No doubt the origin of the troublesome confusion lies in the fact that the verb to 'lie' has 'lay' as its past tense.

Is this a lost cause? I ask because, months after writing the above, I find the following in *The Times* report on Turkey after the earthquake:

> His wife, Aynur, cooks what she can on a camping stove and warms the milk for her ten-month-old baby, Ayae, who lays on a blanket under a tree.

The baby 'lies' on the blanket.

The converse error is just as common.

> When she took Vicki out in her pram, she would lie her on her side.
>
> First lie her on her back on a soft towel.

In each case 'lie' should be 'lay'. 'Lie' is an intransitive verb and cannot take an object.

sat, stood, sprawled

A comparably frequent blunder in verb forms is the misuse of the past tenses of 'sit', 'stand', and 'sprawl'.

> I recently spent a week either sat by my phone or calling my answer machine from work.

The writer means that she spent a week 'sitting' by her phone. And once again the blunder is common. Within a few days I have come across the following two instances, the first from a radio presenter standing in for a celebrated presenter who is on holiday:

> It is a privilege to be sat in her seat.

And the second, according to my newspaper, from a QC addressing his Old Bailey jury:

> I don't suppose you want to be sat in here when there is an eclipse.

In each case 'sat' should be 'sitting'.

The verb to 'stand' is similarly mistreated

> He was stood there like a stuffed dummy.

The writer means that the fellow 'was standing' there like a stuffed dummy. Small wonder that a correspondent in *The Times* writes 'How I mourn the demise of "was sitting" and "was standing" in favour of the hideously inelegant "was sat" and "was stood".' It is not just a case of hideous inelegance, but of elementary grammatical error. We find the same treatment given to the verb to 'sprawl'. 'He was sprawled in front of the TV' should be 'He was sprawling'.

suit

A rather silly practice has recently been cultivated in women's journals of inverting the proper usage of the verb to 'suit'.

> I'm going for a dressy evening look, as I feel Maureen will suit it.

In purchasing clothes the issue is what will suit the customer, not what will 'suit' the clothes. Subject and object are not here interchangeable. The clothes have no choice. The garments with the 'dressy evening look' cannot decide that they would rather clothe Maureen's friend than Maureen. There is no more sense in inverting the usage with the verb to 'suit' than there would be with, say, the verb to 'please'. No one has yet begun to write 'She greatly pleases this kind of holiday' instead of 'This kind of holiday greatly pleases her.'

CHAPTER 6

The Fabric of the Sentence

THE USE OF PRONOUNS

The main building blocks of utterance are nouns and verbs. But we frequently replace nouns by those convenient substitutes which we call 'pronouns'. We scatter our daily talk with pronouns. 'Where is it?', 'How is she?', 'Tell them to be quiet', 'That's the postman.' The words 'it', 'she', 'them' and 'that' are all pronouns. They function as nouns. They save us the trouble of saying 'Where is the newspaper?', 'How is your grandmother?', 'Tell the children to be quiet', or 'The noise at the door is made by the postman.' Stand-in words like these raise few problems in conversation where we know what nouns they are understudying. If you ask 'What is it?' with an unopened Christmas present in your hand, nobody is going to ask 'What do you mean by "it"?' And if you say 'Tell them to be quiet' as your youngsters are performing circus acts in the bedroom above, no one is going to ask you 'What do you mean by "them"?' But in print what the writer is getting at as he or she sprinkles pronouns over the page may sometimes not be clear.

it

Nowhere is this more likely to occur than in the use of 'it'.

> You can never really know the limits of your body; it is always surprising.

What is 'it'? We can guess, but the writer doesn't tell us. For 'it' should refer back to something already referred to ('The tyre is flat; it must be punctured'). On this reading the writer is saying 'The body is always surprising.' But we know that she doesn't mean that. She means that discovering what the limits of your body are is always surprising. She should have said: 'it is always surprising to find out'.

That is the first of the problems raised in the use of pronouns. The reader always needs to know exactly what they refer back to. The good writer will never leave 'it' so placed that the reader is not absolutely certain what the word refers to. There should never be that moment of doubt in the reader's mind produced by a collision between the meaning suggested by the context and the meaning implicit in the grammar.

> Use a make-up sponge to sweep it over the face. Don't overload the sponge or it could look streaky.

Clearly the first 'it' refers to the make-up in use. But the reader's mind receives a little jolt from the second 'it'. The form of the sentence – the grammatical proximity of 'it' to sponge – suggests one meaning, then the brain rules it out as absurd. It can't after all be the sponge that may look streaky. It must be the face. These are reasoning processes which readers ought not to have to go through. The good writer will ensure that they don't have to. It's all a question of the primacy of concepts planted in the mind by the words.

> This is a lovely way to keep fruit for a couple of days. It's delicious for breakfast, lunch or tea.

Here is a case in point. The reader responds to a statement about a 'way' to keep fruit. That is the concept that has the primacy. But the reader is not allowed to continue to hold to the 'way' of keeping fruit as the subject of discourse. For the two words 'It's delicious' plainly refer, not to the way of keeping fruit, but to the fruit itself. Thus time after time it is by the misuse of pronouns that readers are jolted from following logical trains of thought by momentary mental doubts, quickly removed, but nevertheless interruptive.

they / them

The plural pronouns 'they' and 'them' must equally refer back to something previously mentioned.

> Introduce a friend to the AA, and both of you can choose a free gift. They include a travel rug, first-aid kit, sports bag . . .

To use 'they' to refer back to 'a free gift' is bad. Correction is needed: 'The gifts include a travel rug . . .'

Sometimes 'they' can be ill-used in that there seem to be two possible alternative nouns to which the word might refer back.

People's ideas about the 50s and 60s tend to blur together – but they are really quite distinct from one another.

On first reading this one might assume that 'they' refers back to 'people's ideas'. But the context suggests that the writer meant not that people's ideas differ, but that the 50s differ from the 60s. So correction is needed: 'but the two periods are really quite distinct from one another'.

What applies to 'they' applies to 'them'.

Under new proposals up to 200 car spaces may be lost with simply nowhere for them to go.

This conveys the message that there is nowhere for the spaces to go. Nothing has been said directly about 'cars'. The message is about the spaces they occupy. The cars must be specifically mentioned for 'them' to have a reference point: 'up to 200 parking spaces may be lost, leaving simply nowhere for the cars to go'.

this

'This is mine', we say. In relation to that usage the question may arise: What does 'this' refer to? The most common misuse of 'this' occurs when that question cannot be unambiguously answered.

The railway would like to buy the old station building at Market Bosworth, which is used as a garage and workshop. Although it was on sale recently for around £200,000, this is beyond its present means, but it holds hope of some agreement. This may be difficult in the short term.

Here in three sentences are two uses of 'this' and two uses of 'it'. That 'it' was on sale does not trouble us. 'It' there is plainly the old station building. And that 'this' is beyond someone's means does not in itself trouble us. It is clearly the price quoted to which 'this' refers. But for the same sentence to state that 'it' was on sale at a price beyond 'its' present means and that nevertheless 'it' holds some hope will not do. Nor is the last 'this' happily related to what precedes it. The answer to all these problems is simply to economize on pronouns rather than on nouns, and to say: 'Although the station building was on sale recently for around £200,000, the price was beyond the railway's present means, but there is hope of some agreement, though reaching it may prove difficult in the short term.'

One of the facts that complicates the use of 'this' is the double application the word can have. In the one usage it refers back to a single noun, in the other usage to a complete clause. 'He had to take the examination in Physics yesterday. This is not one of his strong subjects.' There 'this' refers directly back to the one word in the previous sentence, 'Physics'. Now change the second sentence. 'He had to take the examination in Physics yesterday. This is unfortunate because he was not feeling well.' In that sentence 'this' refers back to the whole content of the previous sentence. When writing 'this' one should always check exactly what it is that it refers back to. There must be no ambiguity for the reader.

he / him, she / her, I / me, we / us

In turning to these personal pronouns we have to deal with a different kind of error, not so much the error of not making clear to whom the personal pronoun refers, but the error of getting confused between the two forms, subject and object, 'he' and 'him', 'she' and 'her', 'I' and 'me', 'we' and 'us'. When errors occur in this matter the likelihood is that 'him' is used where it should be 'he', that 'her' is used where it should be 'she', and that 'us' is used where it should be 'we'. (Yet, strangely enough, that tendency is reversed with the pronouns 'I' and 'me'.) In certain dialects one used to get the equivalent of 'they hated he' or 'he trusted she', but these are not common errors today. The rule to remember is that the forms 'him', 'her', 'me' and 'us' can never be used as subjects of a verb. Thus 'It is him who is to blame' should be 'It is he who is to blame' and 'We got on well together, him and me' should be 'We got on well together, he and I.' Similarly 'Mum is against him too: both her and Dad want me to leave him' should be 'both she and Dad want me to leave him'. Whereas it is correct to say 'It is we who are to blame', where 'we' is the subject of the verb 'are', it is correct to say 'It is us he blamed', where 'us' is the object of the verb 'blamed'. One has to turn to cheaper magazines to find the crudest such errors in print, and they often occur in letters from readers.

> I'm really interested in plants and have taken down lots of addresses for places me and my friend can visit in the spring.

This should read: 'lots of addresses for places I and my friend can visit'.

Alas, I had just written the sentence above about 'cheaper magazines' when my eye fell on a piece in *The Times*. The newspaper prints a tribute to Charlie Chaplin on the anniversary of his death which reads thus at one point:

> His childhood was unhappy and when Charles was five his mother sent he and half-brother Sydney to an orphanage.

This should be: 'sent him and half-brother Sydney to an orphanage'. The error is curious, for one could hazard a guess that the writer would in no circumstances have written 'His mother sent he to the grocer's shop'. What is it that happens to the human mind to upset it when pronouns are thus partnered with nouns?

There is only one error of this kind that is heard frequently in superficially cultivated circles. It is the misuse of 'I'. For in contrast with what obtains with the other pairs of personal pronouns, it is 'I' that is over-used and not 'me'. Somehow people have got the impression that it is always wrong to say 'you and me'. So we get such tortuous statements as 'They would never threaten you and I' instead of 'you and me'.

> Come immunization day, my mother couldn't get my brother and I jabbed fast enough.

Here is a typical case in print of 'I' used where 'me' would be correct. It is remarkable that people who would never think of saying 'My mother gave I a present' will readily say 'My mother gave my brother and I a present.'

> For you or I it would be an intolerably difficult decision to have to make.

The case after a preposition such as 'for' must always be 'me', 'him', 'her', 'us' or 'them'. It is curious that people are reluctant to commit themselves to the natural construction: 'for you or me'. How deeply this error has corrupted us may be gauged from Norman Lamont's account of how John Major, as Prime Minister, replied in the Commons to accusations of a split between the Chancellor and himself:

> It may be that many people would like to invent divisions between he and I, but there are none.

This should have been: 'divisions between him and me'.

who / whom

This relic of Anglo-Saxon differentiation between the subject case and the object case is still troubling people.

There's a new couple down the road who I'd love to meet.

There's a man at work who I fantasize about.

You need to know who to contact.

In each of these three sentences 'who' should be 'whom', for in each case the pronoun is the object of a verb: 'whom I'd love to meet'; 'whom I fantasize about'; 'whom to contact'. 'Who' is appropriate only where the pronoun is the subject of the verb ('I want to know who lives there').

It is ironic that though the form 'whom' is used far less than it should be, yet people still manage to use it where they should not.

He refused to tell police whom he thinks is responsible for the guerrilla attack.

The pronoun ('whom') used here should not be regarded as the object of 'he thinks' but as the subject of 'is'. Many sentences are made on this pattern. There are two possible alternative corrections. We may change 'whom' to 'who': 'He refused to tell the police who he thinks is responsible'. Or we may make the pronoun the real object of 'thinks' by altering the verb 'is': 'He refused to tell the police whom he thinks to be responsible'. The same treatment could be given in the following case.

The ante-post market for the Sagitta 2000 Guineas has become lively after the winning debut at York last week of Stravinsky, the Aidan O'Brien colt whom many think will follow in the footsteps of his stable companion . . .

This must become either: 'the Aidan O'Brien colt who many think will follow in the footsteps', or: 'the Aidan O'Brien colt whom many think likely to follow in the footsteps'.

The relative pronoun 'whom' must refer back clearly to a noun (or pronoun), and it must be a noun used as a noun, not a noun used as an adjective.

I act for a small husband-and-wife partnership, both of whom are semi-retired and unlikely ever again to be liable to tax.

Here the words 'husband-and-wife' act as an adjective describing the partnership. Strictly speaking, neither husband nor wife has been mentioned as such. If the word 'whom' is to be kept, 'husband' and 'wife' must become genuine nouns: 'I work for a partnership of husband and wife, both of whom are semi-retired.'

USING THE RIGHT PREPOSITIONS

Prepositions, those little words in the architecture of the sentence, are rather like the mortar that holds the bricks together in building. 'I went the cinema my friend the evening the twenty-fifth' is like a pile of loose bricks. When the prepositions are added ('I went *to* the cinema *with* my friend *on* the evening *of* the twenty-fifth') the bricks are fastened together in a meaningful fabric.

A word must be said about the label 'preposition'. In dealing with verbs in the last chapter we finally turned to the part of speech known as the gerund or the 'verbal noun'. The very expression 'verbal noun' can teach us a lot. If a verb can function as a noun from time to time, then basic grammatical labels must sometimes be taken with a pinch of salt. Indeed, the words we were taught at school to call 'prepositions' spend quite a lot of their time not being prepositions at all. Consider the word 'up', how variously it functions. One only has to compare 'He ran up a big hill' with 'He ran up a big bill' to realize that what he did in respect of the hill is very different from what he did in respect of the bill. In 'up a big hill', 'up' is indeed a preposition with a direct relationship to the noun 'hill'. In 'He ran up a big bill' 'up' is what is generally called a 'particle', determining the meaning of the verb 'ran'. This is not a special peculiarity of the word 'up'. 'The bus ran down the hill' might be compared with 'The bus ran down a pedestrian.' Again 'down' is a preposition in the first sentence and a particle (sometimes called an 'adverbial particle') in the second sentence.

What other forms of speech can the word 'up' become? Most commonly perhaps an adverb, as in sentences such as 'A storm suddenly blew up' or 'The winning number came up.' It can also become an adjective, for the railways used to speak of the 'up' line and the 'down' line according to whether the line was used for trains going towards London or away from London. And when we speak of the 'ups' and 'downs' of life we are using the word 'up' as a noun. Finally, in the sentence 'He upped and went away' we use the word 'up' as a verb.

We are here chiefly concerned with prepositions performing their proper prepositional function. As long as crude physical connections are at issue in such expressions as 'to the cinema' and 'with my friend', it is unlikely that the preposition used will be the wrong one. But of course prepositions are used to indicate connections less easily definable than those. And an observer of the way the English language is being used from day to day cannot avoid noticing an extreme carelessness in the choice of prepositions. This is not perhaps so much a matter of logic as of custom. When a reviewer in the *Daily Telegraph* writes 'Many people will be particularly interested by the more speculative pieces', the reader feels a jolt of mental discomfort. Traditional usage would surely require 'Many people will be particularly interested in the more speculative pieces.' Just as we say 'fascinated by' and 'attracted by', so we say 'interested in'.

Now it may be argued that many well-established uses of prepositions are simply the product of convention. But in a sense all verbal meanings are a matter of established convention. It may be agreed that some verbal conventions have more of a philological basis than others. Some verbal conventions are more important than others and no doubt certain verbal conventions are more purely 'conventional' than others. But is there some special reason for treating with indifference the conventions of usage affecting prepositions? I ask this because, so far as the spoken word is concerned, and if BBC Radio 4 is representative of general practice, then it would not be an exaggeration to say that there is an epidemic of prepositional anarchy around. A prominent symptom of the complaint is over-use of the preposition 'to'. There seems to be a campaign to turn it into an all-purpose preposition.

to for *of*

> Remember too – that the secret to getting and staying physically active is to start at a level which is comfortable to you.

> We've discovered the secret to looking good for longer.

Here is evidence from the magazine world of how the usage 'secret of' is being neglected. In these two cases preference should surely be given to 'the secret of getting and staying physically active' and 'the secret of looking good'. Convention has established the usage 'the secret of success' matching the usages 'the riddle of the sands' and 'the enigma of the unsolved cypher'. The substitution of 'to' for 'of' after 'secret' appears to derive from the usage in such sentences as 'Detectives are searching for clues to the identity of the criminal.' By a familiar process of 'constructional transfer' the usage appropriate for 'clue' is applied to the word 'secret'.

And now I have just heard on the radio a speaker telling us that someone 'took a very different view to the whole affair'. Clearly it should be 'a different view of the whole affair'. What makes the mistake worse is the fact that there is a proper use of the expression 'view to' widely different in meaning from the expression 'view of'. One may say 'I bought the country cottage with a view to eventually retiring there.'

Again, I hear on the radio a well-spoken, well-educated woman give this reply to an interviewer: 'I don't know whether I'm the right person to ask that question to.' The established convention is that we ask a question 'of' someone, not 'to' someone, and therefore the speaker should have said 'I don't know whether I'm the right person to ask that question of.'

to for *on*

And now someone has been speaking on Radio 4 about experimentation with GM crops, and insisting that there would be 'no detrimental effect to the environment'. But established convention requires us to speak of the effect 'on' the environment.

to for *in*

> A former Manchester Ship Canal locomotive will celebrate its centenary by being painted to its original MSC livery.

We repaint things 'in' a given colour, not 'to' it: 'celebrate its centenary by being repainted in its original MSC livery'.

> The trick to drawing is measurement.

Even if we condone the dubious use of the word 'trick' (here roughly meaning what was meant above by 'secret'), it surely cannot be followed by 'to'. One might speak of the trick 'in' drawing, but 'trick' is the wrong word anyway.

to for *for*

I read in *The Times* Diary:

> Charges of lack of sympathy to women have been successfully rebuffed by John Casey, Fellow of Gonville and Caius, Cambridge.

The preposition 'to' is again out of place after 'sympathy'. The sentence should read: 'Charges of lack of sympathy for women have been successfully rebuffed.'

to for *with*

We now turn to a misuse which is increasingly damaging our verbal sensitivities, that is, the distinction between 'connected with' and 'connected to'.

> He believed Mr Pettit was connected to drugs.

Here is a clear misuse of 'to'. Mr Pettit may have been connected 'with' drugs, that is to say, he may have been associated 'with' people involved in the handling of drugs. An electric fire is connected 'to' the mains by a plug in a socket. The attachment of one thing 'to' another is a different matter from the association of one thing 'with' another. Cancer of the lung may be connected 'with' cigarette smoking, but cannot be said to be connected 'to' cigarette smoking. But to judge from the English of Radio 4 the habit of using 'connected to' where 'connected with' would be correct is widely prevalent. The word 'to' seems sometimes to have a compulsive grip on speakers. I have even heard a speaker take up a point by saying 'in connection to what we have been discussing' instead of 'in connection with what we have been discussing'.

Here is another case where 'to' appears at the expense of 'with':

> All chief constables have now been ordered to provide to the Home Office confidential reports on corruption in their forces.

It is not established English usage to speak of 'providing food to starving people', but to speak of 'providing starving people with food'. 'All chief constables have been ordered to provide the Home Office with confidential reports.'

to for *after*

What looks like a further misuse of 'to' is displayed in a local journal.

> Then Tom, who has always hankered to run an evening paper, took over the editorship of the *North West Evening Mail* at Barrow.

The verb to 'hanker' actually derives from a verb meaning to 'hang about' and thus gathered its associations of being in search of something. In traditional usage the verb is followed by 'after', though 'for' is also sometimes used. There is no authority for 'to'. The correction is: 'Tom, who has always hankered after running an evening paper'.

to for *from*

Most remarkable of all is this novel practice:

> Much of the decline [of village inns], however, dates to the introduction of greater competition on beer prices by the Thatcher government in the mid-80s.

Why not the established (and logical) 'dates from'?

missing *to*

After the evidence above of over-use of the preposition 'to', it is ironic that we have to draw attention to a failing in the opposite direction. A lax habit is being cultivated in some quarters of omitting prepositions which are really indispensable.

> Some novels are hard to bid farewell.

To find this in print in a review is surprising. The once-fashionable, but quite illogical, ruling against ending a sentence with a preposition can hardly be said to excuse this. Inelegant as it may seem, we must have: 'Some novels are hard to bid farewell to.'

on for *for*

Another over-used preposition today is 'on'. It appears in various contexts in substitution for various other prepositions.

> The Director outlines some of the implications on ministry as a whole.

We speak of implications 'for' ministry, not 'on' ministry. This again appears to be a case of constructional transfer. Because it is our practice to speak of the effects of an event 'on' someone or even the influence of an event 'on' someone, therefore the writer here assumes that one can speak of the implications of an event 'on' someone or something.

on for to

> I wouldn't recommend it on anyone.

This is an even more extraordinary case of constructional transfer. Because we speak of imposing things 'on' people and, more idiomatically, of 'wishing' things 'on' people, the writer here assumes that one can speak of recommending things 'on' people. So we get the over-used preposition 'on' used where the even more over-used preposition 'to' would in fact be proper.

on for *of*

> Economists said the data confirmed that the strong pound, the Asian financial crisis and a slowing domestic economy were taking heavy toll on the sector.

The more regular English usage is to take toll 'of'.

on for *against*

Here is an even more remarkable misuse.

> The Government is continuing its campaign by stealth on the deluded middle classes who elected them.

A campaign 'on' vivisection is surely the same thing as a campaign 'about' vivisection, whether pro or con. Plainly there should be no such vagueness about the above sentence from the hunting lobby. The writer means to persuade us that the government is involved in a campaign 'against' the middle classes. No other word than 'against' would be right here.

redundant *on*

As an extreme instance of the prepositional anarchy from which the media now suffer, let us consider the following passage from *The Times*.

> Hundreds of Ukrainian mercenaries are fighting alongside Sierra Leone's rebels who yesterday made good on their promise to burn Freetown, the capital, to the ground.

There are two idiomatic English usages of the words 'make good'. The one is represented by such statements as 'After a difficult start, he eventually made good', where 'made good' simply means 'succeeded'. The other usage is represented by such statements as 'He made good his pledge to cover all the cost' where 'made good' means 'faithfully kept', generally used of a promise duly fulfilled. The journalist above presumably meant just that: 'made good their promise to burn Freetown'. So what is the word 'on' doing there?

And here is a misplaced attempt to be colloquial:

> Atkinson, 47, of Kilburn, North London, had studied up on art and antiques . . .

'Up' and 'on' are alike out of place. If 'studied' is kept, they must both be removed.

missing *on*

Here is Radio 4's announcement about the discovery of a black box after a plane crash.

> It sheds no light as to what caused the accident.

Light is shed 'on' the objects it illuminates, not 'as to' them.

off

A local authority has sent a receipt for a parking fine.

> Received off . . . Mr Bloggs . . .

Is 'received from' now regarded in local government as an obsolete form?

for

Perhaps 'for' is the common preposition most rarely misused, but the statement below provides an instance:

> Local Tory and Labour leaders share a fierce pride for their city.

This seems to be another case of constructional transfer. Because we speak of affection, fondness or love 'for' a city, the writer wrongly transfers this usage to the word 'pride'. The proper usage is: 'Local Tory and Labour leaders share a fierce pride in their city.'

Radio 4 has supplied another instance of such constructional transfer in a reference to 'a father who has an obsession for sport'. A person may be said to have a love 'for' sport, but we do not use 'for' after 'obsession'. Just as we say that someone is obsessed 'with' (or 'by') a hobby, so we say that someone has an obsession 'with' a hobby. But in the sentence quoted it is difficult to understand why the noun 'obsession' was used at all, instead of the verb: 'a father who is obsessed with sport'.

We are told by a voice on Radio 4 that a certain politician 'has no sympathy for this view'. English has two distinctive usages after the word sympathy. We say that we have sympathy 'with' a friend when we wish to indicate that we share her feelings or convictions in some respect. We say that we have sympathy 'for' the friend when we wish to indicate that we have understanding and fellow-feeling for her in her current situation. It is important not to confuse these usages. You may feel sympathy 'for' a stricken person, because you thereby enter into sharing that person's feelings, but you sympathize (more objectively) 'with' that person's viewpoint. The distinction may be a subtle one, but distinctions between usages have to match in subtlety the workings of the human mind. To lose the distinction in such cases as this is to jettison nuances which are a part of our heritage as thinking beings.

from . . . to

One of the constructions which seems to cause people trouble is the use of 'from' and 'to' in such sentences as 'From saucepans to electric washers everything in the store seems too dear.' That sentence makes its point properly because 'saucepans' and 'electric washers' belong to the same series of items as goods on show in a particular shop. Thus 'everything' makes sense as summing them all up in a generalization about those items. But consider this:

> From frosty pinks to rosy hues, everyone will have a chance to look fashionably made up.

To define people as frosty pinks and rosy hues is not flattering. 'Everyone' here cannot be said to sum up that series of colours in making the generalization. The only possible sequence to 'From frosty pinks to rosy hues' would be something like 'all the colours were fashionable'.

Having looked at a case where a 'from . . . to' construction is improperly followed up, we should also look at a case where the 'from . . . to' construction is itself improperly handled.

> This action plan includes a wide range of activities from working with young offenders to those who suffer discrimination.

The 'from . . . to' construction here itself goes awry. There is no proper balance between what should be parallel items after 'from' ('working with young offenders') and 'to' ('those who suffer'). We need that balance: 'a wide range of activities from working with young offenders to helping those who suffer discrimination'.

from

The preposition 'from' on its own is perhaps less often misused. But the following is noteworthy.

> While Tony Blair has reformed the Labour Party, making its policies more acceptable, the Conservative Party under William Hague has become unrecognizable from the party I used to support so enthusiastically.

We need to consider what prepositions can be properly used after 'unrecognizable'. We can say 'The building is unrecognizable from this distance', but plainly that is not the usage intended above. We can also say 'He is unrecognizable as the man who sold me the car.' And it would appear that this is the appropriate usage for the sentence above: 'The Conservative Party has become unrecognizable as the party I used to support.'

The word 'from' is used after certain verbs of prohibition. A person is prohibited or banned 'from' driving. But that does not justify a statement about Parliament having to decide 'which countries should be forbidden from receiving certain weapons'. We forbid people 'to' do this or that.

at

Sometimes error or awkwardness results from rather thoughtlessly beginning a sentence with a preposition.

> At a meeting called last week by the President of the local Chamber of Trade over 130 people attended.

People do not attend 'at' a meeting. They attend the meeting. To correct this sentence while keeping the first words 'At a meeting' the verb 'attended' would have to go: 'over 130 people were present'.

It seems hazardous to begin a sentence with 'at'. Here a journalist is looking into the background of a newly revealed one-time spy:

> At the house in Kirkham Drive, Hull, where he has lived for the past three years, none of the neighbours knew about his cloak-and-dagger background.

Was it 'at' the house that nobody knew? Did the neighbours all gather there to oblige the journalist, allowing him to economize on prepositions? We cannot know.

There are a few verbs which are often followed by 'at'. We stare 'at' people and we marvel 'at' new inventions. In such cases the word is generally not dispensable even when the verb is passive. If I stare at you, then you are stared 'at', not just 'stared'. That is where the following touch of eloquence about the young goes astray.

> They don't want to be lectured, they don't want to be preached.

The only thing that can 'be preached' is a sermon. There is no alternative to: 'they don't want to be preached at'.

The conversational habit of omitting 'at' after certain verbs which require it should not be followed in print. Where 'It's a nice place to stay' might pass in conversation, in writing one would expect 'It's a nice place to stay at.'

> He reviews restaurants too, and makes most of them sound like places you wish you could eat.

Plainly this should be: 'most of them sound like places you wish you could eat at'. The notion of wanting to eat restaurants might seem unlikely to be often expressed in print, but in fact it is not rare.

> Penang has a mix of Chinese, Indian and Malay people, which, among other things, makes it a fantastic place to eat.

in and out

A common malpractice with 'in' (as with 'at') is that of omitting it. A radio announcer, speaking of the plight of the sufferers from the Turkish earthquake, says that they are finding the emergency tents supplied to be 'places not fit to live' instead of 'not fit to live in'. It is only a living being who can logically be described as 'not fit to live'.

There is a temptation to use 'out' where it is superfluous – for example, 'There are two things you can separate out.' This means no more than 'There are two things you can separate.'

by

At the beginning of this section we cited a misuse of 'by' after the word 'interested'. There is a similar lapse from established convention in a reference to

> Wives or girl friends . . . who don't understand why their partner is so concerned by being bald.

One might be upset, disturbed or moved 'by' something, but 'concerned' is followed by 'at': 'so concerned at being bald'. And another journalist seems equally at sea over the use of 'by':

> Nicholas Owen, of ITN, is in trouble with his friend Sophie Rhys-Jones, by comparing her with Diana, Princess of Wales.

Just as a criminal would not be jailed 'by' robbing a bank but 'for' robbing a bank, so Nicholas Owen must not be said to be in trouble 'by' anything he has done but 'for' comparing Sophie with Diana.

over

We have various idiomatic usages of 'over'. In (a) 'She has changed over the years' the notion of duration is predominant. In (b) 'They exhibited great concern over the whole tragic affair' the word 'over' is the equivalent of 'about' or 'in respect of'. In (c) 'They discussed the latest news over lunch' the notion of simultaneity is present.

> What do you think of the government's handling over the whole affair?

In this question, put by a Radio 4 interviewer, the speaker seems to be trying to combine usage (a) with usage (b) in the same utterance. The effort does not come off. Usage (b) is appropriate only after certain words such as 'concern', 'worry' or 'disappointment' ('He expressed his disappointment over the whole discussion'). In this context the word 'handling' requires to be followed by 'of'.

with

We come now to the treatment of the preposition whose misuse has run riot in contemporary journalism. Journalists, it seems, are prepared to force the preposition 'with' to do numerous jobs for which it is unfitted.

the additive *with*

> She lives in London, with regular travels overseas.

We may accept that the comma after London makes clear that there is no question of cohabitation. Nevertheless since the proper use of 'with' would give us such sentences as 'She lives in London with her grandmother', it seems impossible to justify not writing 'She lives in London but/and travels regularly overseas.'

> We climbed and climbed with a sheer drop as one glanced out of the window.

Here again the word 'with' is asked to do an additive job it is unfitted for. The sentences 'We climbed with heavy rucksacks on our backs' and

'We climbed with great difficulty' show how 'with' should be used. Instead it here introduces an additional piece of information which, as before, might have been properly introduced by 'and': 'We climbed and climbed, and caught sight of a sheer drop as we glanced out of the windows.'

> The statement made clear that there was no agreement on interest rates, with governments likely to go their own way.

Once more 'with' is used improperly to add to the information given. The sentence should conclude: 'and governments were likely to go their own ways'.

There are times when the use of 'with' to add an appendage seems positively forced on the English tongue. Here we have a former ambassador on the subject of the Foreign Office.

> One of the great failures of the diplomatic service has been to cast off its image as bowler-hatted, pin-striped, chinless and with a fondness for champagne.

Why avoid the straightforward natural sequence here: 'cast off its image as bowler-hatted, pin-striped, chinless and fond of champagne'?

the causal *with*

The misuse of 'with' for appending additional information is, however, a mild offence compared to the prevalent misuse of 'with' which treats it as having something in common with the word 'because'.

> As you say, with the noise, you could easily have been persuaded that the gear box was broken.

'With the noise' is here used to mean 'because of the noise'. One wonders what is the rational basis for using the word thus. For the causal element, in various degrees, now seems to intrude into the use of 'with' in many different contexts.

> With a mainly rural constituency it was no surprise when Paddy Ashdown joined the Countryside Alliance march through London.

Paddy Ashdown certainly did not join the march 'with' a rural constituency. He joined it, we are really being told, 'because' he has a rural constituency. Not that there is any need to introduce the word 'because' here. The participle could be used. 'Having a mainly rural constituency,

Paddy Ashdown not surprisingly joined the Countryside Alliance march through London.' This recourse to a participle will often correct misuse of 'with'.

> With trading pretty tough, don't expect a big profits advance this year.

Once more the 'causal' element is predominant in the connotation of 'with'. Yet there is no need to use 'because'. The participle will serve again: 'Trading being pretty tough, don't expect a big profits advance this year.'

Of course there are occasions when getting rid of the offensive 'with' may take much more trouble. Consider the following sentence about life in the Fens.

> Malaria was once a great problem, for example, and with few doctors and endemic poverty the local people often resorted to homemade remedies.

It is bad to combine endemic poverty 'with' few doctors as two equivalent possessions the locals had. The two items require separate verbs to indicate their proper connection 'with' the local people: 'Malaria was once a great problem, for example, and, having few doctors and suffering from endemic poverty, the local people often resorted to homemade remedies.'

the causal / temporal *with*

There is a use of 'with' which is part-causal and part-temporal in its meaning.

> With Gordon's retirement, we have sought to make a few more changes within the team at Headquarters.

The words seem to combine the sense 'since Gordon retired' with the sense 'because Gordon has retired'. The most suitable correction would be: 'Now that Gordon has retired'.

> Now her childhood home is up for sale and, with both her parents dead, saying goodbye is going to be painful.

Here 'with' is used again to give both a temporal and a causal explanation, amounting to 'now that' they are dead and 'because' they are dead. But the participle construction could perfectly meet the need here: 'and, both her parents being dead, saying goodbye is going to be painful'. The same treatment can be given to the following:

> With Edith gone something had to be done about Jack.

Correct this to: 'Edith having gone, something had to be done about Jack.'

with and participle

Some of the most unfortunate misuses of 'with' occur when the word is followed by a present participle.

> With the internet seeming to have an effect on many areas of our lives, it was probably only a matter of time before it was used to organize a railtour.

The causal force of 'with' should be differently obtained: 'Now that the internet seems to have an effect on many areas of our lives'.

Perhaps the most excruciating of all misuses of 'with' can be illustrated by the words of a *Times* correspondent from Washington:

> With it looking almost certain, barring new developments, that the required two thirds of the 100-member Senate will not remove Mr Clinton from office by voting to convict him on the two articles of impeachment, the disagreement among senators is over how quickly to rid themselves of the case.

What is meant here by 'With it looking almost certain' is 'Since it looks almost certain', and that is how it should read. The journalist is operating here on the same level as the person who could write 'With it being wet, I stayed inside' instead of 'Since it was wet, . . .'

Very often the bad combination of 'with' and a present or past participle can be more simply avoided.

> With the plc having increased its authorized share capital to £1,000,000, the relaunch will enable it to raise the money needed to rebuild the line.

All that needs to be done here to make the sentence a perfectly good one is to take out the word 'with': 'The plc having increased its authorized share capital to £1,000,000, the relaunch will enable it to raise the money needed.'

In a more complex sentence the same simple correction can often be made.

> The incumbents of Egremont Castle seemingly had problems providing male heirs, and with Richard de Lucy leaving no son, the superstition developed that no male heir would ever survive to inherit the castle.

If we take out the word 'with' and adjust the punctuation, we are left with a perfectly satisfactory sentence: 'The incumbents of Egremont Castle seemingly had problems in [*sic*] providing male heirs and, Richard de Lucy leaving no son, the superstition developed that no male heir would ever survive to inherit the castle.' This usage of the participle construction in a kind of parenthetical detachment from the rest of the sentence ('Richard de Lucy leaving no son') is one of the most neglected of all English constructions. It is the construction we recommended earlier in getting rid of the absurd hanging participle in 'Having said that, it looks like rain', which we replace by 'That being said, . . .

without

An ugly usage of the word 'without' has now established itself in the press.

> They hoped their partners would know what they wanted without them having to tell them.

This usage exploits what we have called the 'gerciple'. To correct it we must change the gerciple ('them having') into a proper gerund: 'without their having to tell them'. This is one of those cases where that correction can be made straightforwardly. The word 'them' becomes the possessive form 'their', and all is well. Unfortunately, where the error occurs, such a direct change is not always possible.

> Do not believe that Scotland can be given devolution without it then demanding independence.

Strictly speaking, the sentence would be correct if 'it' were changed to 'its': 'without its then demanding independence'. But that usage has an air of pedantic contrivance which we shy away from. Therefore it would be better to get rid of 'without': 'Do not believe that Scotland can be given devolution and not then demand independence.'

Dealing with bad usage of 'without' thus generally means getting rid of gerciples.

> If you, too, find it a trial of strength to pick up a saucepan full of cooked food and drain it without the contents disappearing down the sink, or dropping the pan, Boots has the answer.

This is a useful specimen because it shows the 'without' construction both ill used and properly used. It is correct to write of draining a saucepan 'without dropping the pan' because 'without dropping' is indeed what is meant. It is incorrect to speak of draining a saucepan 'without the contents . . .' because what is really meant is 'without the disappearing (disappearance) of the contents down the sink'. Since the use of the apostrophe ('contents' disappearing') is both awkward and ugly, the need for it must be removed: 'If you, too, find it a trial of strength to pick up a saucepan full of cooked food and drain it without losing the contents down the sink or dropping the pan, Boots has the answer.' The reader will notice that we have brought the two constructions into parallel: 'without losing the contents' and 'without dropping the pan'.

The advice to writers must be to exercise extreme caution whenever the impulse arises to use 'without' to introduce a phrase. Conversational idiom, I suppose, now allows such expressions as 'without anyone noticing' (instead of 'without anyone's noticing') and perhaps 'without trouble arising' (instead of 'without trouble's arising'). On paper, however, such constructions look bad. On the whole they do not appear in good books. And they are avoidable. They are replaceable without straining the language (which sentence is correct, where 'without the language being strained' would be incorrect).

except

This preposition is rarely misused, but error arises when one tries to use it as though it were a conjunction.

> You'll need to pay for these yourself, except if you're hard of hearing.

This instance of generosity on the part of BT is marred by the grammar in which it is expressed. The proper word to use here would be 'unless': 'You'll need to pay for these yourself, unless you're hard of hearing.' There is a construction 'except that' which can function as a conjunction and introduce a clause ('I would love to come along with you except that I have another engagement on the day'). But on its own 'except' must govern a noun or pronoun ('The whole family came except the baby').

CHAPTER 7

Avoiding Grammatical Pitfalls

Our daily utterance in speech may contain a fair proportion of simple sentences or questions such as 'Dinner is ready' or 'What time shall I meet you?' But we also have a lot to say and to write which requires more complex arrangements of words. Daily life inevitably involves us in reasoning which complicates the way we handle words. By 'reasoning' I do not necessarily mean anything very sophisticated. We work through a simple pattern of reasoning when we say 'As a decorative scheme, it just doesn't come off' or 'I prefer the pink wallpaper to the blue one.' The intention here is to consider some of the lines of utterance which are a proportionately significant part of our daily conversation and which can be shown to lead our contemporaries frequently into error. For much of the error in the use of English today is concentrated in a handful of bad practices associated with certain frequently used constructions. When one studies current usage with a microscope, concentrating on the detection of error, one is surprised not just by how much of it there is, but by how limited it is in range. There is a handful of notable constructional defects and they turn up, in many different forms, day after day, by the thousand. Obviously there is a need to make clear what those errors are; and it should be helpful too to illustrate with what ingenious versatility they are committed. Then it becomes possible to look out for them.

As we express views about this or that, as we make plans, as we discuss matters of current interest, as we get involved in professional controversy, we naturally want to know what are the routes our thinking takes which are most hazardous to the preservation of accuracy. Which are the highways of reasoning and indeed the byways of passing reflection most littered with traps? Which are the much-used individual words which sign-post the way to the areas of stumbling and falling? That is at issue here and, at a slightly more sophisticated level, in the next chapter.

FALSE PARALLELS

There are many usages in which item is related to item in such a way as to produce parallelism between them. We see this parallelism at its simplest in the relationship between 'John' and 'my solicitor' in the statement 'John, my solicitor, is ready to see you' or in the statement 'John is here as my solicitor.' The reader may be surprised to discover how much mismatching can be found in usages involving such parallelisms.

Mismatches After *as*

We deal in the next chapter with misuse of 'as' in linking clause with clause ('They went home as soon as they could'). Here we are concerned with that superficially simple construction used when someone says 'As a doctor, I should advise a long rest.' So long as the words 'as a doctor' are firmly anchored to a subject such as 'I', all is well. Alas such simple connections are sometimes hard to find.

> As something of a steam enthusiast, it was good to see steam has now reached Mach 0.45.

There is no word later in the sentence to give meaning to the opening words 'as something of a steam enthusiast'. They require a matching noun or pronoun. Introduce either 'I' or 'me': 'As something of a steam enthusiast, I found it good to see that steam has now reached Mach 0.45', or: 'it pleased me to see that steam has now reached Mach 0.45'. A comparable failure to match the opening words appears in the following.

> As an international holiday resort, every type of cuisine can be found.

The words 'as an international holiday resort' are just forgotten. There is nothing to give them a meaning. A few words appended would provide the matching item needed: 'As an international holiday resort, every type of cuisine can be found in the town.' The words 'the town' provide the matching item for 'as an international holiday resort'.

Often there is a mismatch after 'as' that seems to result from sheer carelessness in writing, carelessness that a moment's thought would have forestalled.

> As the organization which represents the interests of the British-grown timber industry, I cannot let his article go unchallenged.

The writer surely did not intend to identify himself as an organization. He began his letter with something in mind that he then forgot. It would have been better to say at the beginning exactly what he was: 'As spokesman for the organization which represents the interests of the British-grown timber industry'.

There would seem to be a similar forgetfulness in this artist's comment on paintbrushes.

> The behaviour of the synthetic fibre is remarkably effective as a low-cost substitute for animal hair.

It is not 'the behaviour' that is effective as a substitute for animal hair, it is the synthetic fibre. One questions whether the word 'behaviour' is worth keeping: 'Synthetic fibre is remarkably effective as a low-cost substitute for animal hair.' If the original sentence looks like a version of the 'possessive trap', the following observation from the racecourse looks even more so.

> Bought at an auction in Mechelen, Belgium, as a three-year-old by Michael Whitaker, Pion's win pleased David Broome.

We are told here that Pion's 'win' was bought at an auction in Belgium as a three-year-old. So easy it is to slip into the 'possessive trap' and talk about a possession when you should be talking about the possessor. If the first part of the sentence is kept, the subject of the rest will have to be 'Pion': 'Pion pleased David Broome with his win.'

There is an even more common version of the 'possessive trap'.

> His association with Shackerstone, started 58 years ago as a railway junior, has continued ever since.

The strict grammarian will say that it was not 'his association' that started as a railway junior. 'He' started as a railway junior, but 'he' has not been mentioned. The writer is talking about his association and should not forget that. 'His association with Shackerstone, started 58 years ago when he was a railway junior, has continued ever since.'

Mismatch After *although*

Like the word 'as', the word 'although' may be used to introduce a phrase in grammatical parallel. 'Although a heavy smoker, he survived to the age of ninety.' (The opening of the sentence is really an abbreviation of 'Although he was a heavy smoker'.) Care must be taken not to allow a mismatch between the two parts of the sentence.

> Although a strict vegetarian, his only daughter ate meat.

Strictly interpreted, this tells us that the strict vegetarian daughter ate meat. There is no other word than 'daughter' to give grammatical propriety to the words 'although a strict vegetarian'. The only way to rescue the sentence is to introduce the vegetarian and a second verb: 'Although he was a strict vegetarian, his only daughter ate meat.'

Mismatches After Participles

Another source of mismatches is the misconnected participle. We have already seen such failures in looking at present and past participles. They are not hard to locate.

> Handmade by an experienced brushmaker, its Kolinsky sable hairs will hold a generous quantity of colour.

Are we to understand that the hairs were handmade by an experienced brushmaker, or that the entire paintbrush was so made? If the latter was intended, then the above requires correction: 'Handmade by an experienced brushmaker, the brush has Kolinsky sable hairs which hold a generous quantity of colour.'

> Originally designed in 1935 by John Adams, the war and its need for utility delayed wholesale production until 1946.

Here the burden of responsibility for the Second World War seems to be shifted from the shoulders of Adolf Hitler. For the war, we are told, was originally designed in 1935 by one John Adams. The only other possible noun for 'designed' to agree with would be 'production'. Correction involves supplying an appropriate noun to match the words 'originally designed'. This could be inserted towards the end of the sentence: 'the war and the consequent emphasis on utility products delayed production of the piece until 1946'. Alternatively, the sentence could be reworded: 'Originally planned in 1935 by John Adams, wholesale production of the piece was delayed until 1946 by the war and the need for utility.'

Other Mismatches

Many mismatches are made simply by straightforward failure to parallel terms correctly. Sometimes a couple of words will serve to launch a sentence that explodes on take-off.

> Recent parents, our small patch of green had sadly become a wilderness of weeds.

We could allow 'Recent parents, we had no time for gardening', or even 'Recent parents, our neighbours allowed their garden to go to seed.' In each of these statements 'Recent parents' are identified ('we' and 'our neighbours'). But our writer identifies the small patch of green as 'recent parents'. What is meant is: 'As recent parents we had allowed our small patch of green to become a wilderness of weeds.' The longer the sentence, the more easily a mismatch of this kind can pass unnoticed.

> A devout practising Christian throughout his life, the calm of the village church at an early Sunday morning service provided a welcome respite from the hectic pressures of life in the City.

All that is needed here to transform slack writing into correct writing is the addition of the pronoun 'him' somewhere in the latter half of the sentence: 'A devout practising Christian throughout his life, the calm of the village church at an early Sunday morning service provided him with a welcome respite.' Without that 'him' there is nothing to make sense of the opening words 'A devout practising Christian'.

The world of advertising goes in for mismatching on a generous scale. The following is about pottery.

> Sleek and elegant in its simplicity, the clean lines still possess a contemporary modern quality.

What is 'it' that has this simplicity? 'It' cannot be the plural 'clean lines'. Yet those 'clean lines' are the only subject of the sentence, the only item under discussion. To correct the sentence one must either attach 'simplicity' to the clean lines: 'Sleek and elegant in their simplicity, the clean lines etc.' or change the subject of the sentence: 'Sleek and elegant in its simplicity, the pottery has clean lines that still possess a contemporary modern quality.'

DRAWING COMPARISONS AND CONTRASTS

Direct Similarities

like

In no area of statement on paper is there more error than in the making of comparisons and contrasts. Declaring similarities by using the word 'like', or declaring dissimilarities by using the word 'unlike' are processes which seem to bring out the worst in English penmanship. The most obvious failures occur when a comparison instituted by the word 'like' really fails to materialize. If we read 'Like most mothers, she soon tried to teach her child to speak', we recognize that the words 'like most mothers' introduce and define the word 'she'. But if we read 'Like most mothers, the demands of the children were a pressing preoccupation', we look in vain for the word which 'like most mothers' should introduce and define. It does not appear. The sentence illustrates the first kind of misuse of 'like', where the adjective 'like' (for it is usually an adjective) never acquires the noun which it should qualify.

The error is not rare. Consider the following sentence about collecting antiques.

> Like most of the treasured things we surround ourselves with, the fun is knowing their historical context.

The writer starts with the words 'Like most of the treasured things we surround ourselves with' and readers wait for the expected specimen. They await some sequence such as 'our favourite pictures are a constant delight'. But no such sequence appears. We never explicitly hear what these things are which are 'like most of the treasured things' we possess. Instead the writer talks about 'fun', which is not really a treasured piece of household equipment at all. If the opening of the sentence is kept, the conclusion must be totally changed: 'Like most of the treasured things we surround ourselves with, our antiques give delight as we explore their history.'

More common than such elaborately contrived excursions into error are the simple oversights of people who slip up in their use of a pronoun:

> These old horses love their work and, like humans who retire, it can be a shock to the system.

The natural sequence is always the best, and the natural sequence after 'like humans' would begin with 'they'. To introduce 'it' instead after 'like humans' is obviously going out of one's way in asking for trouble. The proper sequence would be: 'These old horses love their work and, like humans who retire, they can suffer a shock to the system.'

When the pedant starts to look for instances of bad usage following the word 'like', he is faced with a seemingly infinite variety. Here is a sentence recording that six kittens had been used in a year in a certain scientific research establishment.

> This was, like laboratories across Britain, the lowest level yet.

'This' presumably is the number cited. It is said to resemble laboratories across Britain. It would be difficult to think of a more disastrous placing of the word 'like'. Neither the number nor the 'level' can be said to be 'like' laboratories. If 'like' is to be kept, the subject of the sentence must be changed: 'This establishment, like laboratories across Britain, thus achieved the lowest level yet.'

The examples we have given may seem to be rather crude, and readers may well feel themselves totally immune from stumbling so badly. But skilled writers sometimes trip up with this same usage.

> Like a husband who has been caught in an adulterous affair, and who tries to repair his marriage with ever more expensive gifts, the relationship between politician and people has become demeaned.

Now indeed this accomplished writer of political diatribes in *The Times* excites our curiosity with his opening words. We are promised reference to someone who is behaving like an adulterous husband, vainly trying to compensate for his infidelities with boxes of chocolates and jars of perfume, chocolates first from Cadbury, then from Belgium, perfume first from Boots, then from Chanel. But alas this rather revolting individual is never named. It turns out that no one is 'like' him after all. What is like him is a 'relationship', and what could be more boring than that? Next time the writer should arrange his words differently: 'Like a husband who has been caught in an adulterous affair, and who tries to repair his marriage with ever more expensive gifts, the politician has demeaned his relationship with the people.'

Other Misuses of *like*

We have dealt so far with failures to achieve correct matchings on either side of the word 'like'. But there is another current misuse of 'like' which is rapidly establishing itself.

> I'm making it sound like we didn't get on.

The correct version of this would be: 'I'm making it sound as though we didn't get on' (or: 'as if we didn't get on'). We find the misuse increasingly in print.

> I feel like my hair makes me look really young.

> You don't want to look like you're plastered with make-up.

> A body that doesn't look like it's swollen three sizes . . .

> As it sounds like you have under twenty per cent grey hair, it should give complete colour.

In each of the above cases 'like' should be replaced by 'as though' or 'as if'. The objection to 'like' used thus is that it is an adjective. 'She is like a mother to me'; 'The pie crust was like cardboard'; such sentences show the adjectival force of 'like' at its most direct. But the word 'like' as used in the faulty sentences above is made to function as a conjunction, hingeing on a verb and linking two clauses together. It links 'I feel' and 'my hair makes me look'; it links 'You don't want to look' and 'you're plastered'; it links 'A body doesn't look' and 'it's swollen'; it links 'it sounds' and 'you have'. This is a function that the adjective 'like' cannot perform.

A slightly different version of such misuse treats 'like' not as the equivalent of 'as though', but as the equivalent of 'as'.

> You get a bill a few weeks later like you would with a Visa.

The same judgement applies to this misuse. It treats 'like' as a conjunction, as a word that can link 'You get a bill' with 'you would with a Visa'. In the same way the substitution of 'as' for 'like' would correct the following sentences:

> *Raw Valley* drew in passengers like never before.

> When I first did Burghley, you could have taken a bold seven-year-old or, like I did, a slightly cobby 15.2 hh, and done well.

The question must be asked here whether this construction has sufficiently established itself to be pronounced acceptable. All one can say is that good writers are not using it.

as with

The word 'like' is so over-used and so often misused that it is ironic to have to point to occasions when avoiding it leads to bad writing. Here we have a comment about 'Tudor Rose' dining trains.

> As with most services of this type, this is very popular.

It is a fairly safe piece of advice to writers to say that if they are just going to begin a sentence with 'as with' they are probably just about to make a blunder. Here the word should be replaced by 'like': 'Like most services of this type, this is very popular.'

> As with the Freud exhibition, Riley's show will include paintings.

The same correction should be made here: 'Like the Freud exhibition, Riley's show will include paintings.'

similar

The word 'similar' (followed by 'to') suffers from the same laxity in usage as 'like'.

> The format will be similar to last year.

This not unusual carelessness requires a very simple correction: 'The format will be similar to last year's.' Short-circuiting a comparison in that way is an error that appears in many guises and at various levels of sophistication.

> The last time I wept was when my cat died. It was uncontrollable, short-term kind of reaction, similar to my father dying.

Here is a fairly crude specimen. The writer compares her misery to the death of her father, instead of to the misery she suffered on his death. She should have written: 'It was an uncontrollable, short-term kind of reaction such as my father's death caused.'

There are examples of this error at a more sophisticated level and they cannot be so easily dealt with.

> Great Eastern generated the fewest complaints, particularly commendable as its service complexity and density is similar to other commuter railways which show far worse figures.

This sentence puts the same error on show, though wrapped about with more words. Great Eastern's performance is being compared with other railways instead of with their performance. One may question too whether 'service complexity' is really a satisfactory equivalent of 'complexity of service', and whether the words 'particularly commendable' should not be more firmly attached to the rest of the sentence: 'Great Eastern generated the fewest complaints, a particularly commendable result, as the complexity and density of its service are similar to those of other commuter railways.' To get rid of the artificial 'those of', rewrite thus: 'a particularly commendable result in that, in the complexity and density of its services, it matches other commuter railways which show far worse figures'.

If two items resemble each other, they can be said to be 'similar'. A BBC news writer commits himself/herself to the absurd comment: 'Both reports are similar.' Since it would be impossible for A to be similar to B unless B were similar to A, the use of the word 'both' is out of place, and it should be omitted.

Direct Contrasts

unlike

Making direct contrasts by using the word 'unlike' is just as productive of error as declaring similarities by using the word 'like'. As is the case with so many misuses that we are examining, this abuse of 'unlike' appears at all levels of simplicity and sophistication.

> Unlike its rival, the Kenwood Chef, the top could be detached and used as a portable hand mixer.

There is the error at its simplest. The 'top' of the mixer, instead of the mixer itself, is said to be 'unlike its rival'. What is meant is: 'Unlike its rival, the Kenwood Chef, it has a detachable top that can be used as a portable hand mixer.'

One persistent version of the error appears in reference to dates.

> Unlike the late 1980s, the economy is starting to slow after the monetary squeeze applied by the Bank of England.

The pedant wonders why anyone should want to contrast 'the economy' with 'the late 1980s'. The only thing that could be properly contrasted with 'the late 1980s' would be another period, say, 'the 2000s'. If 'unlike' is kept, the sentence must be reshaped: 'The economy today, unlike that of the 1980s, is starting to slow.' The slip is not a rare occurrence.

> And, unlike the early 1980s, public finances are healthy enough not to need tightening.

Does the pressure of repeated occurrences of this construction require us to accept it? To anyone in whose mind the word 'unlike' persists in maintaining its adjectival status the idea is unacceptable. The acceptable pattern for these comparisons is 'Unlike 1980, 1990 had a hot summer.' The innovative pattern we are criticizing is represented by such statements as 'Unlike 1980, the weather is hot', where 'unlike 1980' hangs in the air, an incomplete utterance.

The misuse of 'unlike' in comparing dates may be bad, but there are far worse versions of the error. Consider this advertisement from an insurance company.

> Unlike many other plans, if you don't die during its 15-year term, you get a worthwhile cash sum to spend as you wish.

Your custom is sought by a kind assurance that you are 'unlike many other plans'. There is only one kind of sequence that could logically follow 'Unlike many other plans' and that is something that begins: 'this plan of ours' or words to that effect: 'Unlike many other plans, our plan ensures that if you don't die during its 15-year term, you get a worthwhile cash sum to spend as you wish.'

> Unlike the Labour Party, there is not a relationship between financial contributions and the control of policy.

This time there is no attempt to make clear what it is that is 'unlike the Labour Party'. To correct it that body will have to be mentioned: 'Unlike the Labour Party, the Conservative Party allows no relationship between financial contributions and the control of policy.'

Now let us turn to the error locked into a wordier and more complicated sentence:

> Unlike the angry response of western politicians, the Albanian villagers who survived the attack were muted, probably because they were still in shock after the butchery.

The 'Albanian villagers' were unlike the 'angry response' of our politicians, we are told. Only matching items can be drawn together by 'like' or pushed apart by 'unlike'. So the above should read: 'Unlike the angry response of western politicians, the response of the Albanian villagers who survived the attack was muted . . .'.

Other Comparisons and Contrasts

compared with

Not all positive comparisons involve 'like' and not all negative comparisons involve 'unlike'. But the same error of failing to match like with like appears in a variety of constructions. When a man claiming descent from Sir Walter Ralegh was given a jail sentence, a newspaper made this comment:

> Compared with his alleged ancestor, whose tobacco was grown in Virginia, it was a moderate sentence. Sir Walter was executed for treason in 1618.

'Compared with his ancestor . . . it was a moderate sentence' illustrates the same failure in matching like with like as we have found above. The use of the apostrophe 's' could make the comparison valid ('Compared with his alleged ancestor's, it was a moderate sentence') but the more direct correction would be simply to alter 'it was a moderate sentence' to 'he received a moderate sentence'.

Sometimes the misused construction 'compared with' is used unnecessarily anyway.

> The prospect of an economic landline through euroland is adding to pressure on the currency, which has lost 7 per cent of its value against the dollar

> compared with its launch two months ago, and which fell to a new low this week.

The euro is said to have lost 7 per cent of its value 'compared with its launch', but its value cannot be compared with its launch, only with its value at the time of the launch. Yet there is no need for that kind of awkward precision. Simply scrap the construction 'compared with', for the real comparison is between value at one date and value at another. The end of the sentence should read: 'adding to pressure on the currency, which has lost 7 per cent of its value against the dollar since its launch two months ago'.

more than

Making comparisons that involve 'more than' or just a comparative adjective ('bigger than') can produce similar problems. Here, for instance, a slip turns up in a travel piece.

> The food is described as an eclectic mix of Mediterranean and modern British, and is more authentically deserving of that description than many places.

The food, we are told, is better thus described than many other places. Unless the construction is changed there is no escape from: 'is more authentically deserving of that description than the food of many places'. But a writer may well prefer something less clumsy: 'more authentically deserving of that description than food you will find elsewhere'.

The mistake highlights the need for writers to ask themselves before making any comparisons: What exactly am I comparing with what? Failure to face that question squarely results in the error of missing the point in the sequence of thought.

> The Irish economy is growing at almost three times the rate of Britain.

Plainly the writer does not really mean to compare the Irish economy with Britain, but with Britain's economy. In this case the insertion of an apostrophe 's' will correct the error: 'The Irish economy is growing at three times the rate of Britain's.'

We turn to a slightly more subtle comparative misfire:

> Those facing redundancy today face a tougher time than in the previous recession.

This would be correct if those facing redundancy today were the same people who faced it in the previous recession. But they are not. So we cannot say that they are facing a tougher time than in the past. It would be correct, but clumsy, to write: 'Those facing redundancy today face a tougher time than their predecessors did.' It would be better to write: 'face a tougher time than was faced in the previous recession'. After all, the basic contrast is between periods of redundancy.

Personal Likenesses

The kind of error we are dealing with always betrays a streak of illogicality. That is why one cannot accept the notion that it must be regarded as acceptable because so many people are guilty of it. Here, from the world of horse-racing, we have a comment on an expert.

> His knowledge of pedigrees would be the equal of any stud manager in Newmarket.

This error is another version of the 'possessive trap'. The false comparison between one man's knowledge and another man must be replaced by a contrast between one man's knowledge and another's. The apostrophe does the trick: 'His knowledge of pedigrees would be the equal of any stud manager's in Newmarket.'

That kind of false comparison cannot always be rescued by insertion of an apostrophe.

> She knows that the social skills acquired throughout her previous employment, not to mention her day-to-day legal experience, are a distinct advantage over full-time students.

The mistake is really the mistake made in 'Her pupils' skills are better than her children', where what is needed is to change 'children' to children's'. For the 'social skills' are not an advantage over 'full-time students', but over 'those of full-time students'. If an alternative correction is preferred, then it could be: 'She knows that the social skills acquired . . . give her a distinct advantage over full-time students.'

How widely the error is committed may be gauged from these two comments by a judge at the end of a trial.

> Your problems are no worse than hundreds of your fellow human beings who do not behave as you.

> No one hearing the evidence could fail to feel utter disgust at your life-style and others of your social circle.

The pedant is tempted to correct these two sentences with rather ugly additions ('Your problems are no worse than those of your fellow human beings' and 'utter disgust at your life-style and that of your social circle'). But correctness is not all. And evasion of the need to insert 'those of' and 'that of' is always better. We might recommend: 'You have faced no worse problems than hundreds of your fellow human beings' and: 'disgust at the life-style you and others of your social circle have adopted'.

different

The trap which leads to misfires in comparisons operates in other contexts. The word 'different' sometimes lures the writer into it. We find the mistake in a piece on wildlife reserves in Russia.

> The brigade enforces strict regulations on the use of wildlife resources. Its work is very different from the brigades based in main trading centres such as Vladivostok.

The brigade's work must not be said to be different from other brigades, but from their work: 'Its work is very different from that of brigades based in main trading centres.'

> The layout of the boat was slightly different from the previous day's boat.

The layout of one boat must be contrasted with the layout of the other, but we can scarcely use the apostrophe 's' here ('very different from the previous day's boat's') because of the apostrophe already there in 'day's'. Recourse to the expression 'that of' smacks of artifice, so it would be better to recast the sentence: 'The boat was slightly different in layout from the previous day's boat.'

rather than

The use of these words is especially productive of error. 'Rather than' is best followed by a construction that matches the construction preceding it. It is better to say 'I prefer to stay here rather than to go' than to say 'I prefer to stay here rather than going.' On these grounds we criticize the following sentence.

> If someone sustains personal injury while on holiday, through negligence or default of the hotel, and the hotel was booked through a tour operator, it's possible to sue the tour operator here rather than going to the difficulty of finding a lawyer in the USA.

The infinitive 'to sue' preceding 'rather than' should be matched by an infinitive after it: 'it's possible to sue the tour operator here rather than to go to the trouble of finding a lawyer in the USA'.

And here is another example of clumsy recourse to the gerund after 'rather than' where a matching infinitive is called for:

> As teeth became more complex it became advantageous to retain a permanent set rather than continually replacing them.

The sentence should read: 'it became advantageous to retain a permanent set rather than continually to replace them'.

Balancing what follows 'rather than' with what precedes it is not always a matter of rigid parallelism.

> Presumably this is because they want maximum profit now rather than plan for the long term future.

The proper correction here would be: 'they want maximum profit now rather than to plan for the future'. The infinitive can follow 'rather than' even though a balancing noun precedes it, because an infinitive can provide an object for certain transitive verbs ('They want to go') just as a noun can ('They want dinner').

It is alarming to find 'rather than' misused in a literary review of a new book.

> George Eliot's *Journals*, too, would have taken a better form at Oxford rather than they have at Cambridge.

A schoolchild would acquire red ink markings for this. 'Rather than they have' will not do. In fact 'rather' is simply redundant. Omit it.

than

It is not uncommon to find the word 'than' grossly misused where it should not be used at all.

> More than twice as much was spent on tea than on coffee in 1968.

The construction 'twice as much' requires to be followed by 'as'. The word 'than' is totally out of place. Yet one finds the same error in the 'quality' press.

> A study of car prices by the European Commission found that some cars can cost half as much again in this country than in continental countries . . .

A schoolchild who wrote 'My lollipop cost twice as much than his' (instead of 'as his') would be rightly marked down. That is the mistake here. The sentence should read: 'cost half as much again in this country as in continental countries'. And I find this within a few lines in the same paper:

> A report soon to be published by the Organisation for Economic Co-operation and Development is expected to show that the gaps have widened between prices since its last report in 1995 and that goods and services are the most expensive in the UK than most comparable countries.

Again, a schoolchild who wrote 'My marks in Maths are the best than anybody's' would be taken to task. The sentence should read: 'goods and services in the UK are more expensive than in most comparable countries'.

And now I find a political correspondent writing thus of a public opinion poll:

> But nearly four times as many people would discourage others from voting for the Tories than would encourage them.

The journalist is mixing up two constructions. Either 'as many' must go ('four times more people would discourage others from voting for the Tories than would encourage them') or 'than' must go ('as would encourage them').

Logical breakdown can occur when a writer thus mixes up two constructions in the back of the mind.

> Jonathan hadn't been inside her cottage a matter of moments than she knew he was smitten by her lovely house.

The correct version here would be: 'Jonathan hadn't been inside her cottage a matter of moments before she knew he was smitten by her lovely house.' In the back of the writer's mind here was the construction

'No sooner had Jonathan entered her cottage than she knew he was smitten.' But this use of 'than' is firmly linked to the words 'No sooner had Jonathan entered'. It is logical to say 'No sooner did I enter than she left' because the comparative adjective 'sooner' is appropriately followed by 'than'. It is neither logical nor grammatical to say 'I hadn't been there a moment than she left.'

the same as

This is another construction which requires a proper balance to be kept between the items compared. At the simplest level, no problem arises. In 'her hairdresser is the same as mine', 'her' is perfectly balanced by 'mine'. At a more complex level the same balance should be kept: 'She recited her multiplication tables at the same time as she helped with the washing-up.' There 'she recited' and 'she helped' are similarly balanced as grammatical parallels. But consider the following caption to a photograph in *The Times*.

> Drummer boys and Zulu warriors yesterday remember the fallen at the Battle of Isandhlwana 120 years ago in which British forces were overwhelmed on the same day as Britain's defence of Rorke's Drift.

Here the required parallelism is lost. We can correctly say 'They fought the battle on the same day as the reinforcements arrived', but it would be bad to say 'They fought the battle on the same day as the arrival of reinforcements.' 'They fought' can be paralleled by 'reinforcements arrived' but not by 'the arrival of reinforcements'. In the above sentence the error is well cushioned in words but the failure of balance is no less. The sentence should end: 'in which British forces were overwhelmed on the same day as Britain defended Rorke's Drift'.

such as

The word 'such' may be followed by 'that' in statements asserting that something is a consequence of something else ('His anger was such that he sacked the fellow on the spot'). But where 'such' introduces a comparison, it must be followed by 'as' ('It was such a show as I have never seen before').

> This book is certainly entertaining and anecdotal, very funny in places as well as thought-provoking as the author covers such diverse subjects like the problems of access to open countryside, the history of Munros and other tick lists.

Here the word 'like' must be replaced by 'as'. The expression 'such like' is usable only as an idiomatic colloquial way of saying 'et cetera' ('He was always messing about with toy trains and buses, and such like').

PUNCTUATION

The Comma

Correct punctuation is achieved by close attention to meaning. That is especially applicable to the placing of commas. There is a big difference in meaning between 'He said nothing to make his lodger look guilty' and 'He said nothing, to make his lodger look guilty.' The addition of the comma transforms the meaning. Separate items may be linked falsely together if a comma is omitted where it is needed.

> Try not to panic and visit your GP if symptoms persist.

The word 'visit' and what follows it are too closely linked here to what precedes them. As the sentence stands, someone is being advised neither to panic nor to visit the doctor. Clearly that was not intended. The breath that a speaker would take after saying 'panic' needs to be represented by a comma: 'Try not to panic, and visit your GP if symptoms persist.'

> For games lessons we had to wear special togs and goal posts became a symbol of misery for me.

Once more too strong a link is established between the togs and the goal posts, which sound like two items to be worn. A comma must be inserted after 'togs'.

As lack of commas may connect material too closely to preceding words, it may result in failure to mark phrases that call for separation.

> They gathered around the table tasting delicacies and chatting amiably.

Again the natural break after 'table' must be marked by a comma. And quite often the appropriate degree of separation requires the use of commas at either end of a group of words.

> The conflagration had spread to the house next door and for the firemen the whole prospect was a very dangerous one.

The words 'for the firemen' need to be separated by commas at either end: 'and, for the firemen, the whole prospect was a very dangerous one'. It is important not to neglect the second comma in such constructions. Whether the two commas should be used in the case of a single word is now rather a matter of taste than of rule. 'The truth is, however, that not a single member agreed to the proposal.' There, the force of 'however', in announcing a matter seemingly out of line with what has preceded it, requires the prominence that the surrounding commas give. But in the sentence 'The pictures, too, gave me great delight' the intervention of the commas seems fussily interruptive, and they should be omitted.

The Semicolon

The semicolon marks a slightly firmer break in the flow than the comma. The attempt to make a comma do more work than it is fitted to do is one of the faults in punctuation which do occur quite frequently.

> Recovering from the effects of bronchitis is never a quick process, it takes time.

Here the comma is inadequate. The separateness of the clause 'it takes time', which could be a sentence in itself, calls for something more than a comma. It would not be incorrect here to use a full colon, but because of the very close connection between the main clause and what follows, a semicolon will suffice. 'It' harks back to the subject of the sentence, 'Recovering'. This closeness of connection between the separated clauses is what determines the choice of semicolon. 'My husband gave me a necklace; my daughter gave me a box of chocolates.' That is correct, for although the subject of the first clause is 'My husband' and the subject of the second is 'my daughter', the sequence is so close that there is no need to use a colon.

The Colon

The colon stands between the semicolon and the full stop in the forcefulness of the break it indicates.

> Lots of people spend hard-earned money on the lottery: very few of them ever benefit from it.

The contrast here between 'lots of people' and the 'few', and their respective experience makes the colon desirable. Very often the colon could be replaced by a full stop. It would be grammatically satisfactory here, but it would break up the prose too jumpily.

There is another and now perhaps more common use of the colon. It is placed after a general statement in order to introduce a series of specific instances. 'The board had twelve members in all: a chairman, a vice-chairman, a secretary and nine other elected representatives.'

The Apostrophe

In the use of the apostrophe mistakes are made on every side. The apostrophe followed by 's' is required where single nouns are used in the possessive case ('Tom's book', 'the rainbow's end'). The general rule is that this applies even to nouns which already end in 's' ('St Thomas's church', 'Dickens's novels'). But this general rule is broken where it might produce an awkward sequence of letters. Thus we write 'Xerxes' rule', not 'Xerxes's rule'. Indeed in William Blake we find the lines 'What was the sound of Jesus' breath? / He laid his hand on Moses' law.' What happens with these special singular names is that they are treated as plural nouns ending in 's' are treated. ('The parent's attitude' refers to one parent; 'The parents' attitude' refers to more than one parent.)

The general rules are not all that difficult, yet retailers display notices for 'Potato's', 'Turkey's' and 'Newspaper's', and a stylish magazine reads:

> In fact, if her vegetables aren't cooked just so when she dines out, chef's had better be prepared for them to keep coming back until they get it right.

This mistake matches those of the retailers. The ordinary plural of a noun like 'chef' requires no apostrophe. The sentence illustrates the fact that apostrophes are more often put in where they are not wanted than missed out where they are wanted.

> Some of my mates' friends get on my wick. Can I dump them without chucking her too?

This is an interesting specimen of error. When we get to the end of the first sentence we assume that the writer is speaking of the friends of several mates ('my mates' friends'). Only after reading the second sentence do we realize that he has misplaced the apostrophe. There is only one 'mate', so he should have written: 'Some of my mate's friends'.

Mistakes are still frequently made with the words 'its' and 'it's'. The apostrophe is needed only when 'it's' is short for 'it is' ('It's time to go') or 'it has' ('It's disappeared'). Yet one reads in a gardening magazine:

> It's deep red flowers look quite different in full sun or shade.

This should be: 'Its deep red flowers look different'. I have before me a dozen sentences culled from recent journals all making this elementary mistake of inserting an apostrophe into the possessive 'its'. Perhaps more remarkably still, I have a letter from a garage drawing attention to the fact that my car is now three years old and needs an MOT.

> Of course, if any work is needed to get your vehicle through its' test, we won't start without your permission.

Trying to understand how this extraordinary form 'its'' came about, one can only conclude that someone remembers from schooldays that a word ending in 's' must have its apostrophe after the 's' ('Members' coats can be left in the cloakroom').

In forming plurals of words which normally do not have plurals the temptation to use apostrophes should be resisted.

> It was far too late for us to call on the Jones's.

That should be: 'to call on the Joneses'. The following illustrates a comparable error.

> . . . unless you know the basic do's and don'ts it can end up looking a mess.

The apostrophe is needed in 'don'ts' because 'don't' is the equivalent of 'do not'. It is not needed in 'dos' which is an idiomatic plural of 'do'. Comparably easy to find are instances of apostrophes inserted after numbers in recording dates or scores. It is quite wrong to write of 'the fashions of the 1960's' or of 'the 60's'. The apostrophes are not needed. We refer to 'the 1960s' and 'the 60s'. 'A building dating from the 1750's' should be 'A building dating from the 1750s'. Similarly we do not refer to 'a score of two 5's and two 3's' but 'of two 5s and two 3s'. It should go without saying that such headings as '51,516 Thank you's' are also improper.

The Hyphen

Hyphens are used to knit words together into a single unit. In sentences such as 'The accommodation was rent-free' a noun ('rent') is tied to an adjective ('free'). 'Free' is one of a group of adjectives which are frequently used thus to form new adjectives ('pain-free', 'trouble-free'). The adjective 'dependent' is added to nouns in compounds such as 'insulin-dependent' and 'wheelchair-dependent'. In all these cases the hyphen is necessary. But it goes without saying that a compound which in its early days is hyphenated may become so established that the hyphen disappears. In my 1933 dictionary 'world-wide' is hyphenated. In my recent dictionary 'worldwide' is a single word. One should be wary of trying to initiate change in this respect. When in doubt, hyphenate. The same applies obviously to compounds in which prefixes are attached to nouns in such expressions as 'pre-Reformation history', 'post-Reformation history' and 'counter-Reformation movements'. All the compounds above function as adjectives. There are also prefixes attached to nouns which produce compound nouns, such as 'hyper-inflation' or 'pseudo-philosophy'.

There are compounds involving gerunds that function as nouns, such as 'jam-making' and 'bottle-washing'. It is helpful to distinguish these compounds from those which combine the noun with a present participle to form a kind of adjective, such as 'cancer-causing agents' and 'question-begging answers'. It is risky to experiment with this kind of formation.

> The lonely walk can be hard going, but there are no route finding problems.

If 'route finding' is used at all, then it should be hyphenated, but it would be better replaced by: 'there is no difficulty in finding the route'.

Compounds in which the noun is tied to a past participle also function as adjectives. Thus we speak of an 'air-cooled engine' and a 'family-run business'. We also have long-established compound adjectives made up of an adjective and a past participle, such as 'bald-headed', 'sure-footed' and 'long-legged'. When words are piled up together in impromptu combination, it is necessary to hyphenate them.

> This means that the jacket as a whole doesn't have the suit of armour like feel of a saturated double Ventile one.

There is no escape here from a sprinkling of hyphens: 'doesn't have the suit-of-armour-like feel'.

It is chiefly in the compounds made by fusing two nouns that problems arise. The recent fashion for making more and more of these compounds is fully explored in chapter 11. Here we are concerned with the proper use of the hyphen in such innovations.

> The material is notable for its durability and its frost resistance.

The two nouns 'frost' and 'resistance' thus combined in a compound noun technically need to be hyphenated together. However, we are now inundated with totally hyphenless compounds, in the literature of the business world especially. In one paragraph I read of 'a solutions strategy', 'implementation teams', the 'knowledge base', the 'service sectors', 'implementation activities' and 'Global Solutions teams'. In this area the battle for the adjective as well as for the hyphen seems to be already lost.

One must hope that it is still possible to resist the neglect of the hyphen in more general usage where accumulation of nouns is not an epidemic. However, I have recently seen references to 'British made beef', to a 'seven night cruise' and to the 'cat loving public', which seem to cry out for hyphens as the hunted hart for the waterbrooks.

There is, of course, a distinct use of the hyphen in print which merely indicates that a word has been split in two to preserve the neatness of the printed page. It is important to keep a watchful eye on such computerized hyphenation. Failure to do so, according to correspondents in *The Times*, has produced ambiguous combinations such as 'pronoun-cement', 'brains-canner', 'not-ables' and 'bed-raggled'.

CHAPTER 8

Presenting a Case

The expression 'Presenting a Case' is used in its most general sense. You are presenting a case if you say 'In my opinion, the house is dingy as well as ugly.' That is reasoning at a very straightforward level, reasoning in which point is added to point. At a slightly more complex level of reasoning, you might say 'John will miss the bus if he doesn't hurry up.' That is reasoning by which a somewhat less obvious connection is established between two different points. From that level of directness to the level of sophistication at which managers or lawyers argue their cases, a few easily definable constructional patterns form the frameworks of reasoning.

We dealt in Chapter 1 with some of the words which can easily be misused in the reasoning process. There our concern was with the exact connotation of the words touched upon, and the importance of using the right ones. Here our concern is with the deployment of words used in reasoning. We are particularly concerned with the function of certain very frequently used terms which act as links or hinges in connecting point with point. Thus the expression 'as well as' established the link by which point was added to point in the sentence 'In my opinion, the house is dingy as well as ugly', and the word 'if' was the hinge on which point was connected with point in the sentence 'John will miss the bus if he doesn't hurry up.'

In the latter sentence the connection was established between two verbs, 'miss' and 'hurry up', each with its own subject. The word 'if' established the connection and is appropriately called a 'conjunction'. The clause 'if he doesn't hurry up' is a clause subordinate to the main clause 'John will miss the bus'. In respect of the interplay of point with point, the arrangement of words can easily go astray. That is so whether the related points are located within a single clause or in different ones.

We are to look now at the various constructions by which one point is related to another point in argument.

ADDITION

The most straightforward of such constructions are those by which we add point to point cumulatively. The accumulation may be effected by direct aggregation ('I came, I saw, I conquered'), but more often we use linking terms. The simplest is the word 'and' ('I came and I saw'). But there are also much-used expressions such as 'besides', 'as well as' and 'in addition to'. (It should perhaps be added here that in literate English there is no place for the word 'plus' as a substitute for 'and'.)

and

This is perhaps the most used of all link-words. A frequent mistake in the use of 'and' is introduction of what may be called the 'dual-function and'.

> Self-esteem builds up independence, self-reliance and also hikes up those resilience reserves.

The word 'and' here is introduced as though it is going to complete the sequence beginning 'independence, self-reliance' with another noun. Instead of which it introduces a sequence with a different construction. The word 'and' cannot serve two purposes at once. Unless the construction is changed, two 'ands' are needed, one to serve each purpose: 'Self-esteem builds up independence and self-reliance, and it hikes up those resilience reserves.' The following sentence goes astray similarly.

> Life is frustrating for all of us, but we cope using insight, patience, and by turning the other cheek.

The words preceding 'and' ('using insight, patience') lead us to expect a third noun ('using insight, patience, and common sense'). But in fact 'and' is used to connect 'using' with 'turning', while the other sequence ('insight', 'patience') is left hanging in the air. Correct either by using a second 'and': 'but we cope using insight and patience, and by turning the other cheek', or by introducing another verb: 'but we cope, using insight, showing patience, and turning the other cheek'.

When 'and' is used to link two items within a clause, care should be taken to ensure that there is no ambiguity. I read the following in my newspaper:

> Alan Clark, former minister and MP for Kensington and Chelsea, said the confrontation about the party's direction was 'deplorable'.

The reader abreast of current affairs would have had no difficulty here. But the forgetful or the ignorant would not know whether Alan Clark were still an MP or not. The words 'former minister and MP for Kensington' could stand if he had ceased to be an MP, but if the word 'former' applies only to the word 'minister', then another comma would be needed: 'former minister, and MP for Kensington'.

There is a tendency sometimes to insert what is really a redundant 'and' before a relative clause.

> The matter was recently the subject of a Parliamentary Question raised on our behalf by Eric Illsley MP and which resulted in an answer from the Secretary of State.

The word 'and' is here unnecessary and indeed awkward. Moreover, to say that the question 'resulted in' an answer is surely unnatural. The sentence should read: 'a Parliamentary Question raised on our behalf by Eric Illsley MP, which provoked an answer from the Secretary of State'.

in addition to

The various constructions we are here concerned with make the same requirement, namely that parallelism should be preserved between the items joined together by the linking expression chosen.

> In addition to his expertise as a wine-taster, Garrard was a skilful and far-seeing economist.

Here there is no exact parallelism between the two items which the expression 'in addition to' combines together. There must be a noun to balance 'expertise': 'In addition to his expertise as a wine-drinker, Garrard had great skill and far-sightedness as an economist.'

along with

Similar errors occur after 'along with' (and 'together with').

> Along with a complete redecoration of the premises we have added a new floor.

Since the 'redecoration' was not 'added', proper parallelism breaks down. If the construction is to be kept, there must be a noun to balance 'redecoration': 'Along with the redecoration of the premises, we have effected the construction of a new floor.' But obviously it would be much better to change the construction: 'We have both completely redecorated the premises and added a new floor.'

as well as

The same rule about preserving parallelism applies to the use of 'as well as'. One could say 'He has a knife as well as a fork', where 'knife' balances 'fork'. One could say 'He has a habit of drinking too much as well as (of) smoking too much' where 'drinking too much' balances 'smoking too much'. But such parallels are not always preserved.

> The court was told that his route coincided with that of Miss Smith and that he was known to carry a knife on occasions, as well as having a collection of them.

It would be correct to say 'he was known to carry a knife as well as a cosh'. It would likewise be correct to say 'he was known to carry a knife as well as to take dope' where 'to take dope' matches 'to carry a knife'. There is no such parallelism in the sentence quoted. We should be able happily to break up such a sentence into the two balancing halves joined by 'as well as': 'he was known to carry a knife' and 'he was known to have a collection of them'. So the correct version would be: 'he was known to carry a knife on occasions as well as to have a collection of them'.

The temptation that writers succumb to when using 'as well as' is to follow it by a gerund. Whereas this is perfectly satisfactory if the gerund balances a previous one ('He was fond of fishing as well as shooting'), it is poor style to use it without such a parallel.

> He was a lively host and a brilliant raconteur as well as being an indefatigable public servant.

The word 'being' destroys the sequence and, ironically enough, is redundant anyway. It should be omitted.

not just / only . . . but also

This is another construction whose function is to draw items together in parallel. 'It is not just beautiful, it is also valuable', we say, or 'It is not just raining, it is also very windy.' The relationship between 'beautiful' and 'valuable' or between 'raining' and 'very windy' is one where the parallelism intensifies a statement. The parallelism is crucial to the construction.

> The furniture is not just well-made, but also its design is up-to-the-minute.

The parallelism breaks down here because the sequence beginning 'not just well-made but also' is never completed. Instead a new subject and a new verb ('its design is') are brought in. The reading should be: 'The furniture is not just well-made, but also up-to-the-minute in design.'

What applies to 'not just' applies to 'not only'. There is need to preserve parallelism between what follows 'not only' and what follows 'but also'.

> The endangered gorilla families have found themselves in danger not only from the warring people, but have also had their habitats encroached on by refugees fleeing deep into the forests.

Again parallelism breaks down. It is like saying 'I bought not only a pound of butter but have also been given a free voucher for soap flakes.' The words 'not only from the warring people' need to be balanced: 'in danger not only from the warring people, but also from refugees fleeing deep into the forests and encroaching on their habitats'.

besides

Once more we have a construction that draws items together in parallel and where sometimes due sequence breaks down.

> Besides a two-year guarantee the Pakka Jacket features an integral hood, studded stormflap over the full-length zip, side-adjusted hem, shaped back, hood drawcord tidies and extra arm extension.

There is stark incongruity here between the first item and the succeeding ones. The word 'besides' generally introduces an addition closely related to the other items ('Besides a flat in Mayfair, he has a country house in Gloucestershire'). But the sentence above is almost like saying 'Besides a flat in Mayfair, he has a sly expression and a sarcastic tongue.' There is no grammatical error, but the verb 'features', properly applied to the various aspects of the make-up of the garment, is incongruously applied to the two-year guarantee, as though it were also part of the fabric.

ALTERNATION AND SEPARATION

The expressions we have touched upon link point with point accumulatively. We turn to expressions which link point with point so as to indicate distinctions of various kinds. Such is the word 'or' ('You can sleep upstairs or you can have a bed down here').

or

There is a misuse of 'or' comparable to the misuse of 'and', which produces what we may call the 'dual-function or'.

> One can hire pedaloes, motorboats or try waterskiing.

It would be correct to write 'One can hire pedaloes, motorboats or water skis.' But 'or' cannot stand as the link to a third item that can be hired and at the same time serve as the link between hiring something and trying something. One 'or' must be allotted to each function: 'One can hire pedaloes or motorboats, or try waterskiing.'

apart from

A converse construction to that serviced by 'in addition to' is the construction serviced by 'apart from'. We call it a 'converse' construction because that is what it ought to be. It separates where 'in addition to' combines. 'Apart from my youngest sister, we all love pancakes.' That represents the proper use of 'apart from', which distinguishes an exception from a general rule or statement. Unfortunately the construction is often used for the very opposite purpose.

> Apart from a huge fertile plain in the east, the centre of the island has a large mountainous backbone.

The fertile plain does not constitute an exception to a general statement about the island. No such statement has been made. Two facts are stated which need to be connected by 'and' or 'but': 'There is a huge fertile plain in the east, but the centre of the island has a large mountainous backbone.'

Sometimes 'apart from' is allowed to drift so far from its proper function that it stands for virtually the opposite of what it should stand for. Here is a recommendation for a camping stove.

> Apart from the ultralight weight, it's superbly made and the design is excellent.

Far from being a disadvantage, the ultralight weight is plainly an advantage. 'Apart from' is here being used, not to introduce an exception, but to introduce a further positive corroboration of the general drift. Scrap 'apart from' and change the construction: 'Ultralight in weight, the stove is also superbly made and the design is excellent.'

former / latter

The word 'former' relates to the first of two things just mentioned and the word 'latter' to the second of the two. The word 'latter' should not be used when more than two items have been mentioned.

> Of the sitting-room, the dining-room and the study I thought the latter the best furnished.

That is strictly incorrect. Since it would be too strained to say 'I thought the last-named the best furnished', the wording should be: 'I thought the study the best furnished.'

> Some horses require a quiet corner and no changes to routine, others relish being stimulated. If your horse is the latter, stimulate his senses . . .

The words 'former' and 'latter' should refer back to nouns. It would be correct to say 'There is provision for the meat-eater and for the vegetarian: if you are the latter, please inform the housekeeper.' There 'if you are the latter' refers directly back to 'vegetarian'. It would be poor usage to say 'Some people are carnivores, others will not eat meat: if you are the latter, please inform the housekeeper' because there is no direct reference back to a single noun such as 'vegetarian'. In the sentence above ('If your horse is the latter') there is likewise no direct reference back to a single noun. If the word 'latter' is to be kept, the sentence should read: 'There is the horse which requires a quiet corner and a fixed routine, and the horse which relishes being stimulated. If your horse is the latter, stimulate his senses . . .'

CAUSE AND EFFECT

The next group of terms to be investigated is a group of terms concerned with reasoning about cause and effect.

because

The word 'because' has a clear function, yet is often misused. It is correct to say 'He left because he wanted promotion.' It is not correct to say 'His departure was because he wanted promotion.' The difference is that in the first sentence 'because' hinges properly on the verb 'left'. That is its proper function as a conjunction. In the second sentence 'because' is made to hang on the noun 'departure', which is grammatically inadmissible. Yet I read just such a sentence in a political piece about a recent public opinion poll.

> The growing gap between this pessimism and the stability of voting intentions is because the public is still giving the Government the benefit of the doubt.

One should not write 'The gap is because . . .' but 'The gap is caused by . . .' The simplest recipe for getting out of this bad habit is to shift back the verb 'is': 'There is this growing gap between pessimism and the stability of voting intentions because the public is still giving the Government the benefit of the doubt.'

What is virtually the same mistake may occur without the intervention of the verb 'to be'.

> The 34-year-old Ulsterman has always been interested in the media and during a three-month break because of injury from early May looked into the long-term future.

Just as it is improper to say 'His three-month break was because of injury', so it is not permissible to speak of a 'three-month break because of injury'. The correct version would be a 'three-month break caused by injury' or a 'three-month break due to injury'. All uses of 'because' on this pattern mark a writer badly.

Writers need also to be wary of 'because of'. The words often lead one into bad constructions.

> This is because of splinter groups coming down and attacking my home.

The gerciple ('splinter groups coming down') is unfortunate and unnecessary. The more straightforward construction is better: 'This is because splinter groups come down and attack my home.' And here is someone in *Cosmopolitan* explaining why it is always difficult to get over being rejected in love.

> But that's not because of her or him, that's because of oneself asking, 'What did I do wrong?'

The tongue-twisting 'because of oneself asking' could be technically corrected by making it even more of a tongue-twister ('because of oneself's asking'), but the reader deserves something more palatable, and of course more straightforward, than that: 'that is because one asks oneself "What did I do wrong?"'

Writers also need to be wary of what one might call 'causational overkill'.

> The reason she left him was because he was an alcoholic.

That is 'overkill'. Either 'the reason' must go ('She left him because he was an alcoholic') or 'because' must go ('The reason she left him was that he was an alcoholic'). The same kind of 'overkill' occurs at a conversational level in such sentences as:

> Just because he never goes out doesn't necessarily mean that he is ill.

This should be 'The fact that he never goes out doesn't necessarily mean that he is ill', which can be quite properly reduced to: 'That he never goes out doesn't necessarily mean that he is ill.'

> The highlighting is caused because each individual hair is lighter at the tip than at the shaft.

This is like saying 'His death was caused because he was ill.' The duplication represented by the two words 'caused because' is quite illogical. Clumsy as it may seem, if 'caused' is kept, then there is no escape from some such sentence as 'The highlighting is caused by the fact that each individual hair is lighter at the tip than at the shaft.'

due to

This is one of the most ill-used constructions in general use today. 'Due to' is not interchangeable with 'because of'. We may write 'Because of the weather, the match was cancelled', but it would be incorrect to write

'Due to the weather the match was cancelled.' The reason is that 'due' is an adjective and, as such, has to agree with a noun. One can say 'The cancellation was due to the bad weather' because there 'due to' hinges on the word 'cancellation'. In this respect the misuse of 'due to' is as easily found as any misuse explored in this book.

> Due to the diversity of designs and number of bottles produced, it is still possible to pick up Lalique bargains.

> Due to the ever-increasing number of visitors, the company decided to appoint a full-time warden.

> Due to increased use of the locks several pounds were low, even though water was being back-pumped.

In each of these three sentences the words 'due to' are misused. In all cases they could be replaced by 'owing to' or 'because of'. Neither of these two constructions requires to be attached to a noun as 'due to' does. The consequent advice to writers is: Never start a sentence with 'due to' without first checking that it is going to be grammatically correct. In fact it very rarely is. Always consider 'owing to' or 'because of' as your alternative.

It is not only at the start of a sentence that the words 'due to' present risks for the writer.

> The Rail Tour has been put back to November 28 at the request of EWS due to initial problems with the loco.

The words 'due to' are again incorrectly used. It is the attempt to attach 'due' to a verb instead of a noun that is wrong. A 'postponement' might be 'due' to certain problems. But 'due to' cannot hinge on 'has been put back'. Again the words could happily be replaced by 'because of' or even 'owing to'.

There is a tendency to attach the word 'due' to the wrong word, thus producing a slight illogicality.

> The lower than normal number of birds seen could be due to last year's mild winter.

We have a subtle complaint here. When I say 'The top-storey flat makes access difficult', I really mean that the top-storeyness of the flat makes access difficult, or in other words, 'The fact that the flat is on the top storey makes access difficult.' Thus what the writer means in the sentence above is: 'The fact that a lower than normal number of birds are seen could be due to last year's mild winter.' 'The fact that' is a slightly clumsy construction, but what the writer is talking about is not 'the number' but 'the lower-than-normalness' of the number. We mentally bind adjective and noun tightly together in such familiar usages as 'The hot weather is due to an anti-cyclone', where the heat is what is due to the anti-cyclone. (The 'weather' is there, anti-cyclone or not.) But where the adjectival element is increased to 'The hotter than normal weather is due to an anti-cyclone', logic would seem to prefer: 'The abnormal heat is due to an anti-cyclone.'

Oddly enough, the word 'due' is misused in a totally different context from that of reasoning about cause and effect. I have just heard some advice given on a radio programme on the subject of Income Tax.

> If you're due some money back, you must apply at once.

But if money is due to you, that does not make you 'due' some money. Money can be 'due', or a railway train can be 'due'. That is the proper use of 'due'. Just as it would be improper to say 'It is five o'clock. You are now due a train to Paddington', so it is improper to say 'You are now due an income tax rebate.')

cause

It was made clear above that care has to be taken to avoid attaching 'due' to the wrong word where a noun and an adjective are involved. The same problem arises with the verb to 'cause'.

> Dull hair can be caused by product build-up, chemical treatments, sun damage or environmental pollution, so it's not surprising so many of us suffer from it.

The 'hair' is not caused by any of these factors. It is the 'dullness' of the hair that is caused by them. The slight touch of illogicality represented by the above careless usage ('dull hair') will be avoided by good writers. Change the subject of the sentence: 'Hair can be made dull by product build-up.'

One can find even more awkward examples than the above of the way the verb to 'cause' can become detached from its proper mooring. Consider this remark about a railway viaduct.

> The lattice wrought iron structure is designed to minimize weight on the unstable ground caused by mining.

Just as the hair, whether dull or not, was not caused by product build-up, so too the ground, whether firm or not, was not caused by mining. One must spell out exactly what was caused by the mining. If 'caused by mining' is kept, then 'instability' must be mentioned. It is probably better to change the construction: 'The lattice wrought iron structure is designed to minimize weight on the ground rendered unstable by mining.'

PURPOSE AND RESULT

Closely related to reasoning in terms of cause and effect is reasoning in terms of purpose and result.

in order that / to

The words 'in order' can be followed by 'to' or by 'that'. It is not good to follow them by 'for'.

> The current account requires a balance of $2,000 in order for transactions to be free.

'In order' is really redundant here. One might say: 'in order that transactions may be free', but that would be clumsy. All one needs is: 'The current account requires a balance of $2,000 for transactions to be free.'

> In order for the AA to get to you as quickly as possible it would help if you have your membership card ready when phoning our call centres.

Again 'in order' is redundant. All one needs is: 'For the AA to get to you as quickly as possible'. The best correction would be: 'To enable the AA to get to you as quickly as possible'.

result

Used as a verb or a noun, the word 'result' often introduces a bad construction.

> The failure to start on time resulted in them losing the title.

Reference has been made to the bad usage I have called the 'gerciple'. The verb 'result' all too often lures writers to use it. It would be correct to turn 'losing' into a genuine gerund ('resulted in their losing the title') but it would be equally satisfactory to use the verb 'cause' followed by an infinitive: 'caused them to lose the title'. The error is not rare. The following is advice to women on matters of style.

> Attempting to imitate may result in you not getting the look you wanted.

This time use of the genuine gerund is to be recommended: 'Attempting to imitate may result in your not getting the look you wanted.'

> The opportunity came about as a result of David reading an announcement of the Club's forthcoming cruise.

Here the same bad construction follows 'result' used as a noun. Again one can turn 'reading' into a genuine gerund: 'came about as a result of David's reading an announcement'. But the construction could be happily changed: 'The opportunity arose because David read an announcement'.

One can safely say that all writers should exercise extreme care in using the construction 'as a result of'. There is no shortage of evidence to support this advice.

> Premenstrual outbreaks can occur as a result of water retention putting pressure on both sides of the pore and follicle duct.

In this particular instance the option of converting the gerciple into a genuine gerund is not on offer ('as a result of water retention's putting pressure on'). Therefore the construction must be changed. And, as so often when this usage 'as a result of' faces us, the question arises: What is wrong with the word 'because' that people avoid it? It offers the most natural alternative here: 'Premenstrual outbreaks can occur because water retention puts pressure on both sides of the pore and follicle duct.'

Here is another, and very different, misuse of the verb 'result'.

> The dining room is a blue-grey violet that resulted by a happy accident.

The expression 'that resulted' normally occurs in such sentences as 'There was a tragic accident that resulted in two deaths.' The accident resulted in deaths. But the blue-grey violet did not 'result' in anything. It was itself the result. We would not say 'There were two deaths that resulted by a tragic accident.' Nor should we say that blue-grey violet 'resulted' by accident. We may correct here by turning the verb 'result' into a noun: 'The dining room is a blue-grey violet colour, the result of a happy accident.'

resulting

Writers should be wary of using the participle 'resulting'. It must keep the adjectival status it clearly has in such usages as 'The resulting conflagration destroyed the house.' There the word 'resulting' qualifies the noun 'conflagration'. It is lax usage to say: 'The house caught fire, resulting in its destruction' because 'resulting' cannot happily hinge on the whole previous clause.

> Many of the older oaks have been pollarded – the tops have been removed for a variety of uses, resulting in the growth of many almost horizontal branches.

What does the word 'resulting' qualify here? It does not qualify 'oaks' or 'tops' or 'uses'. Instead it is made to hinge on the whole of the previous part of the sentence. In short, it has been forced to do a job a participle is unfitted for. It is better not to use the participle: 'Many of the older oaks have been pollarded – the tops have been removed for a variety of uses, and many almost horizontal branches have grown as a result.'

It is rarely felicitous, though not incorrect, to use the word 'resulting' in such sentences as 'There was a party downstairs and the resulting noise was disturbing.' The construction has to be handled with extreme care.

> In Amsterdam there are literally thousands of cafés to choose from. The downside is that many of these rely on tourist trade and not regular customers, so the resulting meal can be very disappointing.

Clearly no meal should be said to be the result of reliance on the tourist trade. One cannot bypass the chef in the kitchen.

in an effort to

The words 'in an effort to' sometimes form a convenient alternative to other constructions expressing purpose ('in order that', 'so that'): 'He persevered in an effort to make money.' But, like 'so that' and 'because', 'in an effort to' must be connected with a verb (here 'persevered'). A journalist, writing of a plan to turn a sensational murder case into entertainment, speaks of:

> . . . the creation of five screenplays in an effort to make a drama that would not offend viewers.

This should be: 'five screenplays created in an effort to make a drama'. The grammatical mistake of linking 'in an effort' to the noun 'creation' is the same mistake made in linking 'because' to a noun in 'The exam failure was because of sheer laziness.'

CONDITIONS

if

The problems that arise with the word 'if' are similar to those arising with 'because'. It is correct to say 'He will die if he goes on smoking like that', because the word 'if' links directly with the verb 'will die'. It is incorrect to say 'Workers are threatening a strike if their demands are not met.' This will not do since, as is the case with 'because', it is incorrect to make the word 'if' hang on a noun like 'a strike'. The workers are definitely 'threatening' something, and the threat is there without any condition. It is the 'strike' that is conditional. Therefore it would be correct to say 'The workers are threatening to strike if their demands are not met.' For there the conditional 'if' is properly attached to the verb 'to strike'. Below we have a comment about a new Chairman of the Arts Council.

> His first task is to restore the Council's credibility if it is to survive.

This Radio 4 announcement illustrates the bad usage glaringly. The words 'if it is to survive' are made to hinge on the noun 'credibility'. Yet there is no such thing as a 'credibility if it is to survive'. If the words 'if it is to survive' are to be kept, a verb must be provided to make sense of them: 'His first task is to restore the credibility the Council will need if it is to survive.'

> The authorities are drawing attention to the possibly horrendous consequences if the worst predictions prove true.

Here again the clause 'if the worst predictions prove true' is anchored to the noun 'consequences', though a clause beginning with 'if' should always be anchored to a verb. In the sentence 'He will pay the price if the worst predictions prove true' we learn that someone will pay a price 'if' the worst predictions prove true. But in the sentence above the authorities are 'drawing attention' to something whether predictions prove true or not. The solution to the problem is to supply a verb for the 'if' clause to be anchored to: 'The authorities are drawing attention to the horrendous consequences that will follow if the worst predictions prove true.'

Another, less serious, misuse of 'if' is its replacement of 'whether' in indirect questions. This replacement has been gradually taking over. Here is a sentence about day nurseries.

> Your local authority's Early Years Advisor should be able to tell you if one exists in your area, if you're eligible for consideration and how long the waiting list is.

Not so very long ago this would have been: 'Your local authority's Early Years Advisor should be able to tell you whether one exists in your area, whether you're eligible for consideration amd how long the waiting list is.'

The new usage has established itself to such an extent that one can scarcely claim it to be incorrect. But the reader should note the pedant's (bracketed) preference in such cases as the following.

> You need to check if ('whether') management services are available.

> M. J. Street wondered if ('whether') the after-sales warranty would work when the vehicle battery failed.

It should always be remembered that an alternative conditional construction to the use of 'if' is represented by such sentences as 'Were it not raining, I should certainly go' instead of 'If it were not raining'. There are times when this usage is definitely called for.

> She was sentenced in the High Court to three months and told that her term would be higher if not for her ill health and her admission of guilt.

Here it would be better to write: 'her term would be higher were it not for her ill health and her admission of guilt'.

unless

The word 'unless' tends to be misused in the same way as 'if'. It is sometimes wrongly anchored. 'You will receive higher wages unless you insist on sticking to the restrictive practices' is correct, because the clause introduced by 'unless' hinges on the verb 'receive'. Receiving the higher wages is conditional on the employees' attitude. 'The management is offering higher wages unless the workers insist on sticking to their restrictive practices' is incorrect because it is not the act of 'offering' that will be obliterated if the men stick to their restrictive practices. The offer has been made. The simple correction that is needed is to supply the verb for 'unless' to hinge on: 'The management is offering to pay higher wages, unless the workers insist on sticking to their restrictive practices.'

When 'unless' is linked to a participle ('A child should not go out at night here unless accompanied by an adult') the writer must make sure that there is a proper link, like the link here between 'a child' and 'accompanied'.

> Because some medicines are designed to release their ingredients slowly, tablets should not be crushed unless directed by your doctor.

Here it is said that tablets must not be crushed unless they have been told to be crushed. The word 'directed' must be properly linked to a 'subject': 'Because some medicines are designed to release their ingredients slowly, you should not crush tablets unless directed by your doctor.'

Misuse of 'unless' is a matter of logic as much as of grammar.

> Unless your hair is quite thick, the style is most suited to those with even features.

This is like saying 'Unless you are too fat, roast turkey is the most popular Christmas dish.' The turkey's popularity does not depend on anyone's relative obesity. And if the hairstyle is most suited to women with even features, that is a fact independent of whether a given individual has thick hair or not. 'Unless' is out of place.

DEPENDENCE AND INDEPENDENCE

depend / depending

These words are used today with great laxity. The notion of reliance is present in the basic meaning of the word 'depend': 'He depends on farming for a living.'

> What kind of clothing you take with you will depend on the weather at the time.

The relationship here defined by 'depend' is not a matter of reliance. It is rather a matter of cause and effect. Where that is the case, one should use the words 'determined by': 'What kind of clothing you take with you will be determined by the weather at the time.'

> Some companies will charge more [interest on credit cards] depending on where you live.

Here the issue is not so much of dependence as of correspondence, so the better construction would be: 'Some companies will charge more interest according to where you live.' Thus in deciding whether to use 'depend', one should always consider what the relationship is that the word is supposed to define.

'Depending on' is an even more awkwardly mishandled expression.

> Depending on how long you have been a member, you may or may not be eligible for the hand-out.

This shows the risks of starting a sentence with 'depending on'. What is really meant is: 'Whether you are eligible for the hand-out will depend on how long you have been a member.'

despite

This word enables us to cancel out any question of either dependence or causation. 'Because it was fine, we took a walk.' That is positive causation. 'Despite the rain, we took a walk.' That removes any element of causation. The reader should notice that, whereas 'because' can be followed by a clause ('it was raining'), 'despite' is followed only by a noun ('despite the rain'). The attempt to make 'despite' introduce something more than a noun often leads to error.

> Despite his wife trying to dissuade him from the expedition, he determined to go through with it.

The inadmissible gerciple ('his wife trying') is easily avoided if one remembers that 'despite' should be followed by a noun: 'Despite his wife's attempts to dissuade him from the expedition, he determined to go through with it.'

> Despite the income from voluntary contributions having fallen, the treasurer is confident that the work will not suffer.

The same error occurs here. To avoid falling into it, the writer needs to pause before using 'despite' and ask the question whether 'although' or 'even though' would not be a better construction. Where 'despite' requires to be followed by a noun, 'even though' can introduce a clause ('Even though he was tired, he joined in'). Thus the above should be:

'Even though the income from voluntary contributions has fallen, the treasurer is confident that the work will not suffer.'

Of course, even if 'despite' is properly followed by a noun, it can be misused through a failure in logical sequence.

> Despite his detractors, Kitchener was responsible for laying the foundations of what was to become one of the best governed countries in the British Empire.

The writer here does not really mean that Kitchener got on with his job in spite of his detractors. What is meant is that this fact about him must stand in spite of what his detractors claim. The sentence illustrates the usefulness of asking oneself, before using 'despite', whether 'in spite of' would not be better. The sentence should begin: 'In spite of what his detractors say'.

OTHER CONSTRUCTIONS

although

Where 'although' is properly used, there is always an antithesis. 'Although she was over eighty years old, she picked up a hammer and hit the intruder on the head.' We do not expect old ladies of over eighty to pick up hammers and hit intruders on the head. If there is no such element of surprising contrast, then the word 'although' should not be used. Yet the death of an actor was announced thus on the radio:

> Although he was much loved by the public, he will be sadly missed by the acting profession.

'Although' is the wrong word here. The implication of using it is that popularity with the public normally alienates the acting profession. For it suggests that this particular combination of popularity with the profession as well as with the public represents a surprising reconciliation of opposites. What the BBC newswriter meant presumably was: 'He was much loved by the public and will be sadly missed by the acting profession.'

> Although we have to replace the odd tile after a windy day, everything else feels cosy.

This account of life in a country cottage errs in a slightly different way. The implicit contrast between living where tiles are blown off the roof and otherwise feeling cosy may justify the use of 'although', but the words 'everything else feels cosy' produce a disjointed effect. It is rather like saying 'Although we occasionally suffer from food-poisoning, everything else is eatable.' A possible correction might be: 'Although we have to replace the odd tile after a windy day, in all other respects the cottage is cosy.'

as

This word is used in more than one function. Here we are concerned with its use in joining two clauses together. We see this use at its simplest in such sentences as 'The sun shone as the rain stopped', where it brings two statements together in a relationship. The relationship there is a matter of contemporaneity. (The sun shone at the time the rain stopped.) But in the sentence 'He did as he was told' the relationship is one of similarity. (He behaved in the way he was instructed to behave.) It is generally in sentences of the second kind that errors occur, that is, sentences defining some kind of likeness. The most obvious failures in this respect are in those sentences where the likeness is no real likeness. Such is the case in this BBC Radio 4 account of the effects of a tornado:

> The banana crop . . . has been completely flattened, as have other industries.

Clearly the verb 'flattened' cannot be applied to industries in general. Where the verb used in the main part of the sentence is so restricted in usage, the introduction of a parallel by 'as' cannot work. Either the verb 'flattened' must become a more general verb such as 'ruined', or the construction must be abandoned: 'The banana crop has been completely flattened, and other industries similarly damaged.'

Mishandling an 'as' clause can easily cause a more tangled confusion than that.

> Miss O'Donoghue, 54, admitted a crime born of passion as she attacked her former husband Bill Becket, 53, for 'leaving me penniless'.

This report of a court case makes it sound as though the defendant admitted the crime at the same time as she committed it. In fact the word 'as' is out of place: 'Miss O'Donoghue, 54, admitted that she committed a crime born of passion in attacking her former husband.'

There is a habit of taking an ungrammatical short cut after certain uses of 'as'.

> The Tories were not a selfish party, as they were caricatured.

This is really a short cut for: 'The Tories were not a selfish party as they were falsely pictured to be.'

The most common misuse of 'as' in this respect is its use in a bogus connection with the verb to 'know'.

> Ralph is one of the few grocers to specialize in cucurbits as the members of the pumpkin and squash family are known.

This should be 'as the members of the pumpkin and squash family are called'. In English we say 'Smith was called "Softy".' Therefore we can refer to '"Softy" as Smith was called'. But in English we do not say 'Smith was known "Softy"' and therefore we ought not to refer to '"Softy" as Smith was known'. The correct wording would be '"Softy" as Smith was known as'. No one is going to make that awkward statement. Therefore there is no alternative to '"Softy" as Smith was called.' It is incorrect, illogical and insensitive to misuse 'known' as it is now misused day after day by the press and the BBC.

THE USE OF NEGATIVES

Positive statements and negative statements have to be carefully handled when closely combined in a single sentence. Consider the following sentence on the Government's proposals for lone parents' benefits:

> Its proposals were not coherent and a clumsy way in which to start Mr Blair's welfare reform initiative.

Our use of the word 'and' is such that 'She was not willing and helpful' means that she was neither willing nor helpful. On that basis the above sentence might at first sight be understood to be conveying that the Government's proposals were neither coherent nor a clumsy way in which to tackle the matter. No thoughtful reader would be likely so to misread it, but the construction is clumsy. In order clearly to confine the effect of the word 'not' to the part of the statement preceding 'and', the verb it affects must be repeated: 'Its proposals were not coherent and were a clumsy way in which to start Mr Blair's welfare reform initiative.'

An even more extraordinary mix-up between the negative and the positive occurs in this statement from a railway magazine:

> No major external structure modifications have been made during the rebuilding, the most noticeable being the large roof-mounted silencer and the bogie-mounted sandboxes.

This sounds like a contradiction in terms. One must assume that the 'noticeable' modifications referred to are not 'major'. On that assumption, the sentence is really the equivalent of saying 'No young people attended the performance, the most noticeable being a man of eighty.' If the second half of the sentence is to be rescued, it would probably be best to sacrifice the word 'major': 'Only minor structural modifications have been made during the rebuilding, the most noticeable being the large roof-mounted silencer.'

There are cases where the use of the negative should be avoided. It is more elegant to say 'Three people disapproved of the suggestion' than to say 'Three people did not approve of the suggestion.' In reporting views and attitudes, writers need to remember this.

> Only a quarter of the respondents don't feel satellite will ever challenge terrestrial TV.

Here it would be better to move the negative to where it really belongs in the recorded attitude of the respondents: 'Only a quarter of the respondents feel that satellite will never challenge terrestrial TV.'

A slightly more complicated version of this looseness appears in a comment on a report by the Waterways Ombudsman:

> Eight complainants did not show the internal complaints procedure had been completed.

Once more the negative needs to be shifted to where it belongs. As it stands, the sentence is a most uncomfortable way of trying to say: 'In eight cases the internal complaints procedure had not been completed.'

Our sense of logic is offended by double negatives. At its crudest the double negative cancels itself out. 'I don't want not to go', logically considered, would mean the same thing as 'I want to go.' By the same token the sentence 'She will never change her mind or say yes' means what it says, while 'She will never change her mind nor say yes' would appear to convey the message 'She will never change her mind and not say yes', that is, 'She will never change her mind and fail to say yes.' The truth is that double negatives have a respectable history in English literature. If we lay down strictly logical rules, then someone will come along with a quotation from Shakespeare to show that we are insensitive pedants. That being said, it is best to give logic the benefit of the doubt in making one's judgements.

> The dream of the moneyed country lover is shifting back to the green acres and privacy of the real countryside. But once there, they have no wish to farm nor to become the local squire.

Strictly speaking, logic here requires us to question the word 'nor'. The two items 'to farm' and 'to become the local squire' are equally what 'they' have no wish for. They have no wish for 'either' of them. In short: 'they have no wish to farm or to become the local squire'.

The placing of the word 'no' needs to be watched. It comes as a shock to hear on the radio the announcement:

> It's a No Vote of Confidence.

The vote was a vote and the word 'no' belongs elsewhere: 'a vote of No Confidence'.

There are certain words which are always followed by positive verbs. We do not say 'All the members did not turn up' but 'None of the members turned up.' Thus 'All the supporters we contacted could not have been more enthusiastic' would much better be 'All the supporters we contacted were very enthusiastic.' Sometimes a simple change in word order can improve usage in this respect. 'All twenty-five members of the family were never present together.' The awkwardness there is removed if we say: 'The twenty-five members of the family were never all present together.'

After the word 'any' the same rule against a following negative applies.

> From the beginning of April any member of staff will no longer be permitted to smoke in the office.

Here the proper usage would be: 'From the beginning of April no member of staff will be permitted to smoke in the office.' The tendency to break this rule occurs most often when the word 'any' is open-ended in referring to possible future developments.

> Any future changes in your income will not be taken into account in our calculations.

This should be: 'No future changes in your income will be taken into account'.

CHAPTER 9

Good Style and Bad

STYLE AND SUBSTANCE

We all want to write good English, and we believe that something called 'style' is involved. It will be good or it will not. Yet attempts to define good style are not easy to come by. On the contrary, great writers can be very dismissive of the matter. There is a recorded outburst on the subject by Matthew Arnold.

> People think that I can teach them style. What stuff it all is! Have something to say, and say it as clearly as you can. That is the only secret of style.

Is that all it amounts to? Can we not distinguish between the substance of a book and its style? May we not appreciate the one and dislike the other? No doubt we can think of writers in whose cases to think of separating content from style in discussion would seem almost absurd. Swift and Bunyan might be cited as examples. But there are writers who drive us to speak separately of style and content. There is a celebrated comment on Tennyson made by G. K. Chesterton: 'He could not think up to the height of his own towering style.' That implies that here is a writer, a poet, whose style markedly exceeds in quality what he has to say, so that the reader senses a lack of profundity underneath a loftiness of verbal bearing, a paucity of inner substance underneath an outer majesty that seems to cry out for a matching quality of thought.

Dr Johnson, who had so much to say on the subject of writers and writing, himself insisted in his *Life of Cowley* that 'Language is the dress of thought.' He clearly did not underestimate the importance of the substance. Nevertheless, in his *Life of Addison*, he spoke as though a writer might improve his or her style by modelling it on another's.

> Whoever wishes to attain an English style, familiar but not coarse, and elegant but not ostentatious, must give his days and nights to the volumes of Addison.

What is interesting here is that we have something like a definition of good style – or at least one brand of good style. It will be 'familiar' without being coarse and 'elegant' without being ostentatious. That is to say, if we may be so bold as to try to paraphrase Johnson, it will have a kind of natural simplicity which avoids vulgarity and a smooth dignity that avoids showiness. These qualities depend on two things: the appropriate choice of words and the appropriate arrangement of words. A twofold discipline is required of the good stylist, the discipline which forswears laxity and self-indulgence in the selection of words, and the discipline which forswears laxity and sloppiness in their arrangement.

SIMPLICITY

Avoiding Wordiness

Natural simplicity will avoid unnecessary wordiness. One of the first characteristics of good English is the economic use of words. It is not just a matter of not wasting words but also of using the most natural words available. There are certain words which bear the hallmark of unnecessary artifice.

> Recent correspondence regarding microwave ovens suggests it is time for a change concerning the provision of cookers in motorcaravans.

It would be good advice to any writer to say, 'If you are thinking of using the word "regarding", don't.' We do not write letters 'regarding' microwave ovens but 'about' microwave ovens. Likewise we do not say 'There has been a change "concerning" his attitude', but 'There has been a change "in" his attitude.' So the sentence should read: 'Recent correspondence about microwave ovens suggests that it is time to change the provision of cookers in motorcaravans.'

Economy in writing is much more than a matter of avoiding clumsy connecting words such as 'regarding' and 'concerning'. A correspondent with a feeling for English and a sense of humour has written thus to the press:

> The *Today* programme reported this morning that Tony Blair fears slippage in the time frame of the arms decommissioning process in Ulster. Well, I suppose that's better than a delay.

Of course, 'slippage in the time frame' means 'delay'. But alas, we regularly hear now that the 'time frame' or the 'time scale' allotted for some venture was too limited when what is meant is that someone tried to do something 'too quickly'. Here is a sentence from the world of caravanning:

> The gas locker easily accommodates two 6 kg propane or two 7 kg butane containers, which should keep most motor caravanners going for an adequate time span.

Plainly 'which should keep most motor caravanners going for an adequate time span' means 'which should last long enough for most motor caravanners'.

There seems to be something about this business of speaking on the subject of time – how long something takes or how much something is delayed – that stirs up the pot of verbosity.

> You should understand that any further delay in reaching a decision could well jeopardize the likelihood of maintaining a satisfactory level of public support for the whole venture.

In plain English this seems to mean: 'Postponing a decision could cost public support.' But just as we have to speak of 'time spans', 'time scales', and 'time frames' where once things were done slowly or quickly, so being acceptable or popular is now a matter of 'maintaining a satisfactory level of public support'.

Sometimes the choice of a single word or two sends a sentence spinning from the sphere of simple statement into the world of muddy pretentiousness.

> The fear of gas is firmly entrenched into the minds of virtually all sailors.

Why 'entrenched'? The word has, or ought to have, a powerful connotation from the picture of digging defensive positions in the stress of war. What purpose do hints of that connotation serve here? Does the sentence mean anything other than 'Most sailors fear gas'? Consider, too, the following:

> The HCS provide a much needed volunteer section input to the project.

On any list of overdone words 'input' would have to have a place. Is it needed here? And is the word 'section' needed either? Is a 'volunteer section input' anything more than 'volunteers'? What impulse towards wordiness is it that produces such excess? The following is another such instance.

> Building them in greater numbers is under review.

Surely this simply means 'They are thinking of building more.' Similarly the works manager who announced that results showed a 'product uptake curve' only meant that sales were up. And the employer who reported on an employee that he had 'an informal approach to time-tables' presumably meant that he was unpunctual.

Formulas and Evasions

Sometimes wordiness is not so much a matter of picking up the wrong word here and adding the unnecessary word there, but of settling down to a bilious outflow of emasculated words that cushion the brain against thought and the heart against feeling:

> I should like to assure you that on our part we are determined to do our best to settle the matter to your satisfaction.

Clearly this means 'We shall do our best to meet your wishes.' One should be forewarned of coming excess by the opening words. It is a fairly safe piece of advice that if anyone in print would like 'to assure' you of something, then you are not about to receive a crisp announcement. 'I/We should like to assure you that' is only one of a group of introductory expressions that are presumably intended to soften up readers so that they respond more readily to what follows. These expressions have a personal flavour established by the initial 'We' or 'I' and sustained by the direct appeal to 'you' the reader. Other such formal introductory addresses include 'We are pleased to be able to announce that . . .', 'We are taking this opportunity to inform our customers that . . .', 'We believe it will be of interest to you to learn that . . .', and, most winning of all, 'As one of our most loyal and valued customers, you will no doubt be delighted to hear that . . .'

There are also introductory redundancies of a different kind, the impersonal ones. They are less winning. They do not cajole. They do not try to slide into intimacy with the reader. They do not attempt gently to gain the ear for a quiet word. Rather they clamber up to make a formal pronouncement before the face. Some of them retain a degree of restraint, such as 'It is felt that', 'It gives us great pleasure to record that' and even 'It is regretted that'. Others are more clamant and challenging' such as 'It is generally agreed that', 'It must be accepted that', 'It would not be claiming too much to assert that' and even 'It is surely obvious to everyone that'.

There is, of course, a brand of wordiness which has a purpose. The purpose may be to soften a blow, to make an announcement seem less shocking than it is. We are used to this kind of avoidance of the straightforward expression in talking about death. We say that so and so 'passed away'. A firm advising those in direct marketing about checking up on their lists of customers estimates that, while 12 per cent of the customers change their addresses, '3 per cent may be lost due to mortalities'. In short, they die.

The vocabulary of pregnancy and child-bearing was similarly wrapped about with verbiage in the Victorian age. A pregnant wife might be described as being 'in an interesting condition' and she and her husband might be said to be 'expecting a happy event'. In our own period verbal evasions tend to veil very different events. Industrial firms are said to be 'down-sizing' when they plan to dismiss large numbers of their staff. The process of adding to the numbers of unemployed is one of 'rationalization'. A recently sacked employee has ironically described himself as having suffered 'an involuntary career event'. This attitude of seeming tenderness towards employers is not always reciprocated by employers themselves. *The Times* city diarist gives us this information about a large firm:

> As the latest report and accounts reveals, 'as of December 31, 1998, 177 employees had been terminated'.

The finality of being 'terminated' contrasts with experiencing a passing 'career event'.

The sort of evasive style illustrated here is of course a speciality of political propaganda. At the time when news bulletins were filled with horror stories of the ethnic cleansing of Kosovo by Serbian troops, it was said that nearer home, in Serbia itself, the refugees were described as 'relocated transit Albanians' and their lot was to be 'rehoused as guests in Albanian homes'.

NOUNS AND VERBS

Recourse to Nouns

Since excessive wordiness often results from unnecessary recourse to nouns, it is worthwhile to explore fully the difference between English style heavily laden with nouns and English style heavily laden with verbs. But we must first note how uneconomic a too ready recourse to nouns – especially abstract nouns – can be.

> We shall continue to build on improvements in the efficiency of our operations, maximizing the potential for growth at home and for expansion in the global market-place.

We shall look carefully at the vocabulary of business later in the book. For the moment it is enough to observe that all we learn from this sentence could be learned from the simple statement: 'We shall do our best to be efficient and to expand our business at home and abroad.' This reduces the number of words in the original by about a third. And the nouns 'improvements', 'efficiency', 'operations', 'potential', 'growth' and 'expansion' have all gone.

Business reports abound in such wastage.

> The funding will provide us with the ability to deliver world class training to potential team members.

Whenever a writer is tempted to use such expressions as 'provide us with the ability', he or she should pause. All that is needed here is: 'The funding will enable us to deliver world class training to potential team members.' Just as 'to provide someone with ability to do this or that' is identical with 'to enable someone to do this or that', so there are many abstract nouns which can be attached to verbs in the business of manufacturing similar inflations. 'We are determined to give immediate consideration to the plan' should be: 'We are determined to consider the plan immediately.' 'The review should supply us with full awareness of the extent of the commitment that is required of us' should be: 'The review should inform us how far we need to be committed.'

Fondness for abstract nouns is now such that there are cases where a writer appears to have dragged one into the text by the scruff of the neck. Here is a claim from the nursing profession:

> We have finally taken our rightful place at the policy tables at federal and state level due to increasing public recognition of our essentiality.

That nurses are necessary to society is a fact we are not going to question. But can we not appreciate how important nurses are without talking about their 'essentiality'?

And I have just heard a speaker prophesying ill of likely future developments in the European Community:

> Such an eventuality would result in the gravest consequences for all of us.

This means 'If that happens, it would be bad for all of us.' Plainly the temptation to have recourse to established circumlocutions such as 'such an eventuality would result in' is wasteful.

The Pile-up of Nouns

There is another aspect of the current over-fondness for nouns which has developed over recent decades. The fashion is to pile noun upon noun where once adjectives might have been more used. We find a breakfast cereal announcing itself thus:

> The superior high fibre wheat bran cereal.

The words 'fibre', 'wheat', 'bran' and 'cereal' are all nouns. There seems to be a willingness to expand lists of nouns indiscriminately. We hear of, say, a 'Barn Dance Revival Society', then of a 'Barn Dance Revival Society Conference' organized by a 'Barn Dance Revival Society Conference Coordinator'. The nouns are piled up with reckless abandon. The mind begins to long for an adjective as a thirsty man longs for drink in the desert.

The good writer will restrain the appetite for nouns. One of the excesses in this respect is that of forcing a noun into the garment of an adjective.

> These guidelines cover diet and other lifestyle factors that can help prevent cancer.

Notice what process produces a sentence like this. There is the noun 'life' and there is the noun 'style'. The two have been forced together as a new noun. But then this new noun is forced into an adjectival function by being jammed up against another noun 'factors'. The net result is not anything grossly tasteless, but the good writer is not satisfied merely to avoid the grossly tasteless. And the habit of jamming nouns together does not produce elegance. Consider this complaint about weather conditions that can produce flooding:

> There is evidence of some unsatisfactory forecasting and warning dissemination.

The objection here is not against bad grammar but against tortuous juxtaposition of nouns ill-fitted for mutual attachment ('forecasting and warning dissemination'). Reduction in the number of nouns would certainly make for improvement: 'It seems that forecasts and warnings were not made widely enough known.'

In this respect it is not always good style to use one word where two might have been used. 'Warning dissemination' is certainly not better English than 'dissemination of warnings'. The same may be said of the nouns in the following:

> Oil hydraulics have a number of advantages which include greater corrosion protection.

'Corrosion protection' in itself is scarcely a tenable concept. Nothing is to be gained from not saying: 'protection against corrosion'.

Perhaps even more tortuous is the mental process that produces this comment on the timber trade:

> The modern forestry, saw-milling and wood-processing industry has a good story to tell. It makes an important contribution to the economy by providing rural employment and contributes to the balance of payments by import substitution.

The expression 'import substitution' is grotesquely ill-chosen. If 'import substitution' made an acceptable combination, surely it would be more likely to mean substitution 'of' imports than substitution 'for' imports. Again verbal parsimony is misplaced, as it often is when it economizes on prepositions. The sentence should read: 'contributes to the balance of payments by replacing imports'.

Using Nouns or Verbs

Over-use of nouns and under-use of verbs is a plague in much contemporary journalism, indeed in much contemporary prose of many kinds. Let us consider what are the characteristics of prose which is overladen with nouns, as opposed to prose which is fully laden, or indeed overladen, with verbs. For instance I read in a motoring magazine:

> Plans are in place to increase production of high top models.

The first seven words there include three nouns: 'plans', 'place' and 'production'. If we rewrite the sentence, replacing the nouns 'plans', 'place' and 'production' by verbs, it becomes 'We plan to produce more high top models.' The flavour of the latter sentence is less sophisticated and simpler.

We must not conclude that it is always better to sprinkle a paragraph with verbs rather than nouns. We need to take into account the kind of prose we are writing, its purpose and the readership it is intended for. To exemplify prose heavily laden with verbs perhaps no writer is more useful than Defoe. As a stylist he is simple and direct. His *Journal of the Plague Year*, published in 1722, is a supposedly first-hand account of the outbreak of the plague in London that occurred in 1665. Defoe would have been a child of four or five at the time, but he studied factual documentary accounts of the outbreak, and his book acquires a seeming authoritativeness from its sober direct reportage. Defoe always packed his fictional and semi-fictional work with descriptive and anecdotal detail. In the passage we quote he tells of a poor London citizen who lost his wife and all his children in the Plague. He decided to make for the country, taking two servants and an elderly relative with him. Arriving at a village he takes an empty house.

> After a few days he **got** a cart and **loaded** it with goods, and **carries** them down to the house; the people of the village **opposed** his driving the cart along, but with some arguings and with some force, the men that **drove** the cart along **got** through the street up to the door of the house. There the constable **resisted** them again, and would not **let** them be **brought** in. The man **caused** the goods to **be unloaden** and **laid** at the door, and **sent** the cart away; upon which they **carried** the man before a justice of the peace;

> that is to **say**, they **commanded** him to **go**, which he **did**. The justice **ordered** him to **cause** the cart to **fetch** away the goods again, which he **refused** to **do**; upon which the justice **ordered** the constable to **pursue** the carters and **fetch** them back, and **make** them **reload** the goods and **carry** them away, or to **set** them in the stocks till they **came** for further orders; and if they could not **find** them, nor the man would not **consent** to **take** them away, they should **cause** them to be **drawn** with hooks from the house-door and **burned** in the street.

For other purposes this might perhaps seem to have an excessive preponderance of verbs. But Defoe captures the urgency of the situation and something of the desperate frustration involved in trying to find safety. His flow of verbs renders the prose sinewy, home-spun and compelling, but neither elegant nor rhythmic.

By contrast let us look at the style of the historian Lord Macaulay. He concludes his *Essay on Warren Hastings* with a summary character study whose style abounds in resounding nouns.

> Those who look on his **character**, without **favour** or **malevolence** will pronounce that, in the two great **elements** of all social **virtue**, in **respect** for the **rights** of others, and in **sympathy** for the **sufferings** of others, he was deficient. His **heart** was somewhat hard. But though we cannot with **truth** describe him as either righteous or as a merciful **ruler**, we cannot regard without **admiration** the **amplitude** and **fertility** of his **intellect**, his rare **talents** for **command**, for **administration**, and for **controversy**, his dauntless **courage**, his honourable **poverty**, his fervent **zeal** for the **interests** of the **state**, his noble **equanimity**, tried by both **extremes** of **fortune**, and never disturbed by either.

The prose here is less taut, less plain, and less vigorous, but it has smoothness and some stateliness appropriate to the context. There is also a fine balance in the architecture of the prose and a rhythmic flow quite absent from Defoe's narrative.

Current Over-use of Nouns

In our own age, generally speaking, the tendency is to over-use nouns heavily. This is the temptation which today's writer has to resist. It means that our prose is more likely to suffer from flaccidity than from jerkiness.

Contemporary prose is all too likely to lack vitality and force. At its most obvious the unnecessary preference for nouns can so easily be avoided.

> Health professionals yesterday urged the police to stop using CS spray to subdue psychiatric patients after research showed that it was a frequent occurrence.

We all know that a 'frequent occurrence' is something that often happens. Why do we translate 'after research showed that it often happened', which is the way we think, into 'after research showed that it was a frequent occurrence', which has become the way we write?

There seems to be a small glossary of abstract nouns labelled in our minds as 'for use in print'. Users feel that they must be dragged out and put on paper to prevent what they want to say from seeming too obvious or too easily comprehensible.

> The experts fear a worsening of the danger.

Now the person who put that into print would not have put it like that in conversation. To an acquaintance he would have said: 'The experts fear the danger will get worse.' What in speech 'gets worse' on paper becomes 'a worsening'.

> They can contemplate and accept the inevitability of its disappearance.

The person who wrote that would not have said it. He or she would have said 'They can see and accept that it must go.' In speech we recognize that something 'must go', whereas on paper we have to 'accept the inevitability of its disappearance'.

> Americans have long seen the Middle East, North Africa and sometimes even Western Europe as areas in which vigilance against such [terrorist] attacks is a permanent necessity.

Let us again try to imagine what happened in the mind and possibly even in speech before anything of this got put down on paper. Someone decided that there were areas 'where they would always have to watch out for terrorist attacks'. So the mental glossary of 'writable words' was ransacked and the recommended terms were brought into play. Instead of always having to watch out, there must be asserted the 'necessity' for 'vigilance'.

One begins to wonder whether press magnates encourage their

employees to translate from the language of thought and utterance into this laboured and inflexible idiom.

> A further sinister reinforcement of this attitude may be that smoking among older women has been found to be associated with relative thinness, a possibility that may not have been overlooked by observant teenage girls as well as the tobacco industry.

Older women who smoke tend to be thinner. Teenage girls notice that and so does the tobacco industry. The point is worth making, but do we really need all this stuff about 'reinforcement' of an 'attitude' and something being 'associated' with 'relative thinness' and a 'possibility' that some 'observant' people may not have overlooked?

Reaching for an abstract noun whenever one has something to say becomes a kind of ingrained habit. There was a news item on BBC Radio 4 about an incident in the Balkans in which bodies of Albanians were found, seemingly massacred by the Serbian Security Police. Various versions of what had happened were aired. On this issue the radio announcement ran:

> As the days passed the precise truth became less and less clear.

Why drag in this abstraction 'precise truth', when what the newswriter meant was that 'what had actually happened' became less and less clear as the days passed? There is a strange rooted objection in journalism to the use of such a natural English noun clause as 'what had happened'. If 'what was true' became ever more difficult to determine, that does not mean that 'truth' was becoming 'less clear'. It means that 'truth' was getting harder and harder to arrive at. But the reader will notice that, as we strive to make clear what should have been said, verbs come into play. We use such expressions as 'what had happened', 'becoming more difficult to determine', and 'getting harder and harder to arrive at'.

There is need for a campaign in English education against the over-use of nouns. Pick up any piece of publicity you receive through the post and you will find evidence of this. Today I read:

> Under self-assessment rules, the automatic penalty for the late submission of a tax return is £100.

Suppose we try to reduce the nouns there. 'Under self-assessment rules, you will be fined £100 if you send in your tax return late.' Instead of the noun 'penalty' we have the verb 'will be fined'. Instead of the noun 'submission' we have the verb 'send in'.

Children should be given exercises in schools in translating noun-ridden prose into verby prose. The earliest exercises could take the form of turning 'Our sole aim is your satisfaction' into 'We only want to please you.' Nothing is easier than turning up suitable specimens for this kind of exercise. Replaceable nouns are printed in bold type in what follows. Verbs introduced in their place are also in bold type.

> Our **intention** is to give the matter serious **consideration**.

This becomes:

> We **intend** to **consider** the matter seriously.

> **Consideration** must be given to organizational **developments** which could strengthen the **accountability** of senior management.

This becomes:

> We must **consider** how to **develop** our organization so as to **make** our senior managers more accountable.

> After a whole day of **negotiation** a settlement was arrived at which met with **acceptance** from both parties.

This becomes:

> After **negotiating** for a day, a settlement was reached which both parties **agreed** to.

> Greater customer **care** plus improved **support** for dealers were identified as key **benefits** behind one of the biggest **innovations** in the leisure vehicle industry.

This becomes:

> The leisure vehicle industry has **reformed** its practices so as to **care** more for customers and to **support** dealers better.

> There are too many **concentrations** of dangerous heavy metals in plants that are important **resources** for a wider **range** of waterbirds.

This becomes:

> Too often dangerous heavy metals are **concentrated** in plants that **help** to **sustain** many different waterbirds.

Nouns Doubling as Verbs

We have been concerned here with nouns and verbs as words with contrasting functions. But the English language is rich in words which are both nouns and verbs. Look up a few simple nouns or a few simple verbs in a dictionary. Such nouns as 'love', 'force' and 'taste' are also verbs. Such verbs as 'drink', 'wash' and 'play' are also nouns. We think of 'give' as a verb and 'gift' as a noun, but the Scots have long used 'gift' as a verb. We think of 'author' as a noun, but the Americans use it as a verb. The temptation for writers to use an established noun as a verb or an established verb as a noun can scarcely be considered a practice alien to the language. We have been taking such liberties for a long time. Words as essentially nounlike in their form as 'condition', 'position', 'partition', 'requisition' and 'section' are all used as verbs. We can see this practice extended further and further in our own day. My latest dictionary gives 'rubbish' as a noun only, but we now often hear it used as a verb, meaning to disparage totally ('In an ironical outburst the leader of the Opposition rubbished the Government's new proposal'). There are even cases where an individual's career may furnish us with a new noun-turned-verb. It was during Mrs Thatcher's forceful premiership that the noun 'handbag' was turned into a verb expressive of aggressive diplomacy in action.

Experimentation with words can enrich the language. We have long been manufacturing new verbs from existing nouns and adjectives. 'My wife and I caravan all year round', I read. My older dictionary gives 'caravan' only as a noun; my newer dictionary gives it as a verb too. There are obvious advantages in not having to write 'My wife and I use our caravan all year round.' In the early days of the private car the word 'motor' was used of both the vehicle and the use of it. King George V was known to be fond of 'motoring' and Rowntrees successfully marketed 'motoring chocolate'.

It is true that sometimes verbs newly fashioned from nouns make readers squirm when they are first encountered.

> The Craft Movement Contemporary Craft Fair showcases the original work of more than 100 of the UK's best professional designer/makers . . .

Here is a case in point. The noun 'showcase' somehow seems too thoroughly 'nounish' to be so treated. Yet on reflection we realize that some seemingly most unlikely compound nouns such as 'time-table', 'soft-pedal' and 'steam-roller' have become useful verbs.

Where can we draw the line? I have heard an attempt to turn the noun 'nuance' into a verb: 'I think I should want to nuance that criticism a little.' Presumably this means 'I think I should want to give a subtle change to that criticism.' How free are we in this respect? Was the first person to use the word 'rubbish' as a verb charged with illiteracy? If we are so clever that we thus 'invent' a new verb, we must hope that it will catch on until those who at first squirm to read it begin to use it themselves. After all, what noun would totally resist being converted into a verb? The Victorian Age left us a tongue-twister in the form of a snatch of conversation between a lady and a workman repairing a pan:

> Are you aluminiuming it, man?
> No, I'm copper-bottoming it, mum.

And in conversation it is not only nouns that get turned into verbs. In Shakespeare's *Romeo and Juliet*, when Juliet annoys her father Capulet by resisting his demand that she should marry County Paris, Capulet accuses her of being too proud. She quibbles over the word 'proud' and Capulet loses his temper with her. 'Proud me no prouds' he says in rebuke, turning the adjective 'proud' temporarily into a verb and then temporarily into a plural noun.

USE OF METAPHOR

The pursuit of simplicity and directness does not preclude colour and imagery. The judicious use of metaphor is crucial in the best writing. But metaphor misapplied damages style. And, once a seemingly appropriate metaphor has been seized on, it must be properly followed up. Here is a tribute to the old Nature Conservancy Council.

> Its official enthusiasm for local nature reserve designations on educational and recreational grounds has pumped life into official doorstep conservation.

Now to speak of 'pumping' life or 'breathing' life instead of just using a verb like 'strengthened' or 'revitalized' is to make sensible use of metaphor. But pumping life into a movement is one thing, and pumping life into 'doorstep conservation' is another thing. After all, 'wild life conservation' is conservation of wild life. And on that pattern 'doorstep conservation' would be conservation of doorsteps.

It tends to be with the introduction of fairly well-worn metaphors that writers trip up. We are so used to them that we lose sight of their metaphorical content. Consider this, for instance:

> Among the pantheon of great sporting clichés, the hoary old chestnut that luck is something you make for yourself has always seemed to me one of the more blatantly unsatisfactory.

The Pantheon was a circular temple in Rome. Its peculiarity was that it was dedicated, not to a particular god, but to all the gods. Thus the word has been taken up for a building in which a nation's dead heroes are commemorated. From that usage stems the use of the word for a place that houses the full tally of a nation's poets or artists. The writer of the above sentence may or may not have sensed that the word represents a place in which a number of beings are commemorated, but he assumes that he is free to use it to mean a repository for lots of items or indeed a kind of volume of quotations. This is to stretch the metaphor further than it will go. In other words it is to destroy the metaphor. We can accept the other metaphor, the 'hoary old chestnut', as standing for a sporting cliché. But to picture it taking its place in a pantheon is to turn a good metaphor into nonsense.

In the use of metaphor there must be appropriateness, restraint and consistency. These three requirements make for effective use of imagery. When the metaphorical use of the word 'pantheon' required us to treat a temple or a mausoleum as a thesaurus of quotations, there was a plain lack of appropriateness. One might argue that the imagery of the following sentence fails in respect of both restraint and consistency:

> I cannot believe that he [the Prime Minister] will choose to plunge into such an obvious elephant trap which would sour relations with the countryside up to and well beyond the next General Election.

We may or may not feel that it is over-stretching the image to parallel the passing of a new law with plunging into an obvious elephant trap. But, however that may be, we ought not to be asked to picture either the plunge or the trap 'souring' relations.

One ought not to go in for imagery whose effect on readers depends upon their not taking it too seriously; that is to say, not visualizing what is pictured. It is bad to rely on unresponsiveness by the reader to vivid metaphor, however well established.

> England's leading clubs are positioned today to make a gesture that could soothe the months of nagging warfare that have blighted British rugby since the introduction of professionalism.

Now if the writer had said 'a gesture that could put an end to the months of nagging warfare', we should not have complained. But the word 'soothe' is, or should be, a powerful metaphorical expression, and the sensitive reader balks at the idea of 'soothing' months. And just as we do not 'soothe' months, neither do we 'soothe' nagging warfare. This is what is meant by our demand for consistency in imagery.

When, quite justifiably, seeking to avoid the most obvious and most used verbs, the writer must take care not to use a verb with a metaphorical content that collides incongruously with its context.

> Saladin stopped Richard I from taking Jerusalem, sparking the decline of large-scale expeditions.

The image of 'sparking' derives presumably from starting a conflagration or an explosion. It would seem appropriate enough to the launching of an enterprise or to the outbreak of some catastrophic development such as a war, but surely it is not appropriate to an event which marks the beginning of a decline. One can only recommend a more colourless verb: 'starting the decline of large-scale expeditions'.

WORD AND CONTEXT

We all know that words group themselves for us, not just according to their literal meanings, but according to the kind of context in which they are most often used. We read in a leaflet about some public meeting that 'Proceedings will commence with a statement from the Chairman.' The vocabulary does not strike us as odd. But if we were invited out to dinner with some close friends and our host turned to us as he received us and said 'Proceedings will commence with drinks in the drawing room', we should suspect him of being funny. The appropriate vocabulary for one situation is not the appropriate vocabulary for a very different situation.

Now we must not assume that transfer of vocabulary from its normally appropriate context into a seemingly inappropriate context is always a mistake. It may be intentionally done for a comic purpose, as we suggested with the host's greeting at the party. Samuel Beckett at one and the same time convulses us with laughter and wrings our hearts in his plays and in his novels by juxtaposing snatches of the familiar currencies of contemporary day-to-day usage with situations totally and tragically at loggerheads with the thrust and tone of what is said.

Indeed the forcing together of words from different areas of usage may be highly poetic in effect. Surely there is no more prosaic word in the English language than the word 'satisfactory'. We associate it with the dullest school reports on the most unexciting performances by the most pedestrian of achievers. Yet T. S. Eliot achieves a dramatic, indeed a climactic effect by his use of the word at the end of one section of *Journey of the Magi*, his poem about the coming of the three kings to Bethlehem on the birth of Christ. The poem begins in a conversational idiom as the journey is described, and one word seems to stick out at the end of the sixth line where the camels are described as 'galled, sore-footed, refractory'. The seemingly rather clumsy word resonates in the mind until, over twenty lines later, the speaker tells of the eventual arrival at Bethlehem and what they found there in the words 'it was (you may say) satisfactory'.

It takes a poet to make the word 'satisfactory' so powerfully evocative. We are unlikely to be inspired to comparable strokes of genius in our daily use of words. If we get the wrong word from the wrong context it is likely to be a defacement rather than an enrichment of our utterance. The careful speaker or writer uses words which meld happily together. We do not want business jargon in the privacy of the home. A police inspector, interviewed on the radio about a certain problem said:

> It's a question of getting the message down to that section of the police service which has an interface with the public.

The word 'interface', basically a scientific term for the surface which is common to two different contiguous things, has been found useful in the field of business organization, so useful that it has been over-used. It is now a 'vogue word'. But clearly it is out of place in the policeman's statement. If we cannot talk about the officers who come into personal contact with the public without introducing an 'interface' between them, we need some elementary instruction in the use of our language. It is this practice of dropping a decisively technical word into a humdrum sentence that needs to be disciplined. It introduces a linguistically alien element that discomfits the reader.

> The countryside is a complicated entity, in danger of being overlooked or taken for granted.

The word 'entity' is basically a philosophical term for something which has real and distinctive existence. Perhaps its nearest English equivalent would be 'beingness'. It is quite out of place in a sentence pleading for more attention to the preservation of the English countryside. Words such as 'complicated', 'entity' and 'danger' are weakened by usage which relies on the reader not to take any of them at their face value.

We move from the countryside to the garden for another experiment in verbal misplacement.

> People should experiment more with plants. They are unaware of the potential of their gardens, so they plant the norm.

The non-gardener may be so taken aback by this statement as to feel it necessary to check up in an encyclopaedia just to make sure that there is not a fast-spreading herbaceous perennial called 'norm'. After all, the word 'norm' we are accustomed to means the average level of achievement, the standard of action that can be expected as representing the average. It is not something that can be planted in a garden. To use the expression 'they planted the norm' to mean 'they put in the kind of thing that most people would' is again to introduce a verbally alien note.

The converse error of abusing familiar words that are associated with primal human experiences by exploiting them for commercial purposes is a commonplace of business publicity.

> All the members of our Board join me in urging you, as a valued shareholder, to look seriously at a new and exciting proposal which I am proud to be able to present to you.

Here our complaint is that familiar words are applied with an insensitivity to their genuine meaning that cheapens them. 'Valued', 'seriously', 'exciting' and 'proud' are thrown about like counters of little worth. The request to the reader to study something is what has to be conveyed. It is tasteless to wrap it around with the ambience of seriousness, excitement and personal pride.

It is in translations into English that the gravest misplacements of vocabulary can occur. Such misplacements can be a great source of humour. When we are told of them, we wonder whether they are not perhaps the stuff of fiction. But perhaps it is true that a Hong Kong tailor's shop displays a notice saying 'Ladies may have fits upstairs' and a Greek tailor's shop guarantees 'to execute customers in strict rotation'. And perhaps there really is a hotel in an Austrian ski resort where guests are requested 'not to perambulate the corridors in the hours of repose in the boots of ascension'. Periodically such specimens appear in the press and indeed they illuminate nuances and vagaries in our vocabulary.

It should go without saying in this matter of suiting the word to the context that what is appropriate in speech may be unsuitable on the printed page. Many a construction cited in this book for criticism might well be used in conversation without raising pedantic eyebrows. But there is a gossipy informality in our chatter that can look tasteless in print.

> Perhaps you're picking up on problems in their relationship and are feeling protective towards your friend.

The Agony Aunt must be allowed her due licence of informality, but this slangy construction 'to pick up on', meaning 'to take notice of' or 'to make something of', would be better replaced by some tasteful usage that is none the less homely, say: 'Perhaps you're dwelling too much on problems in their relationship.' But if readers feel indulgent towards the Agony Aunt's chatty idiom, they will be less inclined to look favourably on the following:

> Designers have already picked up on the potential of 'mood-enhancing' room fragrances.

Here the meaning is: 'Designers have already exploited the potential of "mood-enhancing" room fragrances.'

Certain readily used conversational expressions somehow have their constructional defects exposed when they are put into print. For instance we ask 'Was it just my imagination?' when we want to imply that perhaps what we are going to say is not factually correct but a guess on our part. Yet when this expression is put in print the literal meaning of the words is revealed in its bareness.

> Was it my imagination or were gardens in June neglected because of the bad weather?

It would be much better here to drop the colloquialism and say: 'Is my hunch correct, that gardens in June were neglected because of the bad weather?'

Such colloquialisms form quite a significant part of our daily conversations. Someone tells us something that fully confirms a perhaps controversial view that we have long held. 'Indeed', we say, 'that says it all!' But put that into cold print and advertise 'Furniture that says it all' and the expression suddenly has its absurdity revealed.

Words which carry only a slight metaphorical content when we use them in conversation may have that content strengthened when they are put into print. For instance, we might say 'That notion sounds absurd', and we are not thinking of the verb 'sound' in connection with noise of any kind. But put that in print and the effect is different.

> The notion of growing orchids in the bitter cold urban jungle of Chicago sounds as unlikely as snow falling in the desert.

When we have read words like 'cold urban jungle' we are mentally in a verbal world where things are felt. When we move on to expressions like 'snow falling in the desert' we are strengthened in our sense of the felt world, the world in which weather changes and snow may fall. As a result the word 'sounds' gets involved also in the world of sensation, and we think to ourselves that growing orchids and snow falling are both silent processes, and that 'notions' do not produce any sound at all.

HYPERBOLE

Hyperbole is exaggeration indulged in for the sake of effect. It may be deliberate and effective. Poets use it unashamedly. In Shakespeare's *Macbeth*, when Macbeth has murdered Duncan and is horrified at the sight of his own bloodied hands, he cries:

> Will all great Neptune's ocean wash this blood
> Clean from my hand? No, this my hand will rather
> The multitudinous seas incarnadine,
> Making the green one red.

Here is hyperbole on the grand scale. Macbeth's notion that if he put his hand in the sea the world's oceans would turn red is imaginatively powerful precisely because its excess matches the enormity of the deed.

The worst kind of hyperbole is that which establishes itself by such frequent repetition that all novelty and force are lost. The most obvious of all hyperboles are those which we use daily in conversation. 'She's terribly late', we say, when in fact the element of terror is lacking. 'Terribly' has become a substitute for 'very'. 'My dear, it was absolutely devastating! The milkman failed to deliver on two successive days.' The potentially powerful words 'absolutely devastating' are used as little more than a substitute for 'inconvenient'.

Now conversation is one thing and the written word another thing. On paper, the cheapening of richly meaningful words by using them as so many counters to avoid repetition of 'very' or 'most' implies failure to think carefully. It also suggests poverty of imagination. Let us consider a few specimens.

> The hotel is close to a fabulous sandy beach.

The word 'fabulous' (from the word 'fable') strictly defines an imaginary beast such as the Minotaur or some other comparable creature or event with only legendary existence. Hence it is used to describe something so astoundingly remarkable as to be unbelievable or all but unbelievable. To describe someone as having 'fabulous wealth' would convey the possession of riches all but inconceivable. To throw the word around as an equivalent of 'very nice' is to dissipate its meaning. The same applies to the word 'fantastic'. An advertiser tells us that if we use certain dyes 'fantastic results are guaranteed'. The word 'fantastic' (from the word 'fantasy') is applied to beings and things conceived in the world of fancy rather than of reality. Again it is totally inappropriate to use the word thus. Closely related to the misuse of 'fabulous' and 'fantastic' is the misuse of 'incredible' and 'incredibly', words which also seem to belong more to the recounting of marvellous events than of day-to-day doings.

> The display of her work went down incredibly well.

Clearly again the word 'very' would do all that the now weakened word 'incredibly' can do.

The desire to give the highest degree of praise one can to efforts of this kind naturally breeds hyperbole. Here we have a comment on a horse trials event. The writer tells that no one is 'too big to give advice, when asked, or to share their ideals', and adds:

> It is eventing's greatest asset and creates such a good camaraderie amongst competitors, an ideal that I believe is unique to this sport.

Here the words 'ideal' and 'unique' seem to be brought into play chiefly because of the nice noise they make.

The specimens we have been looking at tend to arise from the desire to make something seem more remarkable than it is. By the use of hyperbole the writer exaggerates the emotional impact of what is said.

> Dr Jeff Sampson has just joined the Animal Health Trust as Canine Genetics Co-ordinator. This new post, sponsored by the Kennel Club, will help apply this exciting subject to the world of dog breeding.

Over-use of the word 'exciting' is not uncommon. In contexts like this it is apt to raise an ironic smile. Certainly the subject is one that dog-breeders will find 'interesting'. The writer gains nothing by using the word 'exciting', as though it meant no more than that. A similar, perhaps more justifiable, hyperbolic approach to the reader's feelings is made by the word 'horrifying' in the sentence:

> A horrifying number of pets are put to sleep because they can't be identified and their owners traced.

Just as words to do with stirring the reader's feelings tend to be hyperbolic, so too do words connected with suggestions of great size. It is easy to find examples of words such as 'tremendous', 'immense' and 'enormous' used where 'large' or 'big' would be more appropriate.

Hyperbole is not just a matter of using adjectives extravagantly. A different brand of hyperbole builds up an image in a word or two whose effect is quite disproportionate to what is needed. Here we have an advertiser's enthusiastic account of a new car.

> The sexy aristocrat of the open road. Sleek and swift. Purebred and powerful. With the body of a thoroughbred and the soul of a beast.

The world of cold prose seems to be left behind here. We are in the verbal world where Macbeth's bloodied hands could turn the world's oceans scarlet. The trouble is, however, that the AA journal is not designed for theatrical performance before a hushed and rapt audience. No doubt the psychologist could have some fun explaining the propaganda effect of words such as 'sexy' and 'aristocrat', with their associations of glowing beauty and social superiority, of words such as 'purebred' and 'thoroughbred', with their associations of high breed and grace on display in the fresh country air. And, lest it was all beginning to seem too cultivatedly high-class, there is the expression 'the soul of a beast' to raise associations of untamed power waiting to be unleashed.

Ours not to cavil or complain when the poetic souls of advertisers are let off their leash. But the imaginative efforts do not always come off. Witness the advertiser's question, put before recommending a skin treatment.

> Is your skin tight, tingly and throwing a tantrum?

One can give higher marks for ingenuity than for good taste here. To speak of 'throwing a tantrum' in connection with the conduct of skin is surely to go over the top.

CHAPTER 10

Sound Logic

BACK-REFERENCE

Good writing is logical. The relationship between logic and grammar is close. It is very often by a failure in grammar that a failure in logic occurs. That is one way of putting a crucial fact about good style. And the other way of putting it is this: It is often by a failure in logic that a failure in grammar occurs. Such is the interconnection between the two. It follows that we have already in this book had to criticize the choice or arrangement of words because of their illogicality. For instance, a common error which has both its logical and its grammatical aspects occurs when some such word as 'it' or 'this' is used without clarity as to what the word refers back to, and we cited cases in Chapter 6 that would exemplify this. At the crudest level this is a matter of making sure that such pronouns as 'it' and 'this' are properly anchored.

> All the work is done on anaesthetized animals. It is given a single injection and never wakes up.

The error assumes a grammatical character here. The singular 'it' is used where the plural 'they' is required.

But sometimes the failure in back-reference involves a different kind of lapse in the thought-process, which can only be described as illogical. Here is a journalist reporting on the restoration of a three-mile canal tunnel near Huddersfield:

> Sealed for more than fifty years, it has long been thought of as an impossible restoration.

Plainly 'it', as placed here, must refer back grammatically to the sealed tunnel. But no one has ever thought of the tunnel as a 'restoration', whether possible or impossible. When we say 'It has long been thought difficult to climb Mount Everest', 'it' refers forwards to the words 'to climb Mount Everest'. Using that construction, the journalist could have written: 'it has long been thought impossible to restore it', where the second 'it' refers properly back to the tunnel.

'It' is not the only pronoun that can introduce a failure in back-reference. Let us consider a notice seen in a shop in a tourist area:

> Will customers please leave their rucksacks and any other large baggage at the till. This is due to safety precautions.

The failure in grammar and logic here centres on the word 'this'. What is 'this'? If, as appears most likely, 'this' is the request itself to leave the baggage at the till, then it is not 'due to' safety precautions. Rather it 'is' a safety precaution. The better wording would have been: 'This is a safety precaution.'

We turn to a more complicated failure of logic involving the word 'this'.

> You often feel more depressed and alone, and probably quite angry that no one is making the effort to reach out to you. This leads to physical symptoms, hoping perhaps that you can get the attention and care you need that way.

The grammar suggests that the physical symptoms are 'hoping' for attention. The present participle 'hoping', lacking proper attachment, is required here to do an impossible job. What the writer means, I take it, is: 'This leads to physical symptoms, caused by the hope that they may win you the attention you deserve.'

An even more subtle case of faulty back-reference confuses concepts curiously:

> Salman Rushdie says what he most dislikes about his appearance is 'its infrequency'. Happily those who know him as a regular on the party circuit know this is not quite true.

The question arises: What is not quite true? As it stands, the diarist is telling us that Salman Rushdie did not quite tell the truth in saying that he disliked the infrequency of his appearances. But Rushdie's likes and dislikes are not at issue. All that the diarist is wanting to question is the word 'infrequency'. If the shape of the sentence is to be kept, it must end in some such statement as: 'Happily those who know him as a regular on the party circuit know that "infrequency" is not quite the right word.'

Faulty back-reference by misuse of a pronoun is a simpler error to correct than faulty back-reference involving a verb. When a passage includes some such back-reference as 'and that was what we did', it is important that the grammatical antecedents of the conclusion are appropriate. It is correct to say 'We were told to take our umbrellas, and that is what we did', because the words 'that' and 'did' refer back to the words 'take our umbrellas'. It is incorrect to say 'They planned a picnic for us, and that is what we did' because there is no proper connection between 'that is what we did' and 'they planned a picnic'.

> Society must be assured that anyone that comes to hospital for treatment is only discharged at the point where they are well and it's safe to do so.

Safe to do what? the reader wants to know. And here we come upon a typical instance of misusing the expression 'to do so'. Whereas it is correct to say 'I shall discharge you when it is safe to do so', because the words 'to do so' refer back to the word 'discharge', it is not correct to say 'You shall be discharged when it is safe to do so' because the back-reference of 'to do so' must involve an active not a passive verb: 'No one who comes to hospital for treatment will be required to leave before they are well and it is safe to do so' (i.e. 'to leave'). Oddly enough, it would be correct, though not elegant, to say 'You shall be discharged when it is safe to be so' (i.e. to be discharged). The verb to 'do' is so generalized in its meaning that this kind of failure is not rare.

> The Countrywide Holidays operating manual runs to 90 pages. A smaller company might not have the resources to do this.

Again the reader asks the question: to do what? The only verb to which the verb 'do' can refer back is the verb 'runs'. The pedantic logician would argue that what is said here is: A smaller company might not have the resources to run to 90 pages. But it is the manual that runs to 90 pages, not the Countryside Holidays company, however large. The writer is requesting the reader to thought-read: 'A smaller company might not have the resources to publish one so big.'

There is a similar lapse in this advice about simmering on a camp stove:

> It's not impossible, just so difficult that most users never learn to do it and don't often bother if they have.

If they have what? Again that is the question that arises. One might say 'I trust you have brought your raincoat: put it here if you have', because there 'if you have' refers back to 'brought your raincoat'. But it is not correct to say 'if you have' where there is no such clear use of a verb in the matching tense to refer back to. To keep 'if they have' the sentence above would have to read: 'It's not impossible, just so difficult that most users have never learned to do it and don't often bother if they have.' The alternative is to keep the first part of the sentence and change the ending: 'most users never learn to do it and don't often bother if they do'. Ending a sentence with words such as 'they have' or 'he has' requires the writer to check that what has gone before gives the words proper anchorage.

> Keen judges say the 26-year-old Mancunian is riding as well as he ever has.

In conversation this might pass. But there is no proper anchorage for 'he has', which requires 'ridden' if it is to make sense. Since there is no 'ridden' to refer back to, it must be inserted at the end: 'the 26-year-old Mancunian is riding as well as he has ever ridden'.

The risks involved in ending a sentence with 'they have' or 'he has' apply equally to ending a sentence with 'it will'. Here is a sentence about the placing of memorial plaques on the former London homes of famous people:

> The criteria are there to ensure the fame of the person concerned is lasting – in one or two cases it's obvious it will.

The question naturally arises – will what? We can say 'Perhaps rain will fall: I think it will' because 'will' recalls and reintroduces the rest of the verb, 'fall'. But we ought not to say 'There could be rain tomorrow: I think it will', because in that sentence there is no verb to be recalled to go with the auxiliary verb 'will'. The two parts of the sentence must match in this respect: 'The criteria are there to ensure the fame of the person is lasting – in one or two cases it obviously is.'

There are certain words which cannot generally be used except with some back-reference. The word 'others' is one such. Typical usage is represented by such sentences as 'Some like meat; others prefer vegetables.' It is true that sometimes the process is reversed and the word 'others' is balanced by a forward reference. The usage is rare in prose, because it has a somewhat artificial rhetorical quality, but there is a famous sonnet by Matthew Arnold, addressed to Shakespeare, that begins:

> Others abide our question. Thou art free.
> We ask and ask: Thou smilest and art still,
> Out-topping knowledge.

There 'others' is balanced by forward reference to the word 'Thou'.

> Sometimes artists have a very clear idea of what they want, but others may have an idea and be unsure how to resolve it.

Here there is no proper back-reference. One cannot balance 'sometimes' with 'others'. If 'others' is to be kept, then the sentence must begin: 'Some artists have a very clear idea of what they want.'

An instance of faulty back-reference is sometimes better seen as an instance of faulty forward-reference. Where two parts of a verb are joined by 'and', it is essential that the match is exact.

> That could, and has been, dismissed by Conservative Central Office as 'sour grapes'.

One could say 'That could, and I think will, help' because 'could' can be followed by 'help'. But the auxiliary 'could' cannot be followed by 'has been dismissed'. There is no escape from spelling out the first verb properly: 'That could be, and has been, dismissed by Conservative Central Office as "sour grapes".'

INCONSEQUENTIALITY

All the illogical sentences quoted so far in this chapter called for collection which might have been defined in 'grammatical' terms. But of course it is possible to be extremely illogical while not erring grammatically. Not all the sentences criticized in this present section are faulty grammatically. Sometimes, in a perfectly grammatical sentence, a single ill-chosen word turns the logic of utterance upside down. In this respect we trespassed into the field of logic when illustrating in Chapter 3 how ill-chosen words in combination can produce inconsistency and incoherence. That is also at issue here. The following announcement was made on television.

> Louise Woodward will return home to restart the rest of her life.

There were two possible ways of making this announcement logically: either, 'Louise Woodward will return home to start the rest of her life', or 'Louise Woodward will return home to restart her life.' There was one thing that Louise could not do, and that was to return home and 'restart' the 'rest' of her life, because the 'rest' of her life had never been started, and what has not been started cannot be 'restarted'. QED. Words which place events in time (such as 'restart the rest of her life' above) have to be scrutinized for possible logical lapses. Here is one such:

> Jordan will be living on its nerves tomorrow when King Hussein, 63, undergoes a second bone marrow transplant at the Mayo Clinic in Minnesota in a last-ditch attempt to save him from last week's recurrence of lymphatic cancer.

A moment's thought could surely have prevented this illogicality. It is far too late to save someone from 'last week's recurrence' of a disease. The 'recurrence' has occurred, and that is that. The King can perhaps be saved from some of the possible consequences of the recurrence. It would appear that here the journalist's professional obsession with supposed compression led him astray. He wanted to avoid by way of abbreviation the obvious sequence: 'in a last-ditch attempt to save him from the effects of lymphatic cancer which became threatening again last week'. In fact the alteration of a single word ('from' to 'after') in his version would have given him the brevity he required with correctness thrown in as a bonus: 'undergoes a second bone marrow transplant at the Mayo Clinic in Minnesota in a last-ditch attempt to save him after last week's recurrence of lymphatic cancer'.

Placing events in time clearly sometimes strains the logical faculties. Here is a not uncommon misuse of 'when'. The sentence is about a hoarder who one day turned to crime.

> Cleaning the windows of a financial broker in the heart of Reading was when the turning point came.

It is correct to say 'It was a beautiful summer evening when the turning-point came' because 'when' properly relates to a time. It does not relate to a place such as Reading, or to an activity such as cleaning windows. If the activity were placed in time then 'when' could be used: 'He was cleaning the windows of a financial broker in the heart of Reading when the turning point came.'

There are certain words which tend to lure writers into illogicalities of various kinds. One is the word 'true'.

> The picture of political corruption in government circles there is increasingly true.

A picture cannot increase in truthfulness. Even if we take out the 'picture' and write 'The account of corruption there is increasingly true', the sentence would still be illogical. What changes with time is neither the picture nor the account, but the situation on the ground. The sentence should spell that out: 'The reported political corruption in government circles there is increasingly evident.'

Sometimes an ill-chosen descriptive word can collide in meaning with the word it qualifies. I turn to an advertisement for a mountaineering holiday. The advertisement is headed:

> Are you ready for the most fulfilling challenge of your life?

If someone faces a great challenge, whether it is of climbing a high mountain or running in a marathon, then to take it up and successfully accomplish the testing feat is what brings fulfilment. In short, answering a challenge successfully is what is 'fulfilling'. The challenge itself cannot be 'fulfilling'. In a way the two words 'fulfilling' and 'challenge' cancel each other out. To talk of a 'fulfilling challenge' is like talking of an 'answering question'. As the answer satisfies the question, so the fulfilment answers the challenge. Get the wrong combination of terms and the slide into illogicality is easy. A similar kind of misattachment relates two words in the following:

> Finding the right person to suit your need and budget can often be frustrating.

It is not 'finding' that is frustrating. What is frustrating is seeking and failing to find the right person. Logic requires: 'Trying to find the right person to suit your need and budget can be frustrating.'

> New figures were published yesterday showing an increase of one third in the amount of car travel over the past decade. Mr Strang said they demonstrated the need for change. 'Unless we alter some of these trends, they are not sustainable.'

Surely, if the trends are altered, then they become different trends. So the original trends cannot be 'sustainable' if such an alteration is made. The original trends fail to be sustained precisely because new trends have taken their place. The writer should not have used the construction beginning with 'unless'. What he meant was: 'We must alter these trends, because they are not sustainable.'

We see how logical clarity often depends on the careful selection of terms, especially where a choice between related terms has to be made. Here is a sentence from an article about the superstition that soil is best turned when the moon is in the 'barren' signs of Leo, Virgo, Aquarius or Gemini.

> Evidence of this technique is steeped in history and can be traced back as far as the ancient Greeks and Egyptians.

One wants to say 'but . . . but' at several points in this sentence. Is the practice of turning the soil at a certain time really a 'technique'? Then is it the 'evidence' that is steeped in history? One might justly say of an ancient castle 'Evidence shows that it is steeped in history.' The evidence establishes the fact. And is it the 'evidence' that is traced back? Rather the 'evidence' emerges from the act of tracing back. The sentence would be better without the word 'evidence': 'This practice is steeped in history and can be traced back as far as the ancient Greeks and Egyptians.'

There is a curious tendency to produce an illogical concertina effect when handling certain terms. Here is a comment on a World Cup match.

> An estimated worldwide television audience of one million watched Brazil take an early lead.

The question arises: Is an 'estimated audience of one million' really just the same thing as an 'audience estimated at one million'? An estimated audience is surely a concept rather than a crowd of people in an arena. It seems fair enough to say 'The estimated audience will number one million', but once the audience is a fact that use of 'estimated' is lax. It requires a minimum change in the wording to say: 'A worldwide television audience estimated at one million watched Brazil take an early lead.' A similar laxity appears in the use of the word 'predicted':

> However, Steve's predicted number of ten reached the first jump-off.

Surely the 'predicted number' is one thing, existing in the mind, and the horses that reached the jump-off are another thing, bodily active. What the sentence means is: 'As Steve predicted, ten competitors reached the first jump-off.'

In studying erroneous comparisons caused by misuse of the word 'like', as we did in Chapter 7, we were generally concerned as much with failings of logic as with failings of grammar. The worst instances of this misuse achieve a stark illogicality.

> Like all birds seen for the first time at very close quarters, there are surprises in store for those who might be familiar with gannets passing out to sea in their hundreds of thousands. It was the feet that took me by surprise when I first met the birds at such an intimate distance.

When we ask what it is that is 'like all birds', the passage gives us no answer. The seeming implication that surprises are 'like' all birds is clearly not intended. It is always a mistake to begin a sentence with the word 'like' unless one is absolutely clear what the resemblance is and what creatures or items it exists between. In fact the 'likeness' in the writer's mind here resides in the fact that very often birds look different when you get close up to them. This is a generalization for which use of the word 'like' is not needed. The writer should have started with that generalization. 'When you first see birds at very close quarters, their appearance can surprise you. Those familiar only with the sight of hundreds of thousands of gannets passing out to sea would be surprised to see them close up. It was the feet that surprised me.'

Rhetorical effect must not be bought by sacrificing grammatical and logical correctness. But slackness in construction following the word 'like' may appear at a much less obvious level. The following is from a passage on the demise of the Morse Code.

> Like the keyboard of a typewriter, the sequence of dots and dashes is delightfully random.

Is it proper to describe a typewriter keyboard as 'random'? Surely the machinery is such that everything about its construction and its functioning is planned to the last detail. The writer took an unjustifiable short cut in not saying 'Like the seeming arrangement of letters on the keyboard of a typewriter, the sequence of dots and dashes is delightfully random.'

There is another brand of illogicality which stems from making improper comparisons. Here is an advertisement for holdalls.

> They're available with fine leather handles to match the trim or with leather handles for rougher treatment.

Since no kind of 'treatment' has been mentioned, the reference to 'rougher' treatment is out of place. There can be no answer to the question: rougher than what? Since the alternatives are handles that match the trim or handles that can stand rough treatment, the point should be made without the comparative adjective: 'or with leather handles to stand rough treatment'. We see there how intertwined are the grammatical and the logical aspects of the misuse of 'or'.

Finally, we turn to a case where a sentence disintegrates. Whether we criticize it in terms of logic or of grammar, the issue is the same.

> He opened up Greenland, which wasn't well known topographically. The coastland, the mineral deposits and whether it was feasible to use it as an economic commodity were due to Watkins.

The first question is whether the coastland of any country or its mineral deposits can be said to be 'due to' a person. Clearly they cannot. The subject of the second sentence must be changed: 'Knowledge of the coastland and the mineral deposits . . . was due to Watkins.' The rest of the sentence seems to be almost untranslatable. In its basic structure it is the equivalent of 'whether it was going to rain was due to the forecaster'. To put it in grammatical terms, in no sentence can an opening clause beginning with an indirect question such as 'what is at stake' or 'who will be there' or 'whether it will rain' be followed by the adjective 'due'. A possible correction would be: 'Knowledge of the coastland, the mineral deposits and the possibility of developing them commercially was due to Watkins.'

MISSING LINKS

There is a sometimes subtle kind of illogicality produced by mentally taking a short cut so that a statement is left with a link missing. What happens is that the mind of the writer moves too quickly for full control to be kept on the management of the words being used. The practice might well be called 'verbal leapfrog' or even 'mental leapfrog'. It is illustrated in the following sentence.

> During the mid-1920s he travelled throughout North America painting many commissions.

He may have painted landscapes or he may have painted portraits of distinguished people, but no one can paint 'commissions'. There is no escape from filling out the words: 'painting many commissioned pictures'.

Talking of 'commissions' seems to encourage this kind of carelessness.

> The commissions began to flood in, among them several high-profile pieces which demonstrate the young sculptor's impact in a relatively short space of time.

If an artist is commissioned to make a piece of sculpture, what he makes is a sculpture, not a 'commission'. The 'pieces' this artist made cannot be classed 'among' the commissions that flowed in. The sentence can be rescued by elimination of the words 'among them': 'The commissions began to flood in, some of them for high-profile pieces . . .'

A slightly different instance of confusion between the theoretical and the practical, another confusion caused by verbal leapfrog, occurs in this sentence:

> The contractors were behind schedule and completion of the line by 1871 had become unrealistic.

What had become 'unrealistic' was surely the 'plan' or the 'intention' to complete the line by 1871. No one would say 'My marriage in June of next year has become unrealistic' if what was meant was 'My wish to marry in June of next year has become unrealistic.'

There is a similar short cut in the following comment on women's part in secret work in the Second World War.

> Discrimination and poor training were the main complaints of the women who strove to interpret the Enigma codes and to track German submarines.

It is no more correct to say 'discrimination was a complaint' than to say 'the complaint was discrimination'. The complaint was 'against' discrimination. Either one must correct, somewhat clumsily, by directly supplying the missing link: 'Discrimination and poor training were the main subjects of complaint', or one must start again, perhaps replacing the noun 'complaint' by a verb: 'The women . . . complained mainly against discrimination and poor training.'

We are dealing with a kind of error, seemingly due to haste, which produces confusion of concepts. The mind moves so quickly that it leapfrogs a stage in the verbal process.

> Between 1900 and the late 1930s Siberian tigers plummeted to probably twenty or thirty.

This comes from a sad account of a species under threat of extinction. Clearly the tigers did not 'plummet'. The writer assumes that readers will mentally insert the missing word ('the number of Siberian tigers plummeted'), but it is the writer's business not to leave such gaps.

In conversation allowances can be made for a certain amount of verbal leapfrogging.

> Poor eating habits, such as too many snacks, pave the way for an unhealthy diet and possible weight problems.

We might not jib at that, said in our hearing, but in print it will not do. 'Too many snacks' do not constitute a 'habit', it is eating them that constitutes a habit. The point must be made: 'Poor eating habits, such as consuming too many snacks . . .'

A word which tends to encourage writers to make this particular mistake is the verb to 'include'.

> The charter is expected to include an increase in competitive tendering for council services.

A charter is a document. It contains clauses that state principles and make recommendations. No charter could 'include' anything other than such material. It certainly could not 'include' an increase in competitive tendering. What is meant is that the charter 'includes a recommendation for an increase in competitive tendering'. Let us turn to another example of such carelessness.

> As this was a very special occasion, all tickets were pre-booked and included a complimentary bottle of wine.

Obviously the 'tickets' did not 'include' bottles of wine. They supplied the right of admission to the dinner, but it was the dinner that 'included' the bottle of wine.

While we have questions of cost in mind, let us consider the following notice in a big store with a sale in progress. It was placed over a row of dresses.

> Up to half original price.

The verbal compression here produces a kind of contradiction. The writer who devised the notice had in mind that 'up to' half of the original cost was being defrayed for the benefit of customers. But if the reduction amounted to 'up to' half the original cost, then the maximum reduction on a dress costing £40 would be £20. In short £20 was the least that any customer might pay for a £40 item. No going lower than that – 'down to' half the original price.

Sometimes a missing link can leave a whole phrase floating away without any mooring. Here is an advertisement from a financial institution:

> At the risk of sounding like your parents, do you regularly contribute to a pension plan?

This is like saying 'At the risk of sounding like a beggar, can you lend me a few pounds?' There is no escape from mooring the phrase 'at the risk of sounding' to something in the rest of the sentence. We must know who is taking the risk. 'At the risk of sounding like your parents, we must ask you this. Do you regularly contribute to a pension plan?'

The reader will recognize that we are here often criticizing verbal habits which might be readily acceptable in conversation. Consider this advertisement:

> Double-glazed windows, doors or a conservatory are a major home improvement.

The mind leapfrogs over a step in the sequence of thought. It is the actual fitting of these new features that constitutes an 'improvement'. The 'improvement' resides in the fact that they are here today and they were not here last year. That is the definition of the improvement. If the double-glazed windows were fitted to a house while it was being built, then even the fitting of them would not represent an 'improvement'. And it is the use of the noun 'improvement' instead of the verb to 'improve' that causes the solecism: 'Fitting double-glazed windows, doors or a conservatory can greatly improve your house.' A similar excessive use of nouns has the same unfortunate effect in the following advertisement for climbing clothing:

> Its design combines the experience of world-class athletes and the expertise of our research and development teams.

Neither 'experience' nor 'expertise' is combined in the actual design. The design is rather the fruit of both experience and expertise. The verb 'combines' must give way to another: 'Its design embodies the experience of world-class athletes.'

As a tail-piece to our study of 'verbal leapfrog' we add the following prize specimen from the world of transport:

> To facilitate luggage, special facilities are provided.

There is a certain duplication in saying that 'facilities' are there to 'facilitate' something. We cannot allow the grave omission of a word giving proper meaning to the word 'facilitate': 'To facilitate the handling of luggage'. But if the word 'facilities' is to be kept then 'facilitate' must go. 'To expedite the handling of luggage' would perhaps best represent the meaning, but readers might prefer 'To simplify the handling of luggage'.

WORD ORDER

A slight lapse in word order can mar the strict logicality of a sentence. One or two such lapses will categorize a writer as verbally clumsy. We have seen how desirable it is to take special care in placing 'only' or 'not only' in a sentence. To say 'The piano can only be placed opposite the window' when what is meant is 'The piano can be placed only against the window' is to place oneself as a writer only in the second class.

Another construction which requires particular care over word order is the use of 'both . . . and'.

> A rash of televisions have erupted, cheerfully egging their viewers on to radical change both in the house and garden.

This represents the most common slip in using 'both . . . and'. The writer has two alternatives here, either: 'radical change both in the house and in the garden', or: 'radical change in both the house and garden'. If 'both' comes before the word 'in', then 'in' must be repeated. If 'both' comes after 'in', then 'in' is not repeated. And 'have erupted' should be 'has erupted'.

Sometimes the failure with 'both . . . and' is more complex than that.

> The policy will not be easy to carry out both in respect of cost and how it will affect the environment.

To begin with, 'both' cannot be allowed to introduce one construction ('in respect of cost') while 'and' introduces a different construction ('how it will affect the environment'). We can allow 'both in respect of cost and in respect of its effect on the environment'. And in the right context we could allow 'both what it will cost and how it will affect the environment'. So long as the constructions following 'both' and 'and' match and balance each other, all is well. But in fact the above sentence has another grave error. One cannot follow the negative ('The policy will not be easy to carry out') by the words 'both' and 'and'. The negative construction requires 'either . . . or'. 'The policy will not be easy to carry out either in respect of the cost or in respect of the effect on the environment.'

Like the construction 'both . . . and', the construction 'either . . . or' requires careful attention to word order. It would be correct to say 'Either you attend the meeting or I shall go myself' where the alternatives are 'either you attend . . . or I go'. It would be incorrect to say 'You either attend the meeting or I shall go myself', because the first of the two alternatives is 'you attend', which must therefore be preceded by 'either'. 'You must either attend' would be a satisfactory alternative only in some such sequence as: 'You must either attend the meeting or resign.'

> It takes us just a day or two to complete any job. We can either do the work by mail order or you are welcome to stay on our free customer site.

Here we see the word 'either' misplaced. It is not a case of two alternatives that 'we' have ('We can either do the work by mail order or do it on our premises'). The alternatives are that 'we' do something or that 'you' do something. Therefore 'either' must precede 'we' as 'or' precedes 'you': 'Either we can do the work by mail order, or you are welcome to stay on our free customer site.'

There are times when a writer tries to rescue faulty word order by the use of commas.

> Mr Morris arrived on the island on Friday night and was travelling around in a taxi on Sunday, when the robbery took place, to familiarize himself with the area.

The comma before 'to' prevents the reader from gathering that the robbery was a means of familiarizing Mr Morris with the island. Nevertheless, this phrase ('to familiarize himself with the island') needs to be far closer to the place where it belongs ('travelling around in a taxi'). If the misplaced phrase were pushed back, the awkwardness would be removed. 'Mr Morris arrived on the island on Friday night and, to familiarize himself with the area, was travelling around in a taxi on Sunday when the robbery took place.'

The need thus to reposition a phrase at the end of a sentence recurs in the following.

> Remember that a UK provisional driving licence is unacceptable abroad and you cannot drive a car if you're 17 years old in most countries.

The placing of 'in most countries' almost suggests that a person's age may vary when travelling from country to country. The phrase would be much better placed earlier in the sentence: 'Remember that a UK provisional driving licence is unacceptable abroad and, in most countries, you cannot drive a car if you're 17 years old.' The Automobile Association seems to like to delay the arrival of crucial information.

> French motorway picnic areas featured mobile masseurs during the summer for stressed-out motorists, in an attempt to reduce road rage.

Again the last phrase should be pushed back in the sentence: 'In an attempt to reduce road rage, French motorway picnic areas featured mobile masseurs during the summer for stressed-out motorists.'

Even a small adverbial addition to a sentence, if wrongly placed, can make for uncomfortable reading.

> To the west of the house visitors can wander in the magnificent parkland at leisure, which contains woodland walks, deer parks and a profusion of wild flowers.

There is nothing grossly 'incorrect' here but the placing of 'at leisure' so far from the verb 'wander' is slightly awkward and causes an unnatural separation of the relative clause beginning 'which contains' from the noun 'parkland'. 'At leisure' would be better placed next to the verb: 'To the west of the house visitors can wander at leisure in the magnificent parkland.'

EXACTITUDE

The good writer leaves no reader feeling that the meaning has been inexactly expressed. We are talking here about good style as opposed to criticizable style, not about mere correctness as opposed to error. Inexactitude is not just a matter of confusion existing where there ought to be clarity. There is a kind of inexactitude by which the reader is left feeling that really the surest words have not been used. Sometimes this is quite a subtle matter. Compare these two sentences.

> Following the right-hand path, the walker will soon come to a bridge across the river.
>
> Following its successful restoration, the monument has been moved to a new site.

The first sentence would not make any reader pause and ask: Is that the best way of putting it? But the second sentence makes the sensitive reader inwardly aware that the monument is not 'following' anything in the way that the walker would follow the right-hand path. So why not use the obvious 'after' instead of the journalist's favourite 'following'? And indeed, why not?

We dealt with bad use of the present participle in the appropriate place earlier in this book. Here, however, we are concerned with a question of logical sensitivity in the choice of words and constructions which is not always, though it often is, a matter of grammatical correctness. Here are another two sentences which call for comparison in this respect.

> The path meanders downhill for half a mile, eventually leading to a stile in the wall.
>
> In his haste Seth hadn't shut Martin's bag properly again, leading to Ros and Jack's unscheduled discovery.

Again, while sensitive readers find nothing in the first sentence to stir unease, the use of 'leading' in the second sentence makes them wonder whether the most precise word has been chosen. The 'path' led the way in the first sentence. What is it that is doing the 'leading' in the second sentence? To put it technically, the use of the participle 'leading' in relation to a whole clause ('He stormed out angrily, leading to a family quarrel') instead of in relation to a single noun or pronoun, whether grammatically defensible or not, is never a happy construction. And by 'happy' construction we mean one that is comfortably precise for the reader. The above sentence would be better without the word 'leading': 'In his haste Seth hadn't shut Martin's bag properly again, which brought about Ros and Jack's unscheduled discovery.'

A slightly more complex failure of precision involving the same construction is the following:

> Henry II granted the town its charter and right to hold a guild in 1179, making Preston one of the oldest boroughs in Britain.

Although we are dealing with the same construction here again, the degree of imprecision and the character of the reader's mental discomfort are different. When Henry II granted Preston its charter in 1179, he certainly did not thereby 'make' it one of the oldest boroughs in Britain. That is the achievement of history. Time was required. Now some readers may regard this as quibbling, but the attempt here is to sensitize people to the words they use. If you are sensitive to the proper meaning of the word 'make', then you will be mentally uncomfortable to see it ill-used. We can best recommend the simple, straightforward, natural wording: 'Henry II granted the town its charter and right to hold a guild in 1179, and so Preston is one of the oldest boroughs in Britain.'

There are certain words which seem to lure writers to imprecision. The word 'way' is a case in point.

> Campbeltown Heritage Centre is a fascinating way to learn about the cultural and industrial development of Kintyre.

To describe the centre as a 'way' to learn will not do. A given road may be the 'way' to town. A given technique may be the 'way' to learn the violin. In that sense to visit the centre and study its exhibits may constitute a helpful 'way' to learn more of the place.

> Trains provided a relaxing break from driving on the sometimes congested main roads and were a great way to see the country.

The trains were not a 'way' to see the country. Travelling on the trains may perhaps be said to have been such a 'way'.

Another word which lures writers to imprecision is the word 'any'. Since in itself it is a word of vague reference, it needs to be handled with care.

> In any event, any benefits from most of these proposals are bound to be in the long run.

This sentence might stand as a showpiece of minor laxities. To begin with, it is a pity to repeat the word 'any' so soon with a changing connotation. Secondly, there is a slight logical inadequacy in the new shorthand of writing 'any benefits from these proposals' when what is meant is 'any benefits that may accrue from these proposals'. It is the words 'that may accrue' which fully justify the use of 'any'. Thirdly, the main utterance, which amounts to 'any benefits are bound to be in the long run' misuses the verb to 'be'. We do not say 'the benefit will be' but 'the benefit will arise'. Fourthly, 'any benefits from most' is simply insensitive usage. The reading should be: 'In most cases, any benefits that may accrue from these proposals are bound to arise only in the long run.'

Sometimes imprecision results from careless use of 'when' or 'where'.

> Hindlimb lameness is more common than you realize, particularly when the onset is insidious and subtle and affects both hindlegs the same.

The subject is horses. The sentence illustrates a rather imprecise use of 'when'. Again it is the kind of usage which would be accepted in conversation. But lameness cannot be said to be more common 'when' the onset is insidious. If the word 'when' is to be kept, then what precedes it must be changed: 'You may be slow to recognize hindlimb lameness, particularly when the onset is insidious.'

The following sentence, however, errs more gravely.

> Often a coexisting front leg lameness detracts from an underlying problem behind – vets find that once they have resolved a problem in front, a hindlimb asymmetry then becomes apparent.

To 'detract' is to diminish. We might say of a statesman who has been found guilty of some minor lack of candour that 'it detracts from his high reputation'. The writer of the above does not surely mean that front leg lameness reduces the problem of the hindlimb asymmetry. Indeed it reveals it. What was meant was either: 'Often a coexisting front leg lameness derives from an underlying problem behind', or: 'Often a front leg lameness detracts attention from an underlying problem behind.'

AMBIGUITY

It is possible to write a sentence, on the surface grammatically correct, which nevertheless leaves room for more than one interpretation. Very often this results from use of a pronoun the reference of which is not clear.

> About 15 per cent of kidney transplants in Britain are now provided by living donors, although the level is only half that in Scandinavia and the United States.

Here the pronoun 'that' might be construed in two different ways. In speech the meaning would be determined by the kind of intonation and emphasis placed on the word. The meaning might be (1): that the level of transplants from living donors is twice as high in Scandinavia and in the United States as it is in Britain. Alternatively the meaning might be (2): that the level of transplants from living donors is twice as high in Britain as it is in Scandinavia and the United States. It all depends on how you utter the word 'that'. If, as I suspect, sentence (1) gives us the intended meaning, the reading could be confirmed by moving the pronoun 'that' so as to make its reference unambiguous: 'About 15 per cent of kidney transplants in Britain are now provided by living donors, although that level is only half what it is in Scandinavia and the United States.'

A degree of ambiguity sometimes arises from the fact that some present participles are adjectives in their own right. We say 'That was a very moving story', and the word 'moving' is separate in our minds from the verb to 'move'. Such adjectives seem to drift slightly away from their grammatical mooring in the verbs they derive from. When we say 'I visited him on the following day', the verb to 'follow' is not really in our minds. We think of 'following' as an alternative to 'next'. One case where the adjective has drifted notably from the verb is that of the word 'retiring'. 'She is of a retiring disposition' we say, and we do not mean that she is in the habit of repeatedly signing off from her jobs. Thus, when a bank labels a section of a marketing leaflet 'Retiring Women', we are apt to think of ladies who demurely make themselves scarce, instead of ladies on the verge of retirement.

Where a word has two very different meanings ambiguities can be intentionally produced for comic purposes. The notice 'Refuse Tip' placed at the entrance to a field means something different from the advice 'Refuse tip' given to a waitress. The fact that an 'ocean liner' sails the ocean, whereas a 'bin liner' is placed inside a bin illustrates the complexity of the relationship between the first noun and the second. A 'family wrecker' destroys families but a 'family butcher' does not murder them. (If we were stricter in our use of hyphens we should apply them to 'bin-liner' and to 'family-wrecker'.) Sometimes the simplest word can operate in ways so distinctive that careless use can go disastrously wrong. *Private Eye* managed to get a photograph of an advertisement in which use of the word 'better' proves unintentionally hilarious.

> TRY OUR HEALING SERVICE. . . You won't get better!

With almost any other verb than to 'heal' this use of 'better' would have been unexceptional. 'Try our laundering service. You won't get better.' But with the verb to 'heal' a different meaning asserts itself.

Another special kind of problem can arise in making comparisons. If one writes 'These people give their children more attention than their garden', then the reader knows exactly what it means. But if one writes 'The Browns give their children more attention than their neighbours', the reader may wonder whether the neighbours are getting less attention from the Browns than the Browns' children, or are giving less attention to their children than the Browns are giving. A humorist might detect a hint of that kind of ambiguity in the following.

> Somehow the Hungarians have managed to keep their buildings and countryside in better condition than most of their contemporaries.

The context does not encourage misreading, but in controversy it is just that kind of sentence that an enemy might purposely misread. In this pattern of comparison the safeguard against ambiguity is to add a verb: 'Somehow the Hungarians have managed to keep their buildings and countryside in better condition than most of their contemporaries do.'

LISTING IN SEQUENCE

The logical mind is always offended by failure to preserve due sequence in listing items. It frequently happens in devising plans or programmes in the world of business, or indeed of leisure and cultural activities, that a writer has to formulate a series of points in sequence. The framework of the list may be a single sentence. At the other extreme a single sentence may introduce a series of linked propositions. In either case the successive items in the list must be presented in matching sequence. We touched upon elementary grammatical aspects of this matter when use of the word 'and' was explored in Chapter 8.

At its crudest, failure to preserve due sequence results in such sentences as:

> We enjoyed ourselves bathing in the sea, playing in the sand, and a beautiful picnic tea.

Due sequence is broken by the third item, which should match the other grammatically: 'bathing in the sea, playing in the sand, and eating a beautiful picnic tea'. A slightly more complex instance of this kind of lapse is represented in this sentence from the world of waterways.

> The range of crafts considered by the Guild is diverse: to date this includes boat builder, cooper, cast ironware manufacturer, boaters' clothes maker, ropework and fender making, and woodcarving.

The first four items in the list are craftsmen, but the last three ('ropework and fender making and woodcarving') are crafts. Either 'crafts' must become 'craftsmen' and the last three must become 'rope-worker, fender-maker and woodcarver', or the first four in the list must become crafts: 'boat-building, cooperage, cast ironware manufacturing, boaters' clothes-making'.

In all kinds of listing the relationship between the items listed must justify their being assembled together.

> Telling people anything really contentious is always grounds for not telling them until you really have to. Stag nights, football matches, visits to mothers-in-law, requests to mind the children and shopping trips are just a few examples that spring to mind.

That is a straightforward case of failure in logical continuity. The trouble is that none of the items cited is in fact an 'example' of telling people something contentious. We can see what the writer wanted to say, but he or she did not say it. 'One always tends to put off mentioning a possibly contentious matter such as planning to go to a stag night or a football match, or dealing with requests to visit mother-in-law, mind the children or go shopping.' It is worth noting that in total this version saves four words.

We are concerned now with a much more sophisticated kind of listing than these sentences represent, but the basic danger of not preserving due sequence is just the same. We take as a specimen a document produced by the Campaign for Freedom to Roam.

> Our ten points make up a comprehensive plan which we urge the Government to adopt . . . The ten points are as follows:

- Freedom to roam – a new law to enable the public to walk over mountain, moor, heath, down and common land in England and Wales.
- Restrictions – the freedom is restricted to protect wildlife, farming and other interests.
- Enter at own risk – walkers take responsibility for their own safety with occupier's liability reduced.
- Code of Practice – for walkers, to provide education on how best to behave.
- Wardens and by-laws – where necessary . . .
- No access to back gardens, cornfields or farmyards . . .
- Dogs – no automatic right to roam for dogs.
- No compensation – top legal advice makes it clear that the Government need not pay compensation to landowners.
- No payment for access – access to be free of charge for walkers . . .
- Wilful obstruction – it will be an offence for landowners wilfully to obstruct access where parliament has said it must be freely available.

The failure here to preserve a semblance of continuity is comprehensive. One has only to cite the first words of each 'point' to see how incongruous the list is: 'Freedom to roam', 'Restrictions', 'Enter at own risk', 'Code of Practice', 'Wardens and by-laws', 'No access', 'Dogs', 'No compensation', 'No payment', 'Wilful obstruction'. Perhaps the writer made a crucial error in listing the items as 'points'. They might have been presented as a series of 'demands'. Thus a common construction could have been repeated throughout: 'There should be freedom to roam . . . The freedom should be restricted to protect wildlife . . . Entry should be at the walkers' own risk . . . Walkers should adopt a Code of Practice . . . There should be wardens and by-laws . . . There should be no access to back gardens . . . Dogs would have no automatic right to roam . . . There should be no compensation . . . There should be no payment for access . . . Wilful obstruction by landowners would be illegal.'

The sort of grammatical and logical anarchy represented above can be found frequently enough in the business world.

How *Renewal* can support you as a retailer:

- Enjoy healthy profits . . .
- A high percentage repeat purchase
- High quality attractive packaging
- No quibble money back guarantee if your customers are not satisfied.

Again a common pattern must be adopted. If an initial sentence begins with 'How' ('How to remain healthy in middle life') it must be succeeded by phrases which in each case could connect directly with that introductory formula ('By taking regular exercise . . . By drinking alcohol only in moderation . . . By not over-working . . .'). Thus, if the initial sentence is kept in the above declaration, then it must be logically followed up in the same way: 'How *Renewal* can support you as a retailer: By ensuring that you enjoy healthy profits . . .' But it would probably be better to scrap the word 'How' and begin more directly: '*Renewal* can give you these advantages as a retailer: Healthier profits . . .' and so on.

PART 3

Changing Fashions in Usage

CHAPTER 11

Innovation Good and Bad

Language is a changing medium. Even the meanings of individual words may be transformed within a few decades. New inventions inevitably make demands on language. The word 'mouse' is probably used more often today to refer to the computer device than to refer to the household pest. The word 'tape' is perhaps more commonly used of a device we put into our recording apparatus than of a strip of material. We have of course dealt with changes in usage at many points in this book. We have been compelled to do so by the need to illustrate what goes wrong in current practice. In this chapter, however, we turn our attention to developments in usage which do not necessarily call for blue-pencilling. They include innovations which have enriched the language, providing vividly expressive terms in contexts where traditional vocabulary can supply nothing to match them.

COMPOUNDS

The last few decades have seen a vast increase in our use of compounds. Each decade adds to our vocabulary in that respect. The Second World War gave us 'blackout' and 'hitch-hike'. The developing needs of the office world have given us 'clipboard', 'polyfile' and 'word-processor', and now the general adoption of computers has supplied 'inkjet', 'desktop', 'internet', 'disk-drive' and 'web-site'. We speak of a 'test-tube' baby, and the words would have meant nothing a few decades ago. The words 'hitman', 'frog-man', 'front-man' and 'con-man' are twentieth-century coinages. The world of film-making has given new life to the word 'bit', colloquially used of a minor role in the compound 'bit-part'. I have heard a failing performer on the race-track described as being 'reduced to a bit-part straggler'.

Most popular compounds are self-explanatory. When we speak of 'ring-fencing' an issue, refer to someone's 'know-how', or describe a policy as a 'catch-all' solution, the expressions are not likely to be misunderstood. But when we first hear the expression 'squeaky-clean', used of someone who is above reproach, we perhaps need to have the expression explained. Apparently it comes from hairdressing salons, where hair may be washed so thoroughly that wet strands will squeak when rubbed. There is imaginative insight behind many such innovations in the first place. The sense of humour is often operative too, as in the use of the compound 'joined-up' to mock the elementary level of thinking attained by some public figures.

Just glancing thus at the productivity in new compounds today, one wonders how novel is the escalation in hyphenation. Taking down from the bookshelves volumes from past literature and turning the pages in search of hyphens proves surprisingly unfruitful. Oddly enough, only in the work of one of the simplest of early stylists, John Bunyan, does a quick search yield a harvest. *The Pilgrim's Progress* is peopled with such figures as 'Mr Money-love', 'Mr Fair-speech', 'Lord Time-server', 'Lord Turn-about' and 'Mr Facing-both-ways'. The time is perhaps right for a Ph.D. thesis on 'The Hyphen in English Prose'.

Be that as it may, the intention here is to draw attention to how rich and varied has been the production of compounds during the last century.

VARIETIES OF COMPOUNDS

The *Hag-ridden* Variety

It is fashionable to add to the stock of compounds used for a descriptive purpose. We look here at those in which a noun is tied to a past participle to produce a kind of compound adjective. We use a fund of such compounds conversationally, declaring people 'bone-headed', 'rubber-necked' or 'toffee-nosed'. There is nothing new in the practice itself. And there has been considerable grammatical freedom exercised in forming the compounds. 'Hand-made' pottery is made 'by' hand and 'tailor-made' clothing 'by' the tailor, while 'home-baked' cakes are made 'in' the home, a 'house-proud' woman is proud 'of' her house and a 'self-inflicted' wound is inflicted 'by' the self. In many recently developed compounds the relationship between the two partnered elements extends that degree of flexibility even further.

> These cookers are safety-checked and come with a three-month guarantee.

Here the meaning of 'safety-checked' is 'checked for safety'.

> She explained that I would have to fill out a detailed questionnaire and be risk-assessed before I could be considered for cover.

If I am to be 'risk-assessed', I am to be 'assessed for risk'. We now happily accept the complex relationships between noun and participle represented in such partnerships, and we extend such usages freely, speaking of 'government-sponsored' initiatives and 'welfare-focused' legislation.

Where does one draw the line? Perhaps at the following usage:

> Clarins' formulations are dermatologically and allergy-tested.

The curious relationship between 'allergy' and 'tested' ('tested in respect of possible allergic reactions') is made even less acceptable by being cheek-by-jowl with the grammatically clear relationship between 'dermatologically' and 'tested'.

Even in the case of well-established compounds, the logical basis may be problematic. We hear people speak of a 'Norland-trained' nanny, and we recognize that the Norland Institute did the training. But when we are told that the new kitten has been 'house-trained' we know that the house did not do the training. And again, when we hear that the toddler has been 'potty-trained', we know that the potty did not do the training. Moreover, the 'potty-trained' toddler is habituated to doing something in the potty which the 'house-trained' kitten is specifically trained not to do in the house. Such discrepancies abound in the field of compounds. Although a 'council-built' house is a house built by a council, in the words 'a purpose-built' structure the relationship between noun and participle is totally different in effect. But these expressions do not worry us on grammatical grounds as, for instance, the following does:

> We intend to pass on these bargain-priced motorhomes to our customers.

Such expressions as 'highly-priced' and 'cheaply-priced' apply a qualification to the verb 'priced' which is rationally and grammatically acceptable. The noun 'bargain' cannot operate thus.

The *Deep-seated* Variety

Usage today abounds in compounds that attach an adverb to a past participle. There are terms for personal characteristics such as 'high-handed', 'hard-headed', 'tight-fisted', 'long-winded', 'near-sighted', 'flat-chested', 'heavy-handed', 'large-hearted' and 'soft-spoken'. There are colourful and economic compounds such as 'red-handed' and 'back-dated', 'hard-bitten' and 'soft-centred'. In many cultural and commercial activities descriptive compounds of this kind proliferate to meet practical needs. Thus, for instance, the fashion trade relies on compounds such as 'high-necked', 'long-sleeved', 'double-breasted', and 'wide-brimmed'.

The *Mind-boggling* Variety

Compounds using a noun and a present participle (or gerund) are just as familiar. We speak of 'life-saving' equipment and 'labour-saving' devices, of 'back-breaking' jobs and 'nerve-racking' trials. We define difficult issues as 'mind-boggling' and pernicketiness in argument as 'hair-splitting' or 'nit-picking'. Compounds such as 'mouth-watering', 'eye-catching', 'face-saving', 'time-consuming', 'life-threatening', 'record-breaking' and even 'cringe-making' are very much part of living conversation. For the most part these are used adjectivally, but there are compounds such as 'square-bashing' and 'foot-slogging' that are used chiefly as nouns.

Novelists, of course, have long produced extempore compounds without any intention of adding permanently to the language. One reads of a 'cigar-smoking tycoon' and a 'gin-loving reprobate'. And we must hope that some of the business world's instances of the device are intended to be ephemeral.

> But Ms Trotter Betts hit out at 'process re-engineering programmes', which have reduced nursing output.

All of us alter the way we do things from time to time, if it's only the way we lay the table or the route we take to work, but we do not think of ourselves as being occupied in process re-engineering programmes. However, vapid as such usages may be, they do not worry us on grammatical grounds, as does the following:

These shade-growing plants prefer dappled light.

At this the mind boggles. The concept of a plant which grows shades instead of leaves and flowers is alarming. But by no species of grammatical jugglery can 'shade-growing' mean 'shade-loving'.

It is not desirable to try to give a comparative form to adjectival compounds of this kind.

We must encourage the companies to take a more risk-taking approach.

Nothing is gained by not saying: 'We must encourage the companies to take more risks.'

The *Wide-ranging* Variety

What applies to compounds made from a noun and a participle ('risk-taking'), applies also to compounds made from an adverb and a participle such as 'far-seeing', 'long-standing', 'long-suffering', and 'wide-ranging'. The compounds cannot be happily qualified thus: 'We need more wide-ranging talks.' Better re-write: 'We need to range more widely in our talks.'

The *High-profile* Variety

The same advice is needed for use of this other adjectival compound, manufactured of adjective and noun. There are well-established compounds such as 'first-rate', 'last-minute', 'old-time', 'top-grade' and even 'top-hole'. But no one has tried to intensify these adjectives by speaking of someone being 'more top grade' or 'topper grade' than someone else. Yet, regrettably, one now hears someone described as 'very high profile' and a suggestion made that 'a more low-key approach' is needed to a certain problem.

Nineteenth- and twentieth-century developments added to the stock of compounds using 'single' and a noun: 'single-decker', 'single-parent', 'single-track' and 'single-entry'. Though these are used adjectivally, there are comparable compounds using 'double' that make nouns ('double-time', 'double-talk') or verbs ('double-check', 'double-park').

The *Reader-friendly* Variety

We turn to compounds in which the noun is partnered with an adjective. The form very usefully extends the old practice represented by hyphenless compounds such as 'footloose', 'headstrong' and 'seaworthy'. There are highly economic usages such as 'computer-literate', 'publicity-conscious', 'labour-intensive' and 'market-sensitive'. Advertisers produce self-explanatory compounds such as 'crease-resistant' and 'fade-resistant'. These expressions do not strain the language as does publicizing a food for kittens as 'nutrient-dense' and recommending a beauty treatment for 'blemish-prone' skin.

One may quibble too about the following:

> Completely dishwasher-safe, a pack of two coffee cups and saucers costs £15.

A certain grammatical licence is required to describe crockery as 'dishwasher-safe' when what is meant is that the cups and saucers will not drop to pieces as the dishwasher performs its proper function. We have the word 'waterproof' and have extended that usage in such expressions as 'fire-proof' and 'burglar-proof'. The terms 'dishwasher-proof', 'oven-proof' and 'microwave-proof' all make sense.

> It is machine-washable, quick-drying, and will see off light showers and wind.

Here we have in the same sentence a perfectly natural compound ('quick-drying') and a combination of noun and adjective ('machine-washable') which defies logical interpretation.

The habit of forming compounds by adding the word 'friendly' to a noun is well established. We hear of a 'child-friendly' environment, of a 'customer-friendly' approach in business. The usage is convenient but it ought not to be reversed (as it was in advising parents how to make children 'school-friendly'), and like other such compounds, it ought not to be used so as to extend already existing compounds, as it is in this letter to the press from the Breast-feeding Promotion Group.

> While our objective is a breast-feeding-friendly environment, our counsellors are committed to meeting parents' individual needs.

The tongue-twister 'breast-feeding-friendly' pushes compound-construction too far.

Where 'friendly' is attached to a noun, it generally has a human connotation. Where the relationship is between things inanimate, the notion that they can operate readily together without modification or adaptation is conveyed by the word 'compatible'. Thus we get references to computers as 'IBM-compatible'.

The *Junk-mail* Variety

We turn to compounds which involve two nouns. The Second World War gave us 'Home-Guard' and the establishment of the Welfare State gave us 'home-help'. On the pattern of the older compound 'junk-shop' we have gained the useful words 'junk-food' and 'junk-mail'. The word 'junk' of course retains its pejorative connotation. And there is a certain aural crudity about such double-noun partnerships as 'space-walk', 'disc-jockey', 'bodice-ripper' and 'block-buster'. These compounds seem to retain their hyphens, where 'lifestyle' does not.

Glancing at a fifty-year-old dictionary, I find lots of now-popular compounds missing, such as 'egghead', 'ego-trip' and 'puppy-fat'. The old dictionary gives some general compounds of 'twin' such as 'twin-brother', 'twin-sister' and 'twin-born', and also some technical compounds such as 'twin-plane', 'twin-axis' and 'twin-screw', but it apparently predates the regular use of the terms 'twin-bed', 'twin-set', 'twin-track' and of course 'twin-tub'. To take another source of compounds, 'side', most of those we use today were well-established in this source too but, oddly perhaps, not that most useful word 'side-effect'. Colloquial practice has since given us 'side-kick' and transformed a 'sideboard' from a piece of sturdy furniture to a hirsute section of the male face.

More common, however, than the partnered nouns functioning as nouns are those functioning as adjectives. Some of these, such as 'knee-jerk', represent lively developments. But, alas, there is now a plague of partnered nouns used as vapid pseudo-adjectives.

> We know that losing excess body fat is good news, as are a healthy diet, regular exercise, effective stress-management strategies, and medication if necessary.

The compound 'stress-management', consisting of two nouns, performs an adjectival function here in relation to the noun 'strategies'. The two partnered nouns 'body' and 'fat' are given no hyphen, 'body' being given a kind of adjectival function in relation to 'fat'.

The juxtaposing of two nouns is an increasing practice in contemporary usage, and we shall explore the practice further in the next chapter. Indeed, the juxtaposition of noun with noun is now such a regular practice that the question arises: 'When is a compound not a compound?' To which the answer derived from experience would appear to be: 'When the writer omits a hyphen.'

> The interior of the main saloon follows a similar design theme.

There is evidence that the two nouns 'design' and 'theme' are entering into a stable relationship. And here is a tempting invitation to customers interested in fancy tiles:

> Come to our showroom where our helpful staff will be pleased to assist with your queries, design or theme concepts.

In this case we are faced not so much with a stable relationship as with a *menage à trois*. The noun 'design' is mentally conjoined with the noun 'concepts', and the noun 'theme' enters into the same partnership.

The *Wall-to-wall* Variety

It is possible for a clever compound that sums up a topical notion to get out of date through changing fashions. In the fifties, sixties and seventies the smart home had wall-to-wall carpeting in its rooms. Thus 'wall-to-wall' became a useful and colourful expression to apply to any plan or attitude that was comprehensive: 'We can't afford wall-to-wall supervision for our staff.' In the nineties the fashion for wall-to-wall carpeting was replaced by the fashion for wooden floorboards and this colloquial use of 'wall-to-wall' disappeared.

Compounds which bind three words together are not new to the language. Early in the twentieth century the compounds 'ready-to-wear' and 'off-the-peg' were applied to ready-made suits at a time when bespoke tailoring was beginning to go out of fashion. We have some usefully vivid and economic expressions such as 'hand-to-mouth', 'face-to-face' and now 'eyeball-to-eyeball'. The compounds 'hit-and-run' and 'hit-and-miss' are surely irreplaceable. We now hear books called somewhat inelegantly 'no-holds-barred' biographies. And after the murder of a television personality the BBC announced:

> Staff have been offered round-the-clock grief counselling.

Of the nine words there, five are involved in compounds; three constitute a triple compound and two ('grief counselling') a dual pseudo-compound.

The manufacture of triple compounds can achieve a no-squirm-spared inelegance:

> We've got a quality-of-life policing strategy which has got several legs.

That is police-speak. The compound 'quality-of-life' is an empty term of approval, applicable to almost anything. And to follow the dry verbal artifice of the 'quality-of-life policing strategy' by saying that it 'has got several legs' is to achieve a masterpiece of bathos.

Some Wilder Compounds

In addition to the various forms of compound using the participle of verbs there are a few which use the naked verb in the fashion of 'time-share'. There is something peculiarly unattractive about this kind of combination, but its usefulness is obvious.

> I decided to job-share when I had my second child.

The fashion for this usage was set, one imagines, by the expression 'flat-share', which has now bred 'work-share' as well as 'job-share'. More useful and readily acceptable than these have been the now established and unhyphenated verbs 'brainwash' and 'headhunt'. In all these cases the noun is the object of the verb. One shares work or a flat. If that grammatical connection were generally maintained, then to 'force-feed' would presumably mean to cater for the police. But the freedoms exercised in the verb-based compound are wild. We read an advertisement for cosmetics pressing the case for 'leave-in conditioners', and there is advice in an article on decoupage to 'use a wipe clean surface'.

Occasionally an invention that offends one's literary sensibility may at the same time arouse a sneaking admiration for its brevity, as when someone in direct marketing deals with the problem of the 'gone-aways', the addressees who have moved, gone on holiday, or died. There is a similar concentration in the following now popular usage:

> Both were demonstrative people and touchy-feely by nature.

Fortunately it seems to be the case that, when the seemingly worst horrors of compound-manufacture are perpetrated, there is at least a hint of humour in the air.

> Ask anyone who's been docu-soaped and they will tell you it's like placing a ferret in your trousers.

There are worse horrors even than that to be found in the magazine world.

> Hear how other parents unwind and grab some me-time in the midst of their busy, busy lives.

English Prefixes and Suffixes

The twentieth century was also fruitful in adding to the stock of compounds using native prefixes and suffixes.

up / down

We have long-established compounds using the prefix 'up' ('upbraid', 'uphold') and the prefix 'down' ('downfall', 'downright'). Additions now include 'update', 'upmarket' and 'downmarket'. The verb to 'download' is used in the computer world, the word 'upfront' in business. And there too the verb to 'downsize' has acquired ominous overtones through its use in connection with reorganizations that involve cutting staff. The 'downside' of any plan or action is the disadvantages it may involve. And although, in conducting music, the downbeat is the emphatic one and the upbeat the relaxed one, popular usage has reversed this in making 'upbeat' stand for the positive and the cheerful, and 'downbeat' stand for the depressed and unexciting.

Current uses of 'up' as a suffix include 'carve-up' and 'stitch-up', which seems to have taken the place of 'frame-up'. The development of rocketry has popularized 'count-down'. The colloquialisms 'put-down' (for a humiliating rebuff) and 'climb-down' are economic simplifiers.

in / out

An 'in-depth' study involves intensive research. The Automobile Association speaks of 'in-vehicle' devices. An 'in-house' project is one which involves only the employees of a given institution and is conducted within its boundaries. The compound 'out-house' has been used, not of a shed in the garden or an earth-privy at the bottom of the backyard, which used to be its meaning, but of BBC projects involving contracts with outsiders.

The prefix 'out' used with verbs has a distinct connotation: to 'outlive', 'outdo', 'outrun' or 'outstrip'. The meaning of the prefix is consistent. It is a matter of beating others in some exercise, not of turning them 'out' of some premises. When we read that in the Christmas sales 'men have outshopped women', we recognize the standard usage, however infelicitous. But then we read in a railway magazine that a certain engine has been 'outshopped' from a repair shed, and there is no linguistic justification for that usage. To describe an engine as being 'outshopped' (turned out of the repair shed) is like describing a recovered patient as being 'out-hospitalled'.

The world of protest has given us 'sit-in', indulging laziness has made an adjective of 'drive-in', and buying a car has given us 'trade-in'. A person who opts out of things is a 'drop-out'. A 'fade-out' gradually removes a scene from view. More vulgarly, a 'cop-out' is a failure or an escape from some responsibility.

over

Here is another prefix which can be misused. When we use it in such words as 'overeat', 'oversimplify' and 'overstrain', our meaning is that something is being done to excess. There are dozens and dozens of such compounds in recent dictionaries. We now add it to any word we choose, adjectives ('over-explicit', 'over-indulgent', 'over-sceptical') and verbs ('over-supply', 'over-insure', 'over-tire'). Yet in the gardening world, where the verb to 'over-water' means to provide with too much water, we find the following:

> A cool porch is an ideal place to overwinter tender shrubs.

No doubt in the English climate it would be possible to supply tender plants with too much winter, but clearly that is not the meaning here. What makes the usage utterly unnecessary is that in fact we do use the verb to 'winter' (without any prefix) of looking after farm animals appropriately during the cold season.

Using 'over' as a suffix, we compress verbs and adverbs ('I shall need to think it over') into hyphenated nouns ('It will need a bit of a think-over'). The more established compounds of this kind ('hangover', 'pushover', 'flyover', 'walkover', 'takeover') have shed their hyphens.

on / off

Something which is 'on-line' is directly related to the central project in question, and in the political field, the compound 'on-message' describes statements by MPs and party members which are fully in accord with official party policy. We now hear 'on-target' used as an adjective. 'On' is used in the compound 'hands-on', which is descriptive of immediate practical experience of some technical machinery.

The prefix 'off' occurs in the verb to 'off-load' and in the adjective 'off-peak'. The fashion for skiing has added the compound 'off-piste'. 'Off' as a suffix appears in speaking of giving someone a 'tip-off' and in the word 'spin-off' for a by-product. Air-travel has given us the compound 'lift-off'. If we buy something too expensively, we call it a 'rip-off'. To speak of giving a 'brush-off' to someone whose approach is unwelcome illustrates the imaginative quality of such images, recalling as it does the flicking away of an unsightly crumb or piece of hair from a smart suit.

-ism / -ist

These common suffixes are much used in social polemic. We have long had words such as 'anarchism/t' and 'imperialism/t'. The development of liberal ideologies of recent decades has given us 'racism/t', 'sexism/t', and 'ageism/t'. The word 'abolitionist' came into use in connection with the abolition of slavery and has been used more recently in controversy about the House of Lords. Public controversy has given us 'environmentalist' and 'anti-abortionist', 'unilateralist' and 'devolutionist'. New compounds are readily thrown off in argument. One hears an opponent of proportional representation described as a 'first-past-the-post-ist'.

-free

'Carefree' goes back to the mid-nineteenth century, and 'fancy-free' almost as far. The suffix is now added indiscriminately. There is talk of 'traffic-free' areas and 'stress-free' jobs, 'meat-free' diets and 'car-free' existence, not to mention phases of life that are 'child-free' and others that are 'oldie-free'.

-wise

The word 'otherwise' has been matched in such words as 'contrariwise' and 'lengthwise'. We now hear and read innovative developments of this practice of adding the suffix 'wise'.

> Cost-wise I recommend the bus route; comfort-wise I recommend the railway.

This kind of running coinagery, which some people go in for in conversation, is economic but neither elegant nor grammatically impeccable. When one sees it in print, one feels uncomfortable:

> Celeb-wise, Gwyneth Paltrow, Sharon Stone and Cameron Diaz are setting the standard at the moment.

Which means that these celebrities are setting the standard 'hairwise'.

wrong-

The old compounds 'wrongdoer' and 'wrong-headed' have been joined by 'wrong-foot'. Deriving from the game of tennis, in which a player can make the kind of shot which would put the opponent off-balance, it has proved a conveniently colourful way of defining an action which inconveniences an opponent or a rival.

-babble

This is now used colloquially, added pejoratively to 'techno', 'psycho' and 'pharmaco' as a term for the specialist chatter of the respective experts when viewed as so much hot air.

Latin and Greek Prefixes and Suffixes

ante- / post-

These two prefixes, meaning 'before' and 'after', have been long with us. The word 'antecedent' dates back to the fourteenth century. Used more concretely, the prefix appears in 'antechamber', then in 'anteroom', for a room leading to a more important apartment. On the pattern of the word 'ante-natal' we now have 'ante-nuptial'. It has sometimes been convenient to extemporize with 'ante' in conversation so that words such as 'ante-decimalization' and 'ante-devolution' are born. The prefix 'post' occurs as early as the thirteenth century in the word 'postern' for a back door; the words 'posterior' and 'posthumous' date from the seventeenth century. Although we have several uses of the English prefix 'after' in such words as 'afternoon' and 'aftermath', they are now not nearly so numerous as the words prefixed by 'post' ('post-natal', 'post-war') to which we constantly add ('post-modern', 'post-Thatcher').

anti- / pro-

These two prefixes, meaning 'against' and 'for' respectively, are much used in general vocabulary and in scientific vocabulary. In the case of 'anti-' many of the new additions ('anti-abortion', 'anti-semitic', 'antidepressant' and 'antifreeze') testify to social and technological changes. Political developments add to the stock of words with these prefixes and suffixes. Just as we have 'pro-European' and 'anti-EMU', so we hear talk of 'anti-single-currency' attitudes and 'anti-proportional-representation' views. There are, of course, far more words in our language that begin with 'pro', but the recent tendency in use of the prefix has been to hyphenate it. People will declare themselves 'pro-euthanasia' or 'pro-devolution'. The compound 'pro-life' is used by the 'anti-abortionist' campaigners.

cyber-

This root, from a Greek word meaning to steer or to govern, has given us the words 'cybernate' (meaning to control with a servomechanism) and 'cybernetics' for the branch of science concerned with control systems. In the computer world it has given us compounds, serious and less serious, in connection with use of the internet. We hear of 'cyberspace', of 'cyberporn', of 'cyberphobia', of 'cybershopping' on the internet, of 'cybercodgers' addicted to the internet and of 'cyberchondriacs' who obsessively try to find treatments for their ailments there.

contra-

This prefix, standing for what is against or contrary, early used in such words as 'contradict' and 'contravene', has been less used lately, perhaps because the prefix 'anti-' serves a similar purpose. However, the nineteenth century gave us 'contraceptive' and 'contraception' and now the word 'contrasuggestive' has been used of personalities inclined to oppose prevailing and accepted views. We have a new use in 'contraflow', for the movement of traffic on a motorway.

flexi-

The prefix 'flexi' derives from a Latin verb meaning to 'turn'. Hence the word 'flexible' means easily bent and therefore adaptable and variable. The compound 'flexitime' was introduced for the system by which employees are allowed a degree of freedom over the disposition of their hours of attendance at work provided that they serve the agreed minimum.

hyper-

Of the two Greek prefixes, 'hyper' and 'hypo', the former refers to what is above normal or excessive, and the latter to what is below normal or inadequate. Parallel terms are not numerous in common speech, but in medicine there are the parallels 'hyper-thyroidism' and 'hypo-thyroidism', meaning respectively over-production and under-production of thyroid hormones. The popularity of the Latin prefix 'super' has perhaps restrained the development of new compounds with 'hyper', but we use the words 'hyper-inflation', 'hyper-tension' and 'hyper-sensitive'. Computer experts speak of the 'hypertext' and 'hyper-media'. In some cases compounds with 'hyper' duplicate compounds with 'super' ('hypermarket', 'hypersonic'). The colloquial verb 'hype', meaning to make exaggerated claims in publicity, and the parallel noun, derive from this prefix.

inter-

This prefix, meaning between or among, has been used of late years to add scores of words to the already extensive list. Words such as 'Interpol', 'interface', 'intergalactic', 'intergovernmental', 'internet' and 'inter-nuclear' show how widely it has been used.

maxi- / mini-

We took the words 'maximum' and 'minimum' directly from Latin to mean the most and the least. Although the word 'maxidress' (abbreviated to 'maxi') has been used of a full-length woman's dress, new compounds with 'maxi' are chiefly ephemeral coinages thrown off by advertisers (a 'maxi' savings account). But 'mini' has been well used since the 1960s fashion for the 'miniskirt', and the production of the small car by the Austin/Morris combine.

mega-

This prefix, deriving from Greek, means huge or powerful. It gave us such words as 'megaphone', 'megalithic' and 'megalomania'. It has been a useful prefix in various sciences and technologies ('megahertz' and 'megawatt'), and then too in the world of computing. Recently it has been used colloquially as a popular way of conveying the grandeur or importance of something: a 'mega-match' or a 'mega-star'.

micro-

This Greek prefix, meaning small, gave us established words such as 'microcosm' and 'microscope' and they have been added to in 'microlight', for a small aircraft, and 'microfiche', for a card holding miniaturized print, as well as in more specialized terms such as 'microchip' and 'microdot'.

multi- / omni-

The prefix 'multi' derives from the Latin adjective meaning 'much' or 'many'. The 'multistorey' car park, the 'multistage' rocket, the 'multinational' business and 'multimedia' activities, all these compounds have now generally shed their hyphens. We read of a 'multi-million' pound campaign, and the hyphen survives.

In the case of the prefix 'omni' (from the Latin word for 'all' or 'every') the old compounds 'omnipotent' and 'omniscient' have been added to by such words as 'omnicompetent' and 'omnidirectional'.

non-

This prefix, the Latin word for 'not', is used to nullify what follows. The word 'nondescript' goes back to the seventeenth century and the word 'nonpareil' to the fifteenth. In our own day the practice of prefixing a word with 'non' ('non-alcoholic', 'non-infectious') amounts to a runaway habit. We invent the words as we need them, presuming on an attitude of non-objection on the part of our non-pedantic friends.

-phile / -phobe

An interesting development has been the tendency to use the Greek suffixes 'philia' for love of and 'phile' for lover of a movement or a programme, where the Latin prefix 'pro' has been more commonly used (as in the 'pro-life movement'). A foreign enthusiast for things British is sometimes called an 'Anglophile'. Thus we speak of a political supporter of closer ties with Europe as a 'Europhile'. Correspondingly there is the tendency to use the Greek suffix 'phobia' or 'phobe' for hatred or disapproval of a movement or programme, where once the Latin prefix 'anti' might have been used. Thus we speak of 'homophobia' for the disapproval of homosexual practices and of a 'homophobe' for a person so disapproving. Those highly critical of European union do not call themselves 'Europhobes', which somehow has a distasteful air of wholesale negativity, but call themselves by the anodyne word 'Eurosceptics' instead.

pre-

This prefix (from the Latin 'prae') is in continual use. Whereas it used to be confined to historical references ('pre-Reformation' and 'pre-Restoration'), it has become handy for general use over a shorter term ('pre-Welfare State' and 'pre-decimal currency').

pseudo-

Meaning false or bogus, 'pseudo', long used in the word 'pseudonym', is now prefixed depreciatively to any adjective of choice: 'pseudo-Bohemian', 'pseudo-Elizabethan', 'pseudo-Georgian' and 'pseudo-modern'. The noun 'pseud' is applied colloquially to someone scorned for their charlatanry.

retro-

The words 'retrograde' and 'retrospect/ive' have long been in our language. In his astrological work *A Treatise on the Astrolabe* Chaucer uses the word 'retrograd', meaning 'moving in a direction contrary to the order of the signs'. In Shakespeare's *All's Well That Ends Well* Helena tells Parolles that he must have been born under Mars when the planet was 'retrograde', because he goes so much backward when he fights. So the word came into general use for taking backward steps. 'Retrospective' dates back to the seventeenth century. The space behind the high altar in a cathedral is the 'retrochoir'. The prefix has been used in anatomy and pathology as the converse of 'intro', and meaning 'situated behind' ('retro-ocular' and 'retro-uterine'). On this basis the word 'retrofit' has now come into use for the business of fitting parts to aircraft and other vehicles after they have already been in use. The prefix 'retro' is therefore to hand and in a piece in *The Times* Libby Purves uses the words 'retrophobia' and 'retro-dread' of current attitudes harking back to the evils of Nazism and the Second World War. She gives the words a somewhat within-quotes flavour by half-seriously also coining the word 'yesterphobia'. Thus it becomes difficult to draw the line between innovative compounds with a future and one-off compounds tossed out as *jeux d'esprit*, to add spice and not to be taken too seriously. For instance, in the same article Libby Purves ingeniously coins the word 'unthinkabilia' for those matters raised when people 'think the unthinkable'. The word 'memorabilia', for things worthy of being remembered, is clearly related to the word 'memorable'. It might consequently seem reasonable to treat other words ending in 'able' comparably. But one must exercise discipline in making such coinages. To try to treat 'deplorable' as 'memorable' has been treated would not give us words worth having, except perhaps for comic purposes. Neither 'deplorability' nor 'deplorabilia' would fill a gap in our vocabulary.

super-

Our language abounds in words with this prefix ('superficial', 'supercilious') and modern technology has given us 'supersonic'. From the days of the so-called 'supercinemas' of the interwar years and the 'supermarkets' of the post-war world, the prefix has come into use as an intensifier of quality that could be applied to anything in the advertisement world and the media world. Thus we have 'superglue', 'supergrass', 'superstar' and 'superfine'.

TRENDY USAGE

Euphemisms

There are areas of usage in which fashion changes from century to century, and others in which fashion changes from decade to decade. In areas where delicacy has required oblique terms to be used in polite conversation changes in fashion have been fairly frequent. When an inoffensive but evasive word is used in place of a word which might be considered in some way crude or offensive, we call it a euphemism. An early euphemism for a lavatory was the word 'privy' which dates from the fourteenth century. Since it meant 'private' and then 'private room' it was perhaps a more respectable word than the sixteenth-century word 'jakes' (to which Shakespeare seems to have intended an oblique reference when he used the name 'Jaques' for his somewhat sour philosopher in *As You Like It*).

When Sir John Harington, a courtier, equipped Queen Elizabeth I with a water-closet, it marked the beginning of an age in plumbing. But it was not until the mid-eighteenth century that the word 'water-closet' came into use. It is of course euphemistic in that 'closet' means any small room and the use of 'water' does not openly indicate what the closet contained. Indeed the word 'lavatory' was already in use for an apartment containing apparatus for washing. The addition of the lavatory pan to the wash basin was a logical development. The word 'water closet' had a long life. Early in the twentieth century it was in common use, and the letters 'WC' were printed on toilet doors. But already there had been squeamish Victorians whose euphemism for a visit to the lavatory was 'going to see Mrs Jones' or 'Aunt Jones'. Gradually the term 'WC' gave place to the word 'lavatory'. The double function of the apartment in question was convenient verbally. Indeed for a long time the hostess's welcoming question to a guest, 'Would you like to wash your hands?' was considered to be a polite way of asking 'Do you want to relieve yourself?' But eventually the word 'lavatory' began to seem too crude and direct and the word 'toilet' came into competition with it, though never in the 'best circles'. It has taken over on the public scene. It was in the sixties and seventies that the word 'loo' began to be used in conversation. Its origin is in doubt. The suggestion has been made that it comes from the French word for a water-closet – 'lieux d'aisance' ('place of easement'). Whether seriously or not, it has also been suggested that 'loo' is short for 'Waterloo'. Be that as it may, colloquially it is now the most used term.

An interesting euphemism for sexual intercourse came into use in the earlier part of the twentieth century. The press used it, and it was used in the law courts. To ask a defendant whether he or she had been 'intimate' with a partner was to ask whether the two had had sex. This extremely evasive euphemism became even more absurd when the noun 'intimacy' was used in the divorce courts: 'They went up to a hotel bedroom, m'lud, and intimacy took place.'

Sometimes a shift in usage is intentionally encouraged by lobby groups in order to corroborate a desired change in public attitudes. The most notable instance of this is the use of the word 'gay' by the homosexual community. Fashionable colloquial expressions, such as 'pansy', 'queer', 'poof' and 'nancy-boy', all expressed a disdain that the homosexual community was determined to counter.

Colloquial Fashions

It is not only in the realms of the sexual and the lavatorial that verbal fashions change quickly. They change quickly too in the sphere of usage where new words hover uncomfortably between the category we call 'slang' and the category of respectable usage. One such word is the verb to 'scarper', meaning to depart quickly, to beat a hasty retreat. The general resonance of the word suggests a less than respectable getaway by a person leaving a mess behind. The word appears to have taken the place of a verb popular in Victorian usage which I cannot find in my recent dictionary, the verb to 'levant', meaning to bolt or abscond, used especially of betting men who got away without paying.

Today's trendy words will not necessarily be tomorrow's trendy words. To call attractive young girls 'dollybirds' or 'teenyboppers' nowadays would be to hark back to the sixties, and people no longer talk of 'beatniks' or 'groupies'. Moreover, such is the force of fiction, that sometimes yesterday's supposedly trendy words were in fact little used. For instance, the novels of P. G. Wodehouse preserve an upper-class idiom from the early twentieth century which was perhaps always more used in fiction than in fact. Indeed the act of using the idiom comically in fiction rendered expressions unusable in real conversation, except ironically and within metaphorical quotation marks. Only thus would one declare someone to be 'a bit of a bounder', someone's performance to be 'top-hole' or some welcome suggestion to be 'topping'.

But there are colloquialisms less subject to literary mockery that have a real life for a time. If one reads, say, Anthony Powell's *A Dance to the Music of Time*, which recaptures the England of the inter-war years, one will find terms, then trendy, which have since gone out of use. Where, earlier in the century, English people had visited the 'picture house' and the Americans had visited the 'movies', by the thirties middle-class English people talked of going to the 'flicks' (a word formed from the 'flickering' of the early screens). At the same time a favourite word for denigrating a venture or a business was to call it a 'ramp', meaning that it was a swindle, where twenty years later it would have been called a 'racket'. Today popular usage seems to be replacing these terms by the word 'scam'. In the inter-war years the colloquial expression for mockingly mimicking and satirizing famous people was to 'take off'. The Lord Chancellor in Gilbert and Sullivan's *Iolanthe* perhaps stuck a pipe in his mouth and 'took off' the Prime Minister, Stanley Baldwin. But forty or fifty years later the comedian would 'send up' the Prime Minister of the day.

An interesting twentieth-century development has been the use of the word 'chic'. It came into English in the nineteenth century to mean artistically stylish. Then it began to be used of stylishness and elegance in women's fashions. The noun 'chic' was correspondingly used of modish good taste. But colloquial use of the word outside the world of women's fashions later gave it a rather disparaging edge. For instance, in more recent decades, an attitude of political radicalism which was assumed by a well-to-do middle-class person might be dismissed as 'radical chic'. This implied that the radicalism was assumed as a fashionable pose rather than bred of real experience and deep conviction. And now past fashions can be implicitly discredited by calling them 'retro-chic', while firm resistance to fashion is called 'anti-chic'.

Among the words temporarily fashionable among trend-setters in the post-war world was 'camp', meaning affected and effeminate, vulgarly artificial and showy, used especially of homosexuals. It is an interesting word because it seems to have derived from a fictional tetralogy by the novelist L. H. Myers, *The Near and the Far*, published novel by novel between 1929 and 1940. Although the story is set in sixteenth-century India, that is merely a convenient background for Myers's reflections on the world he knew. And he presented a satirical study of contemporary Bloomsbury in the homosexual Prince Daniyal's Pleasaunce of the Arts, a remote camp of pleasure houses and a hotbed of scandal. 'Everybody in the Camp was always ready to do a friend a bad turn.' The word 'camp' appears to have been taken up by the chattering classes of the period.

An odd colloquial innovation of the sixties was the German word 'kitsch', introduced into voguish patter to mean something tawdry and vulgar, over-consciously modish. Applied at first to art and literature, it became the trendy word for dismissively devaluing attempts to catch up with the fashion in furniture and decoration.

In fashionable social circles the increasing habit of resorting to psychiatrists for treatment and advice led to the need for frequent conversational reference to 'psychiatrists'. A comical habit grew of avoiding the taxing series of syllables, and mentally distancing oneself from the psychological need by referring to a psychiatrist as a 'trick cyclist'. Later the word 'shrink' (derived from 'head-shrinker') took over.

Representing a different level of culture the word 'teddy-boy' came into use in the 1950s. In the early post-war years certain fashions imitative of the Edwardian age replaced what had been the fashions for men in the 1930s. For instance, suit jackets were much longer and looser-fitting, and trousers were narrower. There was a cult among youth to push the Edwardian style to extremes. Hence the name 'teddy-boys' was applied to groups of delinquent and roisterous teenagers and young men. Gradually the word came to stand for youths given to violence and criminality.

The same sub-culture gave us the word 'streetwise', a neat term to describe people, especially young people, who are wise in the ways of the street, which means that they are adept at keeping afloat in an environment that may be poor, unsavoury and criminal. The words 'street credibility', now colloquially 'street-cred', refer to awareness of the style and understanding needed to be at home in the urban counter-culture.

The worlds of the media, of pop music and of fashion supply an ever-changing colloquial vocabulary ('rock', 'rap', 'hip', 'grunge', 'grotty', 'glitch', 'glitzy', etc.) only some of which is taken into general usage.

The world of public life and politics has enriched colloquial vocabulary. Slang words readily become acceptable when they prove to serve a useful purpose. They may be widely taken up because they so exactly encapsulate a concept for which there is no easy alternative expression. Such is the case with the word 'freebie', standing for something provided without charge. Earlier in the twentieth century the abbreviation 'perk' was formed from the noun 'perquisite' to stand for the kind of incidental benefit that a person might gain from a certain employment. Thus waiters' and waitresses' tips were regarded as 'perks'. The word has been used for company cars and benefits such as private health contributions provided by certain employers. But the word 'freebie' has come to stand for treats provided, not so much by employers, as by interested parties anxious to gain influence. Thus, where 'perks' belong to the business world, 'freebies' belong to the political world, the world where Members of Parliament or of local councils may be treated to trips abroad.

During the nineties the fashionable vocabulary of political journalism was affected by the growth of the propaganda industry in the service of governments and political parties. We have been accustomed to use of the word 'spin' in the expression 'spinning a yarn', used of too-ready talkers telling a tale without overmuch scrupulousness as to facts. Hence the word 'spin' was adopted for the propaganda poured out by the publicity experts. The experts themselves began to be called 'spin-doctors'. And because of the sheer weight of the government propaganda machine and the irresistible direction it is supposed to exercise on MPs in the Party, the compound 'control-freaks' was used of its key manipulators.

OVER-USE OF FAMILIAR PHRASES AND EXPRESSIONS

In recent decades there has been heavy over-use of certain originally highly expressive phrases and expressions, most of which have a metaphorical content. It is because they are so expressive that we too often have recourse to them. But as a result their force is dissipated. No doubt the first person in our age to speak of throwing something 'out of the window' instead of merely 'throwing it out' achieved quite a rhetorical effect. (Though one is inclined to ask whether the speaker was really brought up to use the window for this purpose.) But now that the expression has caught on so that everyone speaks of throwing things out of windows instead of getting rid of them or abolishing them, the expression scarcely makes an impact. Familiarity breeds contempt.

at the end of the day

So too now, when we hear someone beginning a sentence, 'Well, at the end of the day', we are inclined to yawn. The phrase 'at the end of the day' is of course used metaphorically in that the reference to fading daylight is introduced because as night falls the day's business has to be tied up. The implication is that the point has arrived at which what is said is final and brings doubt and controversy to an end. Thus the expression 'at the end of the day' has gradually taken over as a substitute for 'finally' or 'ultimately'. The trouble is that it now seems to stand for so many different expressions, such as 'when all is said and done', 'to cut a long story short', 'when push comes to shove', 'what it all amounts to', or even 'to give you my honest opinion'. The speaker or writer should weigh such other possible options before using an expression now so over-used.

the level playing field

Other currently fashionable expressions of this kind derive their metaphorical content from the sports field. Again, though useful and colourful expressions, they are now grossly over-used. People demand 'a level playing field' when they want to ensure that there is no bias favouring the one side or the other where there is competition between the two. Thus we hear a government minister express his determination to play fair in looking at the competing interests of gas, oil and coal:

> Our aim is to put all fuels on a level playing field.

The image of a playing field is quite out of place in such a context. The concept of coal, oil and gas – a solid, a liquid and a vapour – in competition over an area of ground is simply unpicturable. In any case, it is perhaps surprising that this image has become so popular when in games such as football the two competing teams change places in the middle of the game, so that neither can reap the advantage of a field sloping this way or that.

moving the goal posts

It is more understandable that this expression from the football field has become so popular. As a metaphor for unfairly changing the conditions under which rival sides compete, interfering in mid-career with the very standards and criteria by which winner is to be distinguished from loser, the expression is a useful one.

kick for the long grass

We are beginning to hear this expression rather often too. Kicking a ball off the pitch into the long grass at the side is a temporary expedient for getting out of a testing position. Thus it makes a satisfactory image for an expedient move that sidelines an immediate problem for the time being.

blow the whistle

Another useful expression deriving from the sports field is 'to blow the whistle on'.

> The British Marine Industries Federation has already blown the whistle on the decline in the number of inland boaters, attributing it largely to the industry's inability to attract the younger generation.

This quotation excellently exemplifies how a colourful expression can gradually be deprived of its usefulness. When the referee blows the whistle on the football field, he does so to draw attention to some foul or inappropriate behaviour by one of the players, thus temporarily putting a stop to the game. A crucial element in what the expression conveys is the notion of bringing to light some misdeed before the eyes of the public. But the writer of the above sentence has fastened merely on the notion of drawing attention to something, irrespectively of whether it involves anything improper. When enough people have used the expression 'blow the whistle on' merely to mean 'draw attention to', then a useful enrichment of the language will have been dissipated.

the name of the game

Another popular expression which comes from the sports field is less easy to account for. We hear the pronouncement 'that's the name of the game' spoken with some solemnity. In most contexts it appears to mean nothing more than 'that's what matters', 'that's the essential point'. It is a way of laying heavy emphasis on some judgement. But we also hear it used in a more explanatory sense to mean 'Yes, that is what is involved' or 'That is what you should expect.' Thus the reply to 'I've lost two thousand on the Stock Market' might well be 'Well, that's the name of the game.' There are times when use of the idiom seems to represent a way of saying nothing at all.

> Sound project management is clearly the name of the game.

The word 'clearly' rings a bell of challenge here.

the bottom line

An expression which, surprisingly enough, seems to overlap in meaning with 'that is the name of the game' is 'that is the bottom line'. Clearly we are in a different field of imagery here. The expression appears to derive from the world of accountancy. The last line on a balance sheet shows the final profit or loss made by the business concerned. But in other fields the last line of a document is apt to finalize matters with the central point to which argument or discussion has led. The expression is to be avoided simply because it has been cheapened by over-use to the point at which it becomes little more than a verbal gesture. As used by some people it is almost the equivalent of exclaiming 'That's that!' or indeed of emphatically saying 'Amen'. I found this at the end of an earnest article about preserving the Cumbrian environment: 'The bottom line is Cumbria.' There, as elsewhere, the expression seems to be enunciated with the flourish proper to proclaiming a credo.

raising awareness and profiles

We nowadays hear of special occasions organized to 'raise awareness' of this problem or that, this affliction or that. Where once one would have said 'Its purpose is to draw attention to the lifeboat service', we now hear 'Its purpose is to raise awareness of the lifeboat service.' A slightly stronger version of drawing attention is represented by 'raising the profile'.

> The primary objectives are to raise the profile of dogs, and to act as a guide to prospective owners – allowing them to make an informed choice on the pet that will best suit their lifestyle.

To 'raise the profile', it appears, is not only to draw attention to, but also to increase the importance or significance of. But surely, whatever one writes about, one writes in the hope of drawing attention to it and increasing its significance in the eyes of the reader. As for the rest of the sentence, time was when one might choose or make a choice. Now one has to make an 'informed choice'. The insult to our intelligence implicit in the suggestion that, without the help offered, we should naturally make uninformed choices is hard to bear. Why not 'The aim is to rouse interest in dogs, and to help prospective dog owners to choose the right pet'? That reduces the number of words from thirty-five to nineteen.

make a statement

There are some familiar expressions which have become substitutes for thought, and this is one of them.

> Black gingham curtains with an overstuffed heading filled with wadding make a huge and expensive statement.

> A Victorian decoupage screen makes a bold statement at the head of a bateau-lit bed.

Strong sharp shapes are young and make a style statement.

What does all this amount to? Is anything at all said here except that the curtains, the decoupage screen, and strong sharp shapes are good things? Yet the statements abound. We have a 'huge' and 'expensive' one, a 'bold' one, and a 'style' one. So too we have flowers that make statements in gardening magazines and gyrations that make statements in the rock world. Here a controversial new production of Wagner or Shakespeare 'makes a statement', and there a seemingly haphazard collection of junk masquerading as sculpture 'makes a statement'. The literate mind demands an end to the making of statements. But the idiom seems to have bred its offshoots. We read in a magazine:

Kate Butner shows you how to turn a lamp into a style statement.

Plainly this piece of legerdemain is of doubtful value if the transformation is complete and the source of light is lost.

what it's all about

We should also like to hear no more of what this or that is 'all about'. We hear a comment on the thorny question of how the National Health Service should deal with mentally unstable individuals who might pose a threat to others. 'Treatment should not be about coercion.' This means that coercion should not lightly be used in treating patients, whatever their condition. Abuse of the word 'about' in this way is now an epidemic. We hear such monstrosities as 'Good relationships are all about being yourself' and 'Conservatism is all about being able to make choices.' People use the words 'it's all about' as simply a clumsy way of conveying that they think this or that is important without actually making a coherent statement.

window of opportunity

This is currently a popular expression, over-used to an embarrassing extent. The trouble is that, in fact, the image of the 'window' scarcely adds anything to the concept 'opportunity', which in itself refers to something that opens up the view to a future possibility. In earlier decades of the last century the favourite image was not 'window' but 'avenue'.

sing from the same hymn-sheet

This expression has caught on for urging people in a common enterprise to make sure that they are of one mind in what they convey. Since it hints at the chaos produced when a church congregation tries to render two different hymns at the same time, it has forcefulness, but it is over-used.

CHAPTER 12

Current Liberties and Constraints

FREEDOM WITH TRANSITIVE/ INTRANSITIVE VERBS

During the last few decades liberties have been taken in the use of transitive and intransitive verbs, that is with verbs which normally take an object ('like' in 'I like ice-cream') and verbs which do not take an object ('sleep' in 'He sleeps on the couch'). The area of usage we are touching on is one which is like a minefield for the pedagogue. The reason is that historically English usage has allowed such freedoms from time to time that it is dangerous for one to lay down the law. It is easy enough to give examples of comparatively recent changes. In my fifty-year-old *Shorter Oxford English Dictionary* the verb to 'resume' is given only as 'transitive' and no instance of an intransitive use is supplied. Thus it is that fifty years ago one would have said 'The meeting was resumed.' Now we tend to say 'The meeting resumed.' Presumably the English teacher of the inter-war years would have been justified in correcting that as a grammatical error.

Established Liberties

The freedom long exercised with certain verbs may be illustrated by the way we use the verb to 'show'.

> Some of Paul's work was already showing at a Glasgow gallery.

We accept this as an alternative to 'Some of Paul's work was already being shown at a Glasgow gallery.' The following sentence extends that freedom:

> The Andrews' London home in Hyde Park could rent for £1,000 a week.

We substitute 'could rent' for 'could be rented', a practice also applied to the verb to 'sell'. 'The picture was sold for £500' might become 'The picture sold for £500.' Just as this usage seems to be particularly favoured in the relevant trading circles, so the same freedom is adopted by specialists in other areas. Let us turn to the world of horsemanship.

> It looks enormous from the road, though fences jump deceptively easily off a sharp rise.

We know, of course, that it is the horses that do the jumping while the fences remain at rest. But we have always played this trick of verbal reversal. We 'tuck' a notecase away in our pocket and say 'See – the notecase tucks away neatly.' And I see that the Wine Society advertises red wines 'that are drinking beautifully now'. Where do we draw the line with this practice? Usage is very arbitrary. You will hear or read 'The organ was playing as we entered the church', but you will not hear or read 'The violin was playing as we entered the concert hall.' Instead it would be 'The violinist was playing'. The organ appears to be the only instrument that is allowed to play itself. (Is this because the player is hidden away in an organ-loft?)

More Questionable Liberties

The difficulty in laying down the law in this matter can be illustrated by the following sentence in which a mother tells what happened when she dressed up her little girl:

> I noticed how she transformed to suit the costume.

The pedant's first impulse is to want to 'correct' this. My modern dictionary allows only a transitive use of the verb to 'transform'. On that basis the reading ought to be either: 'she was transformed' or: 'she transformed herself'. But in fact the *OED* quotes a sixteenth-century intransitive use of the verb and adds 'now rare'.

A comparable but converse instance is provided by the verb to 'vanish'. Here is a piece about a painting by Canaletto.

> And the delicate steeples which needle the horizon of the eighteenth-century city are mostly vanished in the modern photo, destroyed and never subsequently rebuilt.

Modern practice is to treat the verb to 'vanish' as intransitive only. So my later dictionary defines it. Yet the *OED* cites a fifteenth-century transitive use, meaning 'to cause to disappear'. Thus there is precedent for the converse freedoms exercised with the normally transitive verb 'transform' and the normally intransitive verb 'vanish'. It is plain that it would be foolish to be free with the words 'correct' and 'incorrect' when dealing with this particular matter of usage. All one can do is to call attention to what is happening.

> France warred on these neighbours through the 1790s, while trying to recover internal order and reconstruct.

To 'construct' is a transitive verb and to 'reconstruct' is too. But the writer here has taken with the verb to 'reconstruct' the freedom which traditional usage allows with the verb to 'recover'. You can 'recover' your balance and, if you have been ill, you can just 'recover'. Very well then, the verbal libertarian may ask, why should not a state, after a period of turmoil, just 'reconstruct'? And while we are on this subject, do we have the right to criticize an advertisement using 'erect' as 'reconstruct' was used?

> Tents that erect in thirty seconds.

We may itch to correct this to 'Tents that can be erected in thirty seconds', but again past literature can provide instances of the verb used intransitively. The following sentence too may strike one as improper:

> Motorists shun from flattening animal casualties in daylight.

Checking up in a recent dictionary, I find that the verb to 'shun' is labelled 'transitive'. In that case, one might 'shun' something, but not 'shun from' it. But once more recourse to the *OED* reveals that the verb was used intransitively 400 years ago.

We turn to a now more established though very questionable freedom taken with certain verbs.

> Two years ago fashion editors were eulogizing on the chain store's new chic.

This sentence exemplifies what is today probably the most common and regrettable laxity in use of transitive verbs. To 'eulogize' is to praise enthusiastically. There is no justification at all for the word 'on'. The editors 'were eulogizing the chain store's chic'. The habit of thus treating a transitive verb of speaking as though it had to be intransitive is wholly regrettable. Even when popular usage seems to have established the practice, the purist will feel uncomfortable with it.

> He comes across as refreshingly unacademic even when expounding upon complex subjects.

Although a recent dictionary would justify this, the insertion of the word 'upon' is totally unnecessary. It would be better to write: 'even when expounding complex subjects'. But the habit of inserting these redundancies grows apace. We have sentences such as 'The speaker expanded on the new plan of action', as though the speaker increased in size before his audience. There are appropriate verbs for this context, such as to 'expatiate' or to 'enlarge'.

One wonders to what novelties this practice may lead. I have just heard a radio commentator ask whether a certain political development has 'depleted from' a party's reputation. Perhaps he meant to say 'detract from'. To 'deplete' is firmly transitive and means to empty or exhaust.

Unacceptable Liberties

We have been criticizing the unnecessary intrusion of the words 'on' and 'upon' after verbs which are better treated as transitive. Here is a specimen of the converse error.

> This plant hunter embarked his perilous journey.

This should read: 'embarked on his perilous journey'. For while in its intransitive use to 'embark' was to board a ship, in its transitive use it was to put something on board a ship, the 'bark' being the vessel. Equally unacceptable is the following sentence:

> The process is stripped away of inessentials.

'The process' has not been 'stripped away'. It is the inessentials that have been 'stripped away'. One might say 'He was stripped of his clothes' or 'His clothes were stripped away' but not 'He was stripped away of his clothes.' For all the freedoms allowed in this matter of grammar, it is dangerous to take liberties and here the trick has gone too far. Yet the trick is catching on. Another journalist writes of a passionate love affair: 'It's stripped away of the complicated stuff' when she means that the complicated stuff has been stripped away from it. Headline writers sometimes take too far the freedom granted to them in this respect, anarchically misplacing passive verbs.

> Newcastle Pair Torn Off a Strip by Angry Investors.

This headline illustrates the point. The Newcastle Pair were certainly not 'torn off a strip' by the investors. Why, we may ask, did the headline writer not write: 'Strip Torn off Newcastle Pair by Angry Investors'?

The extempore manufacture of intransitive verbs by the insertion of redundant prepositions is not restricted to verbs of speaking such as 'eulogize' and 'expound'.

> Making the most of what you have and minimizing on waste is the key when you're on a budget.

To 'minimize' is to reduce to the minimum. The intrusive 'on' is out of place.

> Munch on vegetable sticks or a handful of raisins or other dried fruit.

Again the intrusive 'on' is ugly as well as redundant. There is an old intransitive use of 'munch', just as there is an intransitive use of the verb to 'eat'. You can say 'He is eating' or 'He is munching', but you would not say 'He is eating on toast.' Very relevantly I have just heard on the radio a comparable misuse of the verb to 'segregate'. The dictionary definition of the verb is 'to set or be set apart from others'. But the Radio 4 speaker spoke of a plan to segregate something 'off', as though the verb were not a clear transitive one.

Perhaps we may usefully include here three further examples in which the freedom to juggle with generally intransitive verbs is exploited too far.

> Each paper motif must be completely adhered to the furniture surface.

The verb to 'adhere' is intransitive. 'Flattery adheres to power', Gibbon observed. We do not 'adhere' a postage stamp to an envelope. We 'stick' it to the envelope, and thereby the stamp 'adheres' to the envelope. And I read a reference to 'the shoe shops that proliferate Oxford Street'. To 'proliferate' is to grow or increase rapidly. A transitive use of the verb is possible in zoology, where it would mean to produce by proliferation. The notion that shoe shops might 'proliferate' a street is therefore absurd. Avoidance here of the natural intransitive usage ('shoe shops that proliferate in Oxford Street') has led to error. And here is a newish verb even more boldly mistreated:

> A girl aged 12 has been questioned by police over the death of the 16-month-old toddler she was babysitting.

No doubt the girl was 'babysitting', but she was not babysitting the toddler. To try to turn 'babysit' into a transitive verb that takes the cared-for baby as its object will not do.

THE USE OF POSSESSIVES

We have seen how modern English has largely lost the inflexions which enabled the Anglo-Saxons to distinguish one case of a noun from another. There are only a few lingering relics of the old Anglo-Saxon inflexions with us. One is the surviving distinction between the singular noun and the plural noun. In most cases we add an 's' to our nouns to make the plural form. 'Book' becomes 'books', 'father' becomes 'fathers' and so on. The relics of other, 'irregular', inflectional changes from singular to plural are few. 'Man' becomes 'men', 'woman' becomes 'women' and 'child' becomes 'children'. These forms have survived, but not (for general purposes) 'brethren' as the plural of 'brother'. And of course there is a handful of nouns which are the same in the plural as the singular, notably 'sheep' and 'deer'.

Another relic of the old inflexions of the noun is the genitive case which is formed by the apostrophe 's'. We speak of the 'teacher's book' rather than of 'the book of the teacher', thus preserving the distinctive genitive case for the possessive. We have two uses of this possessive case in modern English. We may speak of the 'doctor's treatment of Mary' or of 'Mary's treatment by the doctor'. The doctor's 'treatment' is something that he does. Mary's 'treatment' is something that she receives. The one usage may loosely be called 'objective', the other 'subjective'.

There are certain nouns like 'treatment' which lend themselves either to objective or subjective use in the possessive case, for instance the nouns 'selection' and 'portrayal'. In such cases, generally speaking, the objective usage is the safer. We can be slightly happier with 'the local party's selection of John Smith as their candidate' than with 'John Smith's selection by the local party as their candidate'. It is better to speak of

'Shakespeare's portrayal' of Julius Caesar than of 'Julius Caesar's portrayal by Shakespeare'.

Nevertheless the latter usage is not uncommon. Increasingly the subjective possessive is being used where it would be better avoided. Perhaps the worst instances of poor usage in this respect occur when writers use the genitive case of an impersonal noun.

> The Bill's passage, by 33 votes to 21, came after an acrimonious debate.

Surely this should be 'The passage of the Bill' or, better still, 'The Bill was passed by 33 votes to 21 after an acrimonious debate.' The tendency of journalists to use such constructions as 'The passage of the Bill came' rather than 'The Bill was passed' is to be regretted.

> If the existing power struggle in Beijing survives the Asian depression, it will be one of history's more remarkable achievements.

The great achievements are not 'history's' achievements, they are men's or women's achievements ('one of the more remarkable achievements in history').

We turn to a press comment on the national temper:

> There are two reasons for the mood's sudden turn to the worse.

Once more, though 'the sudden change in mood' would be better, better still would be to use a verb instead of either of the nouns 'turn' or 'change' ('There are two reasons why the mood has suddenly changed').

Although the use of an apostrophe 's' with an impersonal noun can be very tasteless, the more common misuse of the subjective possessive occurs with pronouns. We speak of 'his conversion of the stable into a cottage', where he has effected the change, or of 'his conversion to Buddhism', where he has been affected by the change. Clearly there is no reason to question such usages of the pronouns in the appropriate contexts. 'My present' to you becomes 'your present' from me, the moment it is handed over. But 'my message' to you does not become 'your message' from me, once it is delivered. The difference may be a 'conventional' one, but all language is conventional. So the BBC newswriter was at fault to give us this account of an English mother's acquittal on a charge in a foreign country.

> She has already telephoned them [her children] with news of her verdict.

The court's 'acquittal' of the woman may be said to be 'her acquittal' by the court. But the court's verdict on her is in no sense 'her' verdict. No person in the dock can deliver a 'verdict'.

> The foster-father of Billie-Jo Jenkins has launched an appeal against his conviction for her murder.

The awkwardness of combining 'his conviction' with 'her murder' would not be removed by writing 'his murder of her'. It would be better to write: 'his conviction for murdering her'. The press seem to be fond of this usage:

> A Briton who doused his former girlfriend with petrol and set her on fire pleaded guilty yesterday to her attempted murder.

The addition of 'attempted' makes the usage even more illogical. We have got used to 'her attempted suicide', recognizing that the woman may indeed have 'attempted' the act. But 'his attempted' act against her can no more become 'her attempted' act than his crime can become her crime.

We have already seen that the noun 'selection' lends itself to either the objective or the subjective use. But extreme care should be exercised in opting for the latter.

> Almost all his potential rivals in the Republican leadership are even more conservative. Their selection would be an enormous risk for a party that enters the next House election in 2000 with a slender six-seat advantage.

The uncomfortable use of 'Their selection' should be replaced either by: 'Selecting them would be an enormous risk' or by: 'To select them would be an enormous risk'.

We have referred to other nouns which present the same problems as 'selection'.

> She must have been hurt by her portrayal as a fairly clueless mother.

An improvement on that would be: 'She must have been hurt at being portrayed as a fairly clueless mother.'

One may question whether the word 'purchase' fitly allows of the double usage in question. 'My purchase of a new suit' can scarcely be presented as 'the new suit's purchase by me'. Nevertheless we find this in a railway magazine:

> It has been undergoing restoration at the Gloucester Warwickshire Railway since its purchase by the group.

It would be better to change 'since its purchase' to 'since it was purchased'.

The word 'approval' also resists this usage. 'My approval of a new novel' cannot be paraphrased as 'the new novel's approval by me'. Yet I heard talk on the radio of the Northern Ireland Agreement and the speaker referred to 'its overwhelming approval by popular vote'. She should have spoken instead of how it had been 'overwhelmingly approved by popular vote'.

The HSBC Bank advertises what it calls its 'Choice points programme'. 'You can now spend your Choice points on just about anything you want', it says, and then declares 'We've kept your favourite offers.' But we readers know that they are not 'our' offers, they are the Bank's offers. 'Your' present may become 'my' present when I receive it, but 'your' offer of help does not become 'my' offer when I accept it.

> The Masters of the Devon and Somerset Staghounds have been out on Exmoor as normal putting casualty deer out of their misery despite their ban from hunting for five weeks.

'Whose ban?' we may ask. It sounds as though 'their ban' follows on 'their misery' as an additional burden on the deer. In any case it is not very felicitous to speak of 'banning' either man or beast 'from' doing anything. The simplest solution here would be to replace 'their ban from hunting' by 'the ban on hunting'.

The possibility of confusion arising from such careless use of the possessive pronoun is illustrated in the following:

> Computerized typesetting systems fascinated Kindersley and he worked with Cambridge scientific colleagues on their study.

According to general practice in English usage 'worked with scientific colleagues on their study' would suggest 'on the study they were involved in'. But the context indicates that here 'their study' means the study of the computerized typesetting systems. Better write 'worked with Cambridge scientific colleagues in studying them'.

Finally, there is a particular kind of false economy with words in use of the possessive forms.

> A pathologist is going out to report on the Nigerian Chief's death in gaol . . . and remove suspicions about its circumstances.

Our criticism here is about the use of 'its'. The 'circumstances of his death' ought not to be rendered 'his death's circumstances' or as here 'its circumstances'. As so often error would have been avoided and style improved if the noun 'circumstances' had been avoided: 'and remove suspicions about how it happened'.

NOUNS USED AS ADJECTIVES

A practice has developed of using nouns as adjectives might be used, jamming them up against other nouns. We have long run nouns together in such useful combinations as 'family outing', 'dairy farmer' and 'university degrees'. And new compounds have continued to be established more recently on the pattern of 'jumbo jet' and 'word processor'. Here we look at the practice of sticking nouns together, sometimes seemingly with the intention to add useful compounds permanently to our vocabulary, like 'car registration number' or 'PIN number', and sometimes without any intention to establish what can properly be considered a 'compound'. Thus people talk about 'conflict resolution' and 'safety precautions' without mentally hyphenating the words. And the following usage is not uncommon:

> Nationwide Building Society will press the government to introduce new rules to protect societies against member attempts to force conversion.

Until fairly recently writers would have referred to 'members' attempts' or 'attempts by members'. But now writers jam nouns together in twos and in threes, economizing on both apostrophes and hyphens. Presumably the person who wrote 'member attempts' did not think that a new compound was being established on the pattern of 'gas-works' or even a stable relationship on the pattern of 'fruit salad'. Rather the word 'member' was picked up and treated as a pseudo-adjective. That has become a general practice. We read of a 'business strategy unit', and the three words remain separate in our minds. Since, generally speaking, such combinations are not hyphenated, they can scarcely be called 'compounds'.

Let us consider how the word 'customer' has been treated in this respect. We find that we have a 'customer reference number' on our electricity bill, and we notice that the partnership of nouns is a threesome. But whereas the 'customer reference number' is indeed the customer's own number, what is printed under the heading 'Customer Information' includes no facts about the customer at all, but only facts about the company. Some well-meaning businesses talk sympathetically about 'customer care' as though they were in league with the NHS. Indeed the Halifax no longer employs a clerk or an accountant to let you know what interest is now due to you. Instead you receive a communication from a 'Customer Care Manager'. At least one bank has supplied information to its members as what they call a 'customer convenience', words which surely ought to refer to toilet facilities.

Again we find firms talking about 'customer complaints', and the words do not refer to ailments, but to grumbles. A garage labels one of its doors a 'Customer Entrance'. Thus it seems that though a 'Theatre Entrance' would be an entrance to a theatre, a 'Customer Entrance' is neither the mouth nor any other human orifice. It may be argued that only at the dentist's or in a hospital operating theatre could the expression 'Customer Entrance' or 'Patient Entrance' be said to be ambiguous. I do not know whether there is a hospital which marks a 'Patient Waiting Room', though the usage might not be inappropriate. We have long used the expression 'Car Parking' and are well acquainted with what it means. Now we find notices advertising 'Customer Parking'. It may well be argued that no one is going to misinterpret this and treat the area as a human dump, but a current news item informs us that women shoppers are wanting superstores to provide crèches in which they can deposit their menfolk while they get on with the serious business of stocking up with foodstuffs, unimpeded by masculine attendance. Such a room would surely be more justifiably labelled 'Customer Parking'. And now I read that the Halifax is to open '50 Customer Marketing Areas' throughout the country. The marketing of wives was not unknown in nineteenth-century England, as we know from Thomas Hardy's *The Mayor of Casterbridge*. Whether customer marketing can escape the attentions of the law remains to be seen.

THE PARENTHETICAL ADVERB

Controversy has recently drawn the attention of writers to certain freedoms taken in the use of adverbs. Consider the following two sentences.

> We decided to ask the Smiths to come to our party, and they gratefully accepted.

> We decided to ask the Smiths to come to our party and, surprisingly enough, they accepted.

In the first sentence the adverb 'gratefully' tells us how the Smiths responded to the invitation. It does so by its relationship with the verb 'accepted'. In the second sentence the adverb 'surprisingly' does not tell us in what manner the Smiths accepted. Presumably they themselves felt no surprise in agreeing. Rather 'surprisingly' covers the response of the speaker to the Smiths' acceptance. This is a valid construction. Yet in the journal of the *Queen's English Society* the Membership Secretary was taken to task for writing thus of the loss of members:

> Of these 34 have resigned, 28 have been 'lapsed' . . . nine have gone away and 16 – sadly – have died.

The critic protests: How does one know the state of mind of those who died, sad or not? The complaint is unsound. The adverb 'sadly' modifies the verb 'died' only from the point of view of the writer. It comments parenthetically on the clause which it interrupts, '16 have died'. It is the equivalent of 'sad to say'.

What are the limits to this use of adverbial parentheses?

> Thankfully, when baby is feverish and in pain, many new mums seem to know instinctively what's needed.

The word 'thankfully' is accepted as indicating the feeling of the writer. It is almost the equivalent of 'You will be glad to know that . . .'

> You can easily make sponge from a packet, but baking the real thing takes very little effort and, more importantly, it tastes better.

Here again, we are not being told that the mixture tastes 'importantly'. Rather, 'importantly' relates to the whole clause 'it tastes better' as a fact which the writer is attaching the importance to. 'More importantly' is the writer's parenthetical observation.

Let us turn to a common conversational usage in this respect:

> Our noisy neighbours have mercifully removed to London.

We can take it that the neighbours did not act mercifully in removing themselves. 'Mercifully' is the speaker's ironic comment on the event represented by the whole clause it interrupts.

It is perhaps in this context that we should consider the fairly recent development in usage which gives the word 'hopefully' a distinct kind of parenthetical status. Strict traditional usage requires one to use 'hopefully' in clear direct relationship to a verb ('We looked at the recent developments hopefully'). But recent practice has been to use it as a substitute for a parenthetical 'I hope' or 'we hope'. Thus, instead of saying 'Electricity shares will rise rapidly this year, I hope', someone will say 'Hopefully, electricity shares will rise rapidly this year.' Plainly the electricity shares are incapable of feeling hope. Thus the usage is condemned as barbaric by many grammarians. It is said that in the offices of the *Times Literary Supplement* there is a notice over one journalist's door, reading 'Abandon "hopefully" all ye who enter here.' Nevertheless, it looks as though the usage is here to stay. It has a certain usefulness. It is not markedly different in construction from the usage cited above of 'more importantly'.

POLITICAL CORRECTNESS

What we call 'Political Correctness' has had its main effect on English in two areas of usage: the traditional vocabulary of gender and the vocabulary used in reference to human abnormalities.

Gender

Feminists have called for abolition of the practice of using the words 'man', 'men' and 'mankind' to cover both sexes. Words such as 'person', 'people' and 'humanity' are employed instead. Where past usage has left us with male and female forms for certain roles and posts, feminists have sought standardization. In this respect the current situation is somewhat chaotic. The two words 'actor' and 'actress' survive. So do 'host' and 'hostess', 'waiter' and 'waitress', and even 'proprietor' and 'proprietress'. It would seem unlikely that we shall lose the differentiation represented by 'hero' and 'heroine'; and the words 'master' and 'mistress', in their various usages, seem indispensable. But a large number of feminine terms are being discarded. We do not now hear the words 'authoress', 'poetess', 'instructress' or 'sculptress'. Other feminine forms, such as 'creatrix' from 'creator', have also gone out of fashion. However, interesting survivals of that feminized form are still with us. There is the word 'executrix', still used officially and unofficially. The word 'dominatrix' appears in an article by Libby Purves in *The Times*. In the same paper, in a survey of television programmes, a photograph of Amelia Earhart, who flew the Atlantic in record time in 1932, is captioned 'Amelia Earhart, Aviatrix'. But the word 'doctor' never had 'doctrix' as a matching feminine form in English. The words once used were 'doctoress' or 'doctress', and they have long gone out of use. The favoured present practice is to insert the word 'woman' before the masculine term ('woman doctor') where needed.

Awkward linguistic problems can arise where the attempt is made to change the suffix 'man'. American influence has given us 'chair' for 'chairwoman', though there have been female protests in this country against the implicit dehumanization of the role. But we hear such compounds as 'chairperson' and 'spokesperson'. Traditionally we have distinguished between a 'postman' and a 'postwoman', a 'milkman' and a 'milkwoman'. The attempt to popularize 'person' in cases like these has not proved popular. And it would seem impracticable to eliminate the syllable 'man' in such words as 'craftsmanship', 'horsemanship' and 'one-upmanship'. Compounds which have 'man' as a prefix, such as 'manhole', 'manslaughter', 'manpower' and 'manhandle', also resist adaptation. It is likely that inconsistency and illogicality will be with us in this sphere for some time. For instance, the feminine form 'hostess' is still being used in the partying world, whereas there is talk in the sphere of surrogate motherhood of the 'host mother'. It is interesting that when foreign words are adopted, they do not necessarily come in for homogenization. We still distinguish a 'masseur' from a 'masseuse', but we seem to have lost the feminine 'chauffeuse', used early in the twentieth century. Compounds involving 'master' and 'mistress' were once common enough. 'Schoolmaster' and 'schoolmistress' survive. We used to speak of a 'postmaster' in charge of a post office and a 'postmistress' too; we even had both 'stationmaster' and 'stationmistress'.

There are still a few words in use which distinguish masculine from feminine by the addition of the suffix 'ette' for the feminine version. An 'usher' (a word perhaps chiefly used now of a man showing guests to their places at a church wedding service) is balanced by an 'usherette' (used of the woman who shows you to your seat in the cinema). We describe as 'drum majorettes' the young girls fitted out in uniform for their musical parades. In pre-war Oxbridge it was common to speak (if not to write) of 'undergraduates' and 'undergraduettes'. *Private Eye* has established the word 'hackette' for a female 'hack', a disparaging word for a cheap journalist. The French basis of these usages is obvious. The masculine French ending 'et' becomes 'ette' in the feminine. There are cases where we have taken one of a French pair without taking the other. The French 'coq' (English 'cock') produced the French word 'coquet' (for an amorously inclined gallant) as well as the word 'coquette' (for a flirtatious woman). We have adopted the latter but not the former.

On the whole the flavour of delicacy and femininity does hang around the ending 'ette'. Where the word 'toilet' is now used chiefly for a lavatory, the word 'toilette' is associated with refined feminine attention to personal appearance. Associations of refinement also resonate in the word 'etiquette', whose history is oddly interesting. Deriving from the same word as the word 'ticket', and meaning a soldier's billet for lodgings, then a label for admission, it somehow came to stand for the code of polite behaviour.

Strictly speaking, the ending 'ette' was a diminutive form too. Thus we have 'cigarette' as a small version of 'cigar'. We have also taken over 'maisonette', the diminutive of 'maison' without 'maison' itself. And now the small disk used in computers is called a 'diskette'.

The main linguistic problems arise with the use of pronouns. The singular pronoun 'everyone' has always taken a singular verb. 'Everyone goes home at the same time', we say. But when a possessive pronoun is introduced the official usage used to be masculine. 'Everyone must search his own heart' was the usage, and even 'Everyone must look after himself.' Now people had been unhappy with this particular usage well before the feminists attacked it. A headteacher of a mixed school, addressing his pupils, would generally say 'Every one must lock their own locker properly', using 'their' as a singular pronoun. This practice has now become established. But there are cases where awkwardness can be avoided by use of the plural 'all' instead of the singular 'every'.

> It combines the power every motorist needs with the refinement they expect.

This collision between the singular 'motorist' and the plural 'they' could be avoided by use of the plural throughout: 'It combines the power all motorists need with the refinement they expect.'

The reference to motorists reminds us that we perhaps ought not to leave this topic without mentioning the odd use of feminine pronouns in connection with ships and machines. The practice of treating ships as feminine has lingered on. It has been claimed that this practice has sometimes led to comic misunderstandings, as when a journalist is reported to have described the launching of a liner thus:

> Her Majesty smashed a bottle of champagne against the bows and then she slid gracefully down the slipway into the water.

Certainly in the early decades of the twentieth century no garage mechanic and no motorist with a serious interest in the new automobiles would have spoken of a car's performance or discussed problems in the engine except with feminine pronouns. 'She pinks when she gets down to thirty in top on a hill.' This was a spoken rather than a written idiom. It expressed a kind of knowing familiarity between man and machine.

The converse practice of using the neutral 'it' where human beings are involved is unsatisfactory.

> We feel that the smart employer should be concerned with the general health, morale and efficiency of its workforce.

An employer cannot become 'it'. Use of the plural would eliminate the problem: 'Smart employers should be concerned with the general health, morale and efficiency of their employees.' It is odd that the one context in which the use of 'it' for a human being was once acceptable was in reference to babies. 'Lay the baby on its tummy' surely still sounds unpatronizing, though in the case of older children we should find the neutral pronoun uncomfortable. That is presumably why some journalists try to solve the problem by a quota system. Cheek by jowl, we find such sentences as the following:

> Sometimes teasing can bring a child's morale so low that she sees no way out . . .

> But if the child feels that he's not only failed his tests but failed your expectations too, it's doubly hard to bounce back.

> Unless your child is one of those enviable creatures, a good eater, it's easy to become worried or obsessive about their food.

The question about the use of 'man' and 'men' to cover both sexes may be looked at in the light in which we speak of other living creatures. There has always been inconsistency here. The dictionary will define a 'mare' as a female horse and a 'vixen' as a female fox, but would not define a 'woman' as a female man, rather as a 'female human being'. 'Horse' seems to be used rather as 'man' was used. We speak of 'wild horses' and we do not think we are excluding mares. We speak of the 'swans' on the river, and we do not feel that we are excluding the pens. Contrariwise, we say that we are 'keeping hens' even when a cock is included. The feminine sex takes precedence also in reference to 'geese', where the masculine creature is a 'gander'.

It is not easy to discover what current etiquette requires of us now that there has been a reaction against the feminist pressures of a few decades ago. A recent letter to *The Times* runs thus:

> The use of the ugasp – ungrammatical gender-ambiguous singular pronoun – which pollutes our language in the cause of political correctness reaches new depths of absurdity in your report of September 5 on a case of unfair dismissal. You quote the employer as saying '. . . the applicant does not have to tell us they are pregnant'. A cherished ugasp of a similar type comes from a magistrate I heard addressing a defendant: 'You kicked your victim in the testicles and went on to break their nose.'

Certainly it would seem that pursuit of political correctness in this respect can lead to curious logical dilemmas. It would appear to require one to choose between the kind of statement above, using 'they' ('the applicant does not have to tell us they are pregnant') or such usages as: 'If an employee becomes pregnant, he/she will be allowed the usual period of absence.'

Disability

The political correctness that requires ever more evasive euphemisms in reference to physical or mental abnormalities or deficiencies is difficult to talk about objectively because it directs our minds to tragic human problems. One has to accept that where terms carry a physically, mentally or morally pejorative connotation sheer politeness often requires a certain blanketing of the reality. It would be offensive to describe someone as 'grossly fat' or 'obese', when gentler terms such as 'overweight' are available. It may be, of course, that the overweight are a special case in that putting on weight is sometimes the result of over-eating rather than of an inescapable affliction. A well-rounded woman of my acquaintance, concerned about her weight, received from her GP the brutal verdict: 'There were no overweight people in Belsen.'

We are concerned here rather with afflictions which no one would think of as in any way brought upon themselves by the afflicted. What the King James Bible calls 'the blind, the halt and the lame' we now call 'the disabled' or 'the physically disadvantaged'. The once much-used word 'cripple' has become unacceptable. So too have terms such as 'mental deficiency' and 'mentally defective'. What once was a 'deficiency' is now an 'impairment'. Along with the word 'impaired' the word 'challenged' has been attached to various adverbs, as in 'visually challenged'. Some seemingly less serious inventions of this kind include 'vertically challenged' as an alternative to 'short' and 'follically challenged' as an alternative to 'bald' or 'balding'.

In the educational world care has been increasingly exercised to avoid terminology that might damage sensitive children or depress their parents. Where the use of words such as 'backward' and 'retarded' was common in the earlier half of the twentieth century to describe less mentally able pupils, contemporary teachers speak of children with 'learning difficulties'. A deaf, dyslexic, or mentally retarded child is classed as having 'special needs'. An inattentive child is described as suffering from an 'attention deficit syndrome'.

If we can disentangle our thinking from the emotive elements in this matter, we shall have to recognize that the now discredited words 'mental deficiency' and 'mental defective' were introduced as polite and humane words to replace terms such as 'dementia' and 'feeble-mindedness', which themselves were probably introduced to replace terms such as 'dotage' and 'insanity'. If we go far enough back, the words 'lunacy' and 'lunatic', 'idiocy' and 'idiot' were usable. Wordsworth, a very compassionate man, wrote a moving poem called *The Idiot Boy*. It is the touching story of young Johnny Foy, the darling son of Betty Foy, and the adventure that befalls them when she sends him at night on her pony to fetch the doctor for an ailing neighbour. Throughout the poem the words 'idiot boy' are repeated several times in reference to Betty Foy's devotion to her son, 'Him whom she loves, her idiot boy'. The two words together, 'idiot boy', are made to hold a great weight of sympathy and tenderness. They resonate with compassionate understanding of the boy's lot. Yet nowadays they could not be so used.

It would appear to be the case that attempting to blur the reality of what we are talking about generally works only temporarily. When 'disabled' has had a few decades of use, the direct connection apparent between the word and sometimes gross human deformities will initiate the kind of disgust with the word which recent generations have felt with the word 'cripple'. On the basis of historical experience there is reason to believe that the now respectable words 'impairment' and 'disability' will eventually go the way of 'deficiency'. For in the choice of euphemisms the passing ages run from one at first polite word to another as the full significance of the former sinks home. Today's polite word is tomorrow's impolite word.

We have to live in the real world, not in a philological hothouse. And for the moment the real world requires us to describe a blind or nearly blind person as 'visually impaired' and a person with abnormal mental limitations as someone with 'learning difficulties'. This book, however, is about the use of English. Its statements about usage cannot properly be measured according to the degree of compassion seemingly evidenced for those who suffer appalling afflictions. It is the relationship between word and reality that concerns us here. When a man who has brutally raped, strangled and then carved up a number of young women is described as a person 'with mental health problems', there is a peculiar discrepancy between word and fact which in other contexts would produce humour. What we call the 'discrepancy', that is to say the immense disproportion between the reality and the word defining it, is precisely what political correctness exists to establish. Verbally speaking, political correctness in these matters is the denial of literalness. Instead of trying to match act and experience with commensurate terminology, it determines to create a gap between the two. In this respect it moves in the opposite direction from rhetoric and poetry, which augment meaning by exaggeration and amplification, pressing it home in terminology that brings the maximum intensity and vividness to bear on facts and events defined. By contrast political correctness of this particular brand dilutes and disembodies everything it touches. Regular addiction to its terminology is a form of linguistic anorexia nervosa.

CHAPTER 13

Workaday English

It remains to take a look at some questionable verbal habits now adopted in various spheres of commerce, in certain national institutions and in our cultural life, and to recommend simplifications.

BUSINESS-SPEAK

The term 'business-speak' covers a wide field of usage. One would hesitate before attempting to write about 'science-speak' as though one could generalize about the linguistic characteristics of writers in psychology and physics, medicine and metallurgy *en bloc*. To enter into the linguistic world of any such speciality is a study in itself. Business-speak too is a house with many mansions. Quite apart from the distinguishing linguistic features that mark a given form of commerce, there are linguistic features appropriate to various specialisms such as management and marketing, and to sub-divisions of the former, say, such as those concerned with overall strategy and those concerned with human resources. The general public, however, comes across business-speak chiefly through publicity, whether in the form of advertisements in the press or direct mail. It is to this that we turn our attention.

Publicity and Recruitment

We had something to say about the use of hyperbole in Chapter 9. At the present day a certain group of extravagant terms has been seized on by the business world and they are so over-used that their meaning is dissipated. Consider the following.

The company's growth has been meteoric and Worldcom has very quickly

> established itself as the most dynamic player in the market. Essential to achieving continued success is the recruitment of high quality people and two new fabulous opportunities have been created to play a key part in Worldcom's expansion.

The extravagance here is obvious. 'Meteoric', 'dynamic', 'fabulous' and even 'essential' are, or used to be, powerful words, and their use here devalues them. The sentences are unnecessarily wordy. 'Essential to achieving continued success is the recruitment of high quality people' conveys no more than 'We need to recruit good people' would. That firms intend to remain successful can be taken for granted. Declarations of this kind are now familiar, and we cannot help wondering whether a greater impact might be made by a simple statement, directly noting that the firm is a big one and a growing one, and is making two new appointments to crucial posts.

An even greater extravagance is shown in the following:

> At Ostagon you will be immersed in an innovative, energetic and driven culture, focused around your accelerated development and achievement of personal goals. The experience gained through this programme creates an awesome platform for your ultimate success.

Words such as 'innovative', 'driven', 'focused', 'achievement' and 'goals' are nowadays peppered over statements in the business world as exclamation marks were in the Victorian age. As for the 'awesome' platform, the words might be an appropriate description of the site of a public execution. But, since the platform is represented as a starting-point, one must assume that it is the kind of platform from which one catches the train rather than the kind from which one appears in public for whatever purpose.

The business pages of the press abound in this kind of sticky-toffee-pudding vocabulary.

> Our continued growth has been achieved through our unique ability to create business solutions that integrated expertise and experience across the full range of business needs – strategy, technology, processes and people.

'Continued', 'achieved', 'unique', 'create', 'business solutions', 'integrated expertise', 'strategy', 'processes' . . . The words tumble out of the business-speak thesaurus, and they have all been heard so many times before in this kind of context that they simply do not register at all. They are dead counters.

The epidemic is raging everywhere. Instead of finding a way to improve a business, you have to discover a 'high performance vehicle for adding real value' to it. Instead of having an eye for profit, you have to have 'a proactive response to the market's ongoing consolidation'. Instead of directing a firm's marketing, you have to 'take immediate responsibility for the creation and implementation of a sales development strategy'. Instead of watching carefully for new ways of improving sales, you have to be a 'catalyst for growth' whose 'focus will be to identify opportunities and convert these into a business reality'. Instead of looking for the right man for the job, the employers seek someone who will have the 'credibility to make an immediate and sustained impact'.

Efficient businessmen ought not to be able to endure this waste of verbiage. Its sheer excess simply does not go with the image of the slick and the streamlined which is supposed to characterize modern commerce. It is a vocabulary that belongs, not in the age of the Eurostar, but in the age of transatlantic liners whose rooms were burdened and littered with the unnecessary ornament of the age. It should have gone down with the *Titanic*.

The Personal Touch

We have seen how the verbal excess is sometimes combined with a personal touch in advertisements for posts. The imaginary applicant is addressed in the second person, often with fulsome flattery. The appeals made to would-be employees in such advertisements can reach a pantomimic level of hyperbole. We turn to an advertisement for 'NT Server Product Managers (Hardware and Software)'.

> Standing up in front of a senior level audience, convincing them you're the most knowledgeable server guru alive, leveraging your technology and marketing skills to enthuse customers about the supremacy of our products – by doing these things you'll become the ultimate products champion, bringing confidence and a drive for results to all you do. A proven relationship builder and project manager, you'll probably be straining at the leash of a national remit and keen to upgrade to a truly pan-European environment.

This is the kind of excess which makes the layman gasp. We who would like to be regarded as plain-speaking, we who are quite prepared to talk about people doing their best to make their products popular, do we now need to learn the language of 'leveraging technology and marketing skills to enthuse customers about the supremacy of our products' and all in the cause of winning the ultimate products championship? What sort of people are they who talk like that? It is the same question that arises in our minds when we look at a mediaeval tapestry of knightly jousting or a picture of a gorgeous Elizabethan banquet. What on earth were these people really like behind all this fancery and flummery? And yet, in truth, there is something about this excess which one wants to call its 'innocence'. There seems to be a childish delight in having a go, in discovering and verbally dressing up in grandma's discarded finery that maturer heads have put away in the attic.

And if one tries to enter the mind of the would-be applicant for the post advertised above, the natural question arises: In what idiom shall I respond? To begin 'Dear Sir/Madam, With reference to your advertisement of such and such a date' would seem totally inappropriate to the grandeurs on offer. And to take the advertisement too literally would surely suggest a lack of respectful subservience: 'Dear Sir/Madam, Thank you for the tribute you paid me in the advertisement of such and such a date. I could not agree more and I can only applaud your insight.' The advertisement would surely seem to require adoption of an idiom that does justice to the character of the challenge and yet avoids tedious formalities: 'Now you're talking!' perhaps.

The Worst Excesses

What it all amounts to is that verbosity now runs riot in the kind of publicity material we have been sampling. The first rule of the crudest business-speak appears to be: Never use one word where two will do, or two words where three will do. Do not talk about such things as 'management'. Far better to talk about 'management systems' or 'management issues', better still about 'management systems issues' and best of all about 'management systems issues strategy'. The question arises whether courses in business studies and management ought not to be classified under the 'Modern Languages' umbrella. At the extreme point business-speak seems to be making a lot of noise yet saying nothing at all. Consider the following from a letter to *Marketing Week* usefully preserved in the 'Pseuds Corner' of *Private Eye*.

> Surely marketing is and will always remain a transactional-based function responsible for the designated tangible and intangible interactions between internal and external customers.

However one struggles to translate this into decent English, the verbiage resists the attempt. 'Surely marketing is marketing' might perhaps say it all. Even to add 'and will always remain so' merely compounds the redundancy. To say 'Marketing is a matter of transactions between people' is to function as a dictionary. The pile-up of unnecessary and indeed redundant terms such as 'function', 'designated', 'tangible', 'intangible', 'internal' and 'external' adds nothing but noise. Suppose we try to describe driving a car in the same idiom. 'Surely driving is and will always remain a directional-based function responsible for the designated and co-ordinated operational interactions between internal combustion and external propulsion.'

An interesting feature of business-speak is the way it sometimes reaches out to involve linguistic currencies from other spheres of life in the effort to give an upmarket flavour to simple statements about buying and selling, advertising and marketing.

> Communicating a brand's core equity and being able to leverage a media brand's value as part of a more holistic and integrated sell is something I know advertisers are simply crying out for.

One may be a little sceptical about the notion that people in the business world are crying out for this kind of thing. The wording of the business world proper is evident in talk about being able to 'leverage a media brand's value'. What the writer appears to be getting at is that somehow a brand's worth should be exploited as part of a new kind of 'sell', indeed a more 'holistic' and 'integrated' sell. The words 'holistic' and 'integrated' carry overtones of what is comprehensively health-preserving and thoroughly purified of limitations and peripherals. To try to bring these resonances to bear upon an act of handing over a product in exchange for cash is to plumb the depths of bathos.

Post Office

The world of business-speak, once perhaps a small domain, has now taken over in the former nationalized institutions and colonized the professions. This is the idiom of Post Office Counters:

> Delivering coherent strategies through effective change management, Post Office Counters is a commercially focused customer driven quality retail business.

Do the first seven words say anything at all that is worth communicating? And is it not self-evident that a business must be 'commercially focused' and 'customer driven'?

> With continuous customer service improvement seen as a key to ensuring continued long term success, our business strategy unit has identified a need for an energetic change management professional, to be based in Chesterfield, to support the delivery of the company's strategies within the individual business unit through the integration of new, with existing, initiatives and the management of the planning process within the unit.

What is the difference between seeing continuous customer service as a key to ensuring continued long-term success and believing that it pays in the long run to do your best for your customers? And, while we have long benefited from newspapers on our doormats and milk bottles on our doorsteps, why does every firm in the land now want to start 'delivering' strategies or flexibility, solutions or added value, bottom-line efficiency or integrated expertise? The Post Office, at least, has better material to deliver.

Electricity Industry

We turn to the electricity industry to illustrate the language of company reports. This is how a major supplier of electricity explains that it is going to pay its employees as well as it can:

> National Power's remuneration policy takes account of the changing nature of the business in both the UK, where competition has increased significantly, and overseas. In order to compete and meet these challenges the

Committee has established remuneration levels which will retain and motivate top quality executives but which are sufficiently incentivized to link remuneration to Company performance.

Before commenting on style, let us note an elementary error. One cannot speak of the nature of the business 'in both the UK. . . and overseas', because we do not use the expression 'in overseas'. The word 'in' is on the wrong side of 'both'. Correct the passage to 'both in the UK. . . and overseas'. What exactly do we learn from the two wordy sentences? We might try to put it succinctly. 'National Power's business is growing at home and abroad. It will pay top employees enough to keep, encourage and reward them in an increasingly competitive market.' The words and phrases happily sacrificed include 'remuneration policy', 'changing nature of the business', 'in order to compete and meet these challenges', and 'sufficiently incentivized'.

We may cite a further example of National Power's increasingly lavish output of verbiage.

Activities in the UK have continued to focus on maximizing our operational and commercial performance.

Plainly this means that the firm has gone on trying to do its best.

Banking

We turn to banking to explore the language of direct marketing used to make a personal appeal to the customer. A few years ago a much used word in advertising was 'choice'. It had become an approval noise to be voiced alongside political claims for 'freeing' the population from this or that programme pressed by the rival party. A bank seized on the word.

Midland Choice . . . We are proud to introduce Midland Choice . . . A world of innovative ideas, exclusive offers and awards designed specifically for you. Midland rewards your loyalty . . . as a valued customer and cardholder. It provides us with a means to express our thanks in the most direct way possible for using our credit cards and enjoying the variety of benefits they provide – Midland Choice offers you a wealth of opportunities and special awards. You have only to look through this brochure to get an idea of the quality and range of existing benefits available.

The business-speak we have already encountered reappears here in such terms as 'innovative ideas', 'exclusive offers', 'valued customer' and 'wealth of opportunities'. These expressions derive from the Business-speak All-Purpose Guide to Recommended Terms. But that vocabulary is threaded through with a vocabulary more appropriate to the world of personal communications between friends. We might speak of seizing a 'means to express our thanks in the most direct way possible' if we were writing round to those friends who had sent us wedding presents or indeed sent letters of sympathy to us after a bereavement. That vocabulary is here used in the process of drawing attention to a catalogue of items that are purchased by the 'points' accumulated through lavish use of the bank's credit card. This merging of idioms prompts one to ask the question: Does it take anyone in? Are there customers who feel a warm glow as the bank talks about rewarding their loyalty? Indeed, are there customers who, as they hand over their card at the check-out, are not wondering 'Have I spent too much?', but 'Have I been loyal enough to the bank in being content with this modest trolley-full?' Does the departing customer have second thoughts: 'Ought I perhaps to have bought that extra bottle of claret? It might have earned me a special word of thanks from the bank manager. It would certainly have opened the way to a special award. I should have won increased freedom of choice to plunder that range of existing benefits.'

National Health Service

The NHS is run by a bureaucracy and when the bureaucracy makes its announcements one expects to hear the voice of bureaucracy. Nor is one disappointed. Hear a comment made on BBC Radio 4 by a representative of one of the country regions. The question at issue was the need to avoid overspending. How could the trust economize?

> One of the areas identified was the potential closure of regional hospitals.

Here we have the words 'areas' and 'potential' introduced and a matter of identification touched on all in the process of translating into the language of bureaucracy the statement 'We may have to close some regional hospitals.'

We have come to expect this usage from managers. But, alas, the idiom is not restricted to managers. The caring professionals may not talk like that, but some of them are capable of writing like that. Here is a comment from the *Nursing Standard* on how a nurse valued what she had gained from taking a certain course.

> If she had acquired this earlier, she says, the transition to her desired goals could have been achieved more quickly.

Did the nurse really say 'The transition to my desired goals could have been achieved more quickly'? Did she not rather speak of having got more quickly to where she wanted to be?

The possibilities of using a lot of words to say nothing are explored in many directions in the same journal. Here we have one among a series of paragraphs presented as 'challenges for debate' on the importance of a balanced diet for patients in hospital.

> To measure how nutrition outcomes have been achieved and assessed. Debate assists in clarifying expected learning outcomes for nutrition components of a programme. Reflections on and the use of learning outcomes for the key characteristics of the board's framework will help to determine progress in meeting nutrition education outcomes and will also help to specify the professional and academic standards to be achieved in different programmes and modules at both pre- and post-registration levels.

We seem to drown in a sea of words designed only to fill space. We are in a mental world of 'components' and 'outcomes', of 'programmes' and 'key characteristics' in which no clear line of utterance emerges. What do we know at the end of the paragraph that we did not know at the beginning? By thinking about the use of learning outcomes we are going to make progress in meeting nutrition education outcomes. Is this what the National Health Service is all about?

Dialects of Business-Speak

There are various dialects of business-speak, and some of them go in for brevity, for instance the idiom in use by professionals for publicity purposes within their own field of activity. It is designed to make a quick impact and not to waste words. In this idiom practitioner is speaking to practitioner, and much can be taken as understood. Thus it trims business-speak down:

> TRUEDATA is a proven 7 step data quality framework for dealing with UK domestic and international data within a scalable architecture.

This presents the product with a directness that suggests efficiency. 'Scalable architecture' may be a less than exact image but, like the rest of the sentence, it does not waste words. Nor does the following:

> Our vendor independent approach will allow us to support TRUEDATA with best of breed software as it becomes available and thus free IT resources from time consuming product assessment exercises.

The point to be made here is that business-speak has an in-business dialect which makes a no-nonsense approach that values brevity. And the message is phrased so as to achieve the kind of impact made by headlines and newspaper placards. This dialect extends further the freedoms of the business-speak that is directed at the outside world. Usages such as '7 step data quality framework' and 'best of breed software' illustrate the queer amalgam of influences from business jargon and from literature.

There is also a business-speak dialect far less formal, far chattier and more intimate than the public voice. It tends to be used within the management world rather than in communicating with the public outside. We perhaps feel some reluctance in exploring what is after all an area of intimacies into which outsiders are not expected to intrude.

> If you have any ideas/views; know of the key documents etc. other areas have please let me know. I believe that within the business we have excellent well thought through ideas, there are some key issues/challenges that need to be bottomed out and the task is to pull these threads together into a realistic focused strategy.

Here we have the intimate word-in-your-ear approach. Button-holing fellow workers does not call for the heavy hand of verbal solemnity. If we are to subject the passage to criticism/judgement/analysis, we must appreciate that it was not intended for the pages of the *Financial Times* etc., but for distribution among the office fraternity. If there are grammatical/logical errors/solecisms in it that need to be bottomed out/topped up, then we may overlook them. All the writer was anxious to do was to pull a lot of threads together into a realistic focused strategy.

E-mail

E-mail is of course used outside the business world as well as within it. Academics converse across the Atlantic by e-mail about their studies in this or that abstruse field of research. In such communications appropriate idiomatic shorthands are used which to outsiders may make no sense at all. That is true too of the continuous on-line chat which lightens the daily burdens of the business world. And lovers are increasingly sending billets-doux by e-mail. Here is another sphere of usage into which outsiders can scarcely dare to intervene. We regard Jonathan Swift as a master of English prose. If a model of simplicity, directness and plainness in English prose is called for, then Swift is the writer to whom literati turn. But he was quite prepared to end a letter to his dearest Stella with such messages as:

> I'm angry alomost; but I won't tause see im a dood dallar in odle sings, iss and so im Dd too . . . Lele I can say lele it ung oomens iss I tan, well as oo.

Such mysterious idioms survive in the personal columns of the press on St Valentine's Day. The point to be made is that much e-mail is a kind of private correspondence. And according to the degree of intimacy between correspondents private languages are adopted. This applies to the business world too.

Leisurely pen-pushing is not the only parent of e-mail. It is equally the offspring of the telegram. And the telegram made the maximum demand for brevity: HOUSE BURNT DOWN STOP COME QUICKLY STOP PHONE INSURANCE STOP. The use of e-mail by the business world must be noted because it is another medium which demands brevity.

We have just dealt with communications within the sphere of a given set of business interests. Communication by e-mail is common within limited segments of that world. And, where communication is between people engaged in the same work and perhaps in many cases familiar with each other, the freedoms cited above are further extended. The in-house e-mail dialect of business-speak thus makes a fascinating field of study. As one might expect, the modern liberties taken with nouns and verbs are further extended:

> Please action as below if possible.
>
> What products are available to mailed customers?
>
> Confirm Wilkinson order processed/despatched.

Such terse messages as these three exemplify the point. (We now accept liberties taken with the verb to 'mail', though, if my recent dictionary is comprehensive and authoritative, one could only 'mail' customers by posting them in letter-boxes.)

When records are at issue in in-house e-mail, computerology inserts another vein into the verbal amalgam.

> This is currently not in scope of the programme and needs consideration (eg keep excluded? include in XYZL WN3456? delay until resource resolved?)

Outsiders are likely to have just as much difficulty with this as with the *Journal to Stella*. Yet there is no doubt that the bracketed questions save space by obviating the need to spell out the three options with grammatical clarity. Indeed brackets are used with some versatility in this dialect:

> What do you think is the (business as usual) route by which these things will be addressed?

But perhaps the most interesting feature of in-house e-mail is that, because personal contacts exist between correspondents there is a natural tendency to use conversational expressions which one would not find in externally directed business-speak.

> Please let me know how this is working once it has had time to bed down.
>
> We need another meeting to sweep up any other matters.
>
> Feed this to Robinson.

Usages such as 'bed down', 'sweep up' and 'feed' give the in-house e-mail dialect a vein of refreshing simplicity absent from so much business-speak.

VERBIAGE IN THE ARTISTIC WORLD

Visual Arts

The peddlers of verbiage in the arts are a special breed. They have an inestimable advantage over writers in the fields we have been looking at. They can rely on the assumption that if readers do not understand what they read, they will believe that this is due to their own ignorance and not to any failing on the part of the writer. Writers on the arts are protected from the judgements of common sense by a mystique. The mystique derives from the notion that all worthwhile new developments in the arts meet at first with popular opposition because they are not properly understood. It follows that the cognoscenti can brainwash the public into laying aside the judgements of common sense when face to face with new art. The notion that great art is generally unappreciated by the contemporary world cannot be supported by reference to history. But the artistic world keeps it alive, and it fills the laity with apprehension. If a new work does not make sense to them, then probably that is because they are old-fashioned ignoramuses.

We are not here concerned with the larger civilizational aspect of this attitude. We are concerned with the treatment of the English language which art critics can indulge in on the basis of that attitude. Mystification pays off when the truly great is likely to be the incomprehensible.

It is with these observations in mind that we should approach the field of aesthetic criticism. For it is a field rich in empty verbiage. We may have seemed to some readers to have been over-caustic in our treatment of the business world. Let it be clearly understood, therefore, that the misuse of language in the business world pales into insignificance compared with the misuse of language in the world of the arts. To begin with, business uses a vocabulary with limits. Business may reach out into the field of personal vocabulary or even, as we have seen, into the vocabulary of personal well-being, but these tend to be sporadic incursions into recognizable fields of discourse. Moreover, as we saw above, when a firm brought in the word 'guru' from a different field of discourse, it really meant 'guru'. The concept came in as well as the noise. The world of artistic appreciation criticism knows no such inhibitions. It is not just that in context after context any word will seemingly do, but that whatever meaning that haphazardly chosen word drags along with it from its normal contextual backgrounds can be happily ignored. Let us look at this sphere of the aesthetic at a modest level of discourse where a magazine article deals with restoring an old house.

> Drawing the line between ethics and personal preference has to be considered and controlled, but where an overall scheme of decoration of this type was carried out, the only way it can be interpreted satisfactorily is to return to its nearest state of originality.

The reference to ethics ('the philosophical study of the moral aspects of human conduct') illustrates the point made above about the tendency among aesthetic writers to make forays into alien verbal territory. What it means, if it means anything, to 'consider and control' a line drawn between ethics and personal preference scarcely seems to matter. The grammatical and logical collapse that follows ('where a scheme was carried out . . . the only way it can be interpreted satisfactorily is to return it to its nearest state of originality') is complete. How a scheme can be interpreted by being so treated is incomprehensible.

The point that needs to be made here is, not that the passage makes nonsense, but that the passage can nevertheless be found in print. And that point is worth making. Because, once we have appreciated that the world of aesthetic criticism, at a fairly low level of expertise, can play havoc with meaning and logic, we shall be better prepared to face the horrors of more 'highbrow' utterance. Let us look at an account of the massive sculpture known as the 'Angel of the North', an account for which we are indebted to the 'Pseuds Corner' of *Private Eye*.

> The body of the Angel is trapped. It exists between vulnerability and strength. It is a millennial work witnessing the transition between the industrial and the information ages. This is not a logo, symbol, or even a representation in the traditional sense. It is based on reality; a moment of lived time in which my body was registered in plaster, a moment when biological time was captured in geological time.

If the terms 'vulnerability' and 'strength' are properly understood, then the notion of being 'trapped' between them is untenable. If the millennium marks a transition between the ages of industry and information, that does not mean that a contemporary work of art will somehow 'witness' to that idea. To say something is 'based on reality' adds nothing to our understanding of it. As for 'lived' time, 'biological' time and 'geological' time, the terms reek of imprecision.

Literature

The story of the development of literary criticism during the last hundred years or so is one of increasing specialism. Time was, in the Victorian age, when critics were content to comment on works of fiction on the understanding that, say, Tess in Hardy's *Tess of the D'Urbervilles* was a portrait of a human being such as you or I might meet, and the novelist's ability to render her lifelike was one of his major gifts as a writer. Literary criticism then began to interest itself in the relationship between the fictional content of a writer's books and the actual events of the author's life. In the early years of the twentieth century, therefore, literary studies of authors were often combinations of biographical material from the author's own life and commentary on related material in the fictional output. Various changing emphases on the aesthetic, the social, the psychological and the political aspects of fictional constructions emerged during the mid-century years. These attitudes were superseded in the last decades of the century by theorists who cut away the traditional assumption that literature expressed some kind of reality in exploring the life of humanity. Attention shifted to works of literature as constructs manufactured from words. The business of criticism was not to comment on the world as presented in art form but to examine the linguistic formulations from which works of literature were constructed.

It is necessary to give this brief account of developments in a now very technical field in order to explain how the stage has been reached at which what literary critics say on paper can make seeming nonsense; that is to say, how writers can conceal the true quality of their thinking behind a flow of contrivedly abstruse terminology. The following is a review of a critical work for which we are again indebted to *Private Eye*.

> The first part of her essay concludes with naming the spatialized polity of the (Derridean) sophist – the city of modernity – as necropolis. For, in denying temporality and the spoken word, and 'being' as the gift of an excessive beyond, eliciting an erotic gaze (sight which participates in that which is seen), in favour of spatialized writing and being as the 'given'

> commanded by a panoptic vision, modernity ironically embraces necrophilia where it should affirm only life.

It is not my intention here to try to elucidate this. Half an hour spent with a dictionary, checking up on the meaning of such words as 'spatialized', 'polity' and 'panoptic' will not get one far, for it is not the individual words that present a problem to the reader but the eccentric juxtapositioning of one with another: 'spatialized' along with 'polity', 'spatialized' along with 'writing', and 'excessive' along with 'beyond'.

Taking a glance at this specimen of recent literary criticism, we recognize that this area of study has become a closed world for specialists. But imaginative literature, unlike nuclear physics, is meant to be open to all comers. And if one asked seriously the questions 'Would Shakespeare understand this?' 'Would Dickens understand this?' they would have to be answered in the negative.

Music

It is a common view that music is the most incorruptible of the arts. Yet it has suffered from the regrettable recent developments here explored, the bold exploitation of the public by a seemingly informed use of words that is specious and often nugatory. It is a brand of verbosity that covers near-meaninglessness. We have to distinguish this from wasting words to convey something easily said with far fewer words. What we are here concerned with is rather a matter of using words to say little or nothing at all while seeming to be profound. There is a flavour of bogusness about this kind of utterance which it would be unjust to impute to those whose often wasteful, but scarcely dishonest, manner of speaking and writing we illustrate elsewhere. Let us turn to a programme note about one of Beethoven's major works . . .

> It is what it is, says what it says, offers what it offers, with immediacy, confidence and transcendental pertinence.

Now clearly, once you've started on this 'says what it says' lark, you can really make a meal of it: 'urges what it urges, announces what it announces, bubbles up with what it bubbles up with' and so on. As for the list of qualities: 'immediacy', 'confidence' and 'pertinence' (whether 'transcendental' or not), there is no reason why one should not add several more abstractions, say 'vigour', 'astuteness', and 'determination'. And what makes 'pertinence' 'transcendent'? Why not 'eternal immediacy, infinite confidence and transparently transcendental pertinence'? If music critics are paid by the shovelful of words, we could easily add to the income.

If a writer is seriously engaged in describing a composition intelligibly, that writer is surely limited in the intensity of the nonsense he or she can produce. What is written may be awkward, ill-phrased, even highly ungrammatical, and yet what the writer is trying to say may make sense. Here is a sentence from a programme note on Rachmaninov's third symphony.

> An urgent triplet rhythm takes us into the development with wind meanderings leading to disparate pockets of themes (based on the first subject) eventually coming together in a tramping rhythm with trumpets pealing, alternating with the afore-mentioned xylophone/piccolo/bassoon passage.

It is not elegant prose. If a schoolboy handed it in, one would suggest a re-write. But it is not nonsense. Indeed, having swallowed our reservations about the idea of 'disparate pockets' eventually merging in a 'tramping rhythm', we may feel that the connection between the prose and the matter in hand is firm, and that the sequence of ideas rather clumsily assembled actually helps us to understand the work in question. In the present climate of aesthetic utterance, that is no mean achievement.

Unfortunately music critics do not restrict themselves to elucidation of musical form. Here we have a piece from the Programme Notes for the Huddersfield Contemporary Music Festival, again courtesy of *Private Eye*.

> To ask if the artist has a moral responsibility implies, paradoxically, that the artist is not divorced from the social reality despite there being no empirical evidence that art has a function beyond the aesthetic. But asking the question at all amounts to a confession that society – and art – is in a crisis, and emphasises the inability of the Marxist or any other readily available vision to direct the way to the creation of a value structure which suggests the possibility of hope in the final few years of the twentieth century. The search for meaningfulness is as old as time, but during this climacteric there has never been a greater need for affirmation.

The supporters of the Huddersfield Contemporary Music Festival may be generous people. They need to be. Presumably they purchased their programme notes in the belief that they would find guidance towards full appreciation of the new music. They would probably have been quite content to swallow a few verbal gob-stoppers about the adventures of 'disparate pockets', provided that they thereby got some signposts to the thematic content of the work under review. But what have they been sold instead? A forced question about the connection between morality and art leads to the assertion that 'there is no empirical evidence' to support such a connection. 'No empirical evidence?' Does not Defoe's *Robinson Crusoe* have a moral message? Does not Bunyan's *Pilgrim's Progress* have a moral message? What about Dickens's novels? And, in the sphere of music, what about Beethoven's *Fidelio* and Tchaikovsky's *Eugene Onegin*? These works ooze with moral overtones. As for the statement that 'Asking the question at all amounts to a confession that society – and art – is in crisis', it is totally mistaken. Asking the question as he does merely reveals that the writer is intellectually in deep trouble. The words that follow about directing the way to 'the creation of a value structure' which suggests the possibility of hope are so much empty froth. The 'possibility' of hope is always there. What is needed now is the possibility that careless critics of the arts will learn to use their native tongue.

SPORTSPEAK

One cannot listen to the reports on the radio of football matches and cricket matches without wishing that the sports writers could be persuaded to give advice to the newswriters and to fellow journalists on how to produce lively prose. The same can be said of the reports on matches in the daily press. It is not that sports writers generally deserve the highest marks for economy of utterance, but they have a way of vivifying their prose with metaphor. Now it has to be accepted that there is often a touch of self-conscious irony in their recourse to grandiloquent image and vocabulary. Great commentators on cricket for long relied on the language of heroism on the battlefield. Their presentation of events might endow noble stands at the wicket with the heroism of Horatius on the bridge at Rome or give to the struggle on the field the flavour of epic encounters under the walls of Troy. This tradition seems to justify the grandiloquence still adopted. Here is a comment on the news that an English FA club had just signed a young Italian.

> It also sends a signal down through the English fabric of the game, descending through the Nationwide League into the semi-professional and even amateur roots. Whither the opportunity for our embryonic talents if we are importing the seed as well as the full-grown plant?

The progress of the signal down through the very 'fabric' of the game all but reminds one of how, in Macaulay's ballad, the approach of the Spanish Armada was signalled by beacons right up the kingdom from hill top to hill top until the red glare on Skiddaw aroused the burghers of Carlisle. The question 'Whither . . . ?' maintains the grandiloquent flavour. When, in a previous book on usage, I happened to observe that we had all but lost two very useful words in ceasing to say 'whence' instead of the clumsier 'where from' and 'whither' instead of the clumsier 'where to', a critic pounced on this as a sign of my unfittedness to address the contemporary world on the subject of usage. Who on earth would want to use either 'whence' or 'whither' nowadays? Apparently the sports commentator does. One may argue that the 'fabric' of the game through which the signal is transmitted sounds more like a block of flats than a living thing and that therefore the reference to 'roots' (instead of perhaps 'basement'?) and the quick change of metaphor to that of seed and plant is a little wayward. But the prose is alive. And the idiom is with us daily. I turn to this morning's *Times*.

> After all the subterfuge and the paranoia of the reign of Glen Hoddle, the sheer boldness of Kevin Keegan swept through the England camp like a river of hope yesterday. The caretaker English coach did not just flout convention by naming his team to play Poland a day early, he nailed it to a tree.

We are learning about the end of a 'reign'. As the news in the previous specimen seeped down through a fabric to its roots, so the newcomer's boldness sweeps here through a camp like a river. Now, if you have ever put up a tent in Wales or in the Yorkshire Dales, you will know that when a river sweeps through the camp it is not exactly a symbol of hope. But water is refreshing and it could be that the picture here is of a camp in the Sahara or in the desert of Arizona. The image of the new caretaker is of one who flouts convention. Indeed the picture of him, nailing to a tree – not convention (as the grammar suggests) – but the list of his chosen team, brings back associations of Martin Luther taking on the whole might of Rome. That the writer is not unconscious of the implicit similarity with mighty historical events becomes obvious in what follows.

> A small crowd gathered round the proud old oak outside the team hotel to peer at the 11 names he had written in black capital letters on a white sheet and felt the thrill of a visceral challenge pass through them. Keegan could not have made it much more stirring if he had been a medieval knight.

The pathetic convention is employed to make the old oak 'proud' of the privilege it has been granted. After all, we are in a world where black capital letters on white paper can send the thrill of a visceral challenge coursing through the veins of grown men. And now the cat is out of the bag. We are not picturing a humdrum contemporary in action, but a mediaeval knight. Later in the piece the knight himself speaks. He does so with a different idiom.

> I see the team playing on a wonderful pitch. I see us winning and I see people cheering when we come off. But that is me.

Here is someone who can make simple words, framed in simple rhetorical repetitions, touch the heart, like Martin Luther King's repetitive words 'I have a dream'. They are the words of a visionary, but a visionary with his feet on the ground.

JOURNALESE AND MAGAZINE-SPEAK

This book has relied greatly on quotations from the daily press and from magazines. It may therefore seem to the reader to be superfluous to devote a special section to issues that have been with us throughout the book. But a glance at certain journalistic habits may not come amiss in this survey of the current scene.

Verbal Ostentation

We have just looked at the kind of hyperbole found in sportspeak. Some readers may even feel that we have been too tender in our treatment of sports writers in this respect. After all, the touch of hyperbole and the taste for avoiding plain, direct utterance are not features peculiar to sportspeak. The same kind of ironic over-statement that the sports writers use may be found in many different contexts. Here is part of an account of a well-decorated home in a magazine on style.

> But the *coup de grâce* could be her bathroom, whose cupboards belie a mundane function. Instead they resemble one of those charming Victorian screens pasted with nostalgic snapshots . . .

A 'coup de grâce' is originally an expression from battle. Literally a 'stroke of mercy', it represents the final blow which puts an end to the opponent's life and suffering. Hence it is used of momentous acts which terminate a struggle, then, less seriously as here, of the final touch which comes as a climax to what has been done or said. Just as one senses the authorial smile behind this expression, so too it is there behind the consciously sophisticated way of saying that in appearance the cupboards belie their mundane function. Even advertisers rely on not being taken too seriously in their adventures with words.

> Shimmer the summer away with Pastel Lumière Eyeshadows from Bourjois – fabulously strong, long-lasting colours . . .

The notion of a woman 'shimmering' her summer away asks not to be conceptually analysed any more than the claim that the colours are 'fabulously' strong.

But when the hint of humour is lacking, such artificial verbal poses may fail to come off. In a journal directed at the field sports community a writer lets off steam about the threats from the Green movement. He has just come across a piece of scientific research which throws doubt on some of the claims of the environmentalists.

> We can but hope that this incident marks a new era when there will be further stirrings in the scientific thickets to apply correctives to the miasma of humbug with which we are at present enveloped.

The writer might argue that a simpler and more direct sentence would not have conveyed the sense of outrage which expressions such as 'miasma of humbug' reveal. Nevertheless, by being too indigestible, the image of correctives to a miasma that emerge somehow from stirrings in the thickets turns almost to parody. The result is that, where readers are meant to receive the image of a righteously wrathful opponent of non-sense, they receive instead an image of someone all but frothing at the mouth uncontrollably. In short, the thing becomes comic.

The kind of verbal finery we are exploring does require a certain degree of sophistication in the writer, for the vocabulary is rich in artifices. Because of this, it cannot afford to lapse grammatically. To hear a lout being noisily ungrammatical is not hair-raising. But to hear the smart, supposedly educated person on a platform being ungrammatical is embarrassing. So too the user of verbal finery cannot afford to trip up in elementary grammar. Yet it happens. Here we have a writer praising alfresco meals taken in various places, and he describes lunch at a club in St Tropez where a mist of water is sprayed from concealed piping.

> This cooled the air but was sufficiently well judged and fine enough so as not to militate against a post-prandial cigar.

We are in a sophisticated world where one can measure the degree of atmospheric interference that might mar enjoyment of a post-prandial cigar. How inappropriate, then, to commit a grammatical howler that might disgrace a schoolboy by saying 'sufficiently fine enough so as not to militate' instead of the correct 'fine enough not to militate'. One or the other, 'sufficiently' or 'enough', is redundant. And that 'so as' represents a lapse into illiteracy.

In this respect a kind of moral code comes into operation when one is picking holes in other people's writing. A modest writer slipping up with a difficult word or concept does not seem fair game, as does the sophisticated writer slipping up when showing off. So when a third leader in *The Times* comes a cropper, while dealing with a literary subject and ostentatiously dropping names of writers and works, conscience allows one to record it for posterity. The topic is the lighthearted question whether the dawn of a new century will turn today's avant-garde writers into yesterday's men. After attributing to Keats Browning's oft-quoted lines, 'Oh, to be in England / Now that April's there', the writer continues:

> But for the *Times Literary Supplement*, Eliot's *Prufrock* was 'of the very smallest

> importance' and, in *The Waste Land*, he was rebuked for neglecting 'the limitations of his medium'.

Eliot was not rebuked in *The Waste Land*, but in a review of the poem. The mistake is the error we called 'verbal leapfrog'.

Overstatement

We turn to a less sophisticated brand of verbal finery where hyperbole is used to express enthusiasm. Our conversation and our private letters abound in simple and 'innocent' forms of overstatement. How else can we express our grateful appreciation of our friend's cooking and hospitality? Words like 'wonderful', 'superb', and 'delightful' fall from our lips or are penned in our letters of thanks. When we have to pay tributes to people on occasions of celebration, we tend to use a ready vocabulary of praise. And when journalists have the duty to report achievements in competitive events, they tend to tap a familiar vein of overstatement.

> Once again Mrs Ronnie Wallace's Anchor Herd stallion, Icecream, won an impressive collection of silverware at the Exmoor Breed show, at Exford on the moor.

A few lines below this, we read:

> Also well laden with trophies was Vera Lipsombe, from Wootton Courtenay, near Minehead . . .

Talk of winning an impressive collection of silverware and of being laden with trophies is the product of three motives. The first motive is the wish to say something different from 'The horse came first'; the second motive is the wish to say something that takes up a little more space than 'The horse came first'; and the third motive is to say something that expresses more enthusiasm than 'The horse came first.' We see the same three motives in operation when we read how a certain competitor 'crowned a marvellous season' with a win, how another 'followed up earlier triumphs' with a victory, and how a third 'belied his age with a scintillating performance' to claim first prize. The sports writers we cited above used imagery to create a definable verbal ambience, but the over-used expressions here do not carry authentic feeling and drop into the mind as dead counters.

The trouble is that certain kinds of writing are the product of the necessity to pen sentences when the material available for utterance would be more appropriately put in note form. In reading reports of competitive events, one can often sense the struggling mind of the writer adopting this device and that in order to put in seemingly natural prose the ordered list of winners and losers.

Experimentation

Adventurousness in the choice of words is tempting, but purposely pushing a verb into a new usage by a kind of colloquial inventiveness may come off or may fail to come off. Consider the use of the verb 'guarantee' in the following.

> The pursuit of ratings is now such an all-consuming matter that bagging a face that will guarantee the cover of the *TV Times* has become almost more important than signing the best actor for the part.

The usage is neither precise nor grammatical but there is a touch of verbal legerdemain about translating 'a face that is sure to appear on the cover of the *TV Times*' into 'a face that will guarantee the cover of the *TV Times*'. With this kind of experimentation one does of course run the risk of seeming illiterate rather than clever, as we see in this use of the verb to 'muster':

> The sheep gave me as filthy a look as a sheep can muster to display their displeasure at being kept waiting.

The verb to 'muster' has been primarily used of collecting together bodies of men for military or other duties. Thus the notion of assembling personnel is basic to the usage. The fact that failure to assemble enough people for a given purpose produced the usage 'Is that all you can muster?' should not be the basis for eliminating the basic meaning of the verb in its connection with gathering numbers together. In short the experiment does not come off and the writer should have been satisfied with: 'gave me as filthy a look as a sheep can give'.

Fanciful coinages manufactured by journalists with a sense of humour can brighten sober prose. Some decades ago the word 'couth' was used in print. It was intended to mean the converse of 'uncouth'. As 'uncouth' means 'lacking in good manners', so 'couth' was used to mean 'civilized and cultivated'. Whoever it was that first used 'couth' thus provided others with an entertaining word to drop in conversation. But etymologically the usage does not make sense. Although the current meaning of 'uncouth' is 'lacking in good manners', the word 'couth' once meant 'known'. We find the word in Chaucer. There is a point in his narrative poem *Troilus and Criseyde* at which an exchange of prisoners is planned between the Trojans in Troy and the besieging Greeks. The news of this plan spreads rapidly. 'This thing anon was couth in every street' Chaucer tells us. And we do not need to look as far back as that for use of 'couth', meaning 'known'. It still survives in Scotland.

That said, the joke was a good one and produced some imitations. 'They behaved perfectly, which gruntled me no end', I read in a magazine. Here again the joke depends on assuming that 'gruntle' must be the converse of 'disgruntle'. The reasoning is that if being 'disgruntled' is being displeased and put into a bad mood, then 'gruntled' must mean pleased and satisfied. But this is to ignore etymology and history. In fact the verb 'gruntle' is the frequentative form of 'grunt' (as 'prattle' is the frequentative form of 'prate') and is not therefore the opposite of 'disgruntle' (to put in a bad temper) but a near equivalent.

There are certain other words which exist in a seemingly negative form for which the converse positive form is not used. We speak of a clumsy, physically unprepossessing person as being 'ungainly', but the positive form 'gainly', meaning 'graceful', has long dropped out of use. We use the words 'scrutiny' and 'scrutinize' for close examination and we describe a taxingly unreadable personality as 'inscrutable', but the word 'scrutable' has also gone from common use. Used in journalism, the two words 'gainly' and 'scrutable' give a piquancy to the text.

No doubt the temptation to use or adapt archaic or rarely used words comically will always find takers.

> Your swash has never been buckled until you've experienced Errol Flynn in full doublet and hose as Robin of Locksley.

'Swashbuckling' is a colourful word, but to talk of buckling a swash is really topsy turvy. It would be nearer the point to talk of 'swashing the buckle', for the 'swash' was the clattering stroke of sword on metal. A 'swashbuckler' was one who made a noisy display by striking his own or his opponent's shield with his sword. It is safer philologically to make such jokes with purely imaginary words, as the writer of the following does.

> On behalf of her mates she keeps alert (surely this country's got enough lerts, perhaps she should be a loof instead?).

Slang

Usages which exploit slang or crude colloquialisms may brighten journalism or cheapen it. Perhaps the following advertisement manages to do both.

> Let Direct Line guide you to a bright career as the glammest gran on the block.

We all know what 'glammest' must mean, though we may never have met it before. 'Glamorous' is not an adjective that can be turned into 'glamorousest'. Evading the usage 'most glamorous' in the interests of brevity and of sustaining a tone of informal chatter serves its purpose.

One may feel less indulgent towards the comparatively recent usage of the verb to 'forget' in a piece about the treatment of children.

> Forget shouting at them to clear up.

As a substitute for saying 'Don't do this' or 'Stop doing that', 'Forget doing it' has a certain colloquial freshness at first, but that kind of freshness soon palls, and one begins to sense that, after all, desisting from doing something is one thing and forgetting to do it is another and very different thing. But the usage is part of the 'Listen-to-me-being-informal' idiom which is to be heard all around us.

> Disclosing tablets can be a fun way of testing that all the plaque has been removed.

Too many liberties are taken here in the advice for looking after a child's teeth. Using 'fun' as an adjective and defining tablets as a 'way' are no doubt devices for keeping up a light-hearted tone, but the price paid in verbal 'finish' is too high. On the other hand one can see what is gained in briskness and conciseness by the following opening:

> Spring is the ideal time to dejunk your wardrobe.

The word 'dejunk' carries the suggestion of someone who means business and it doesn't convey the tone of a person from whom the polite might shrink, as does the following:

> I take real pleasure in slobbing around in T-shirts with holes in.

We are not, of course, expected to want to join her, and she makes sure of that. There is no verb to 'slob', but the noun 'slob' means someone unattractively coarse and crude. To suggest that you enjoy indulging in the coarse and the crude sounds too much like a challenge. One feels the need for a word to define the practice of verbal slumming.

> When you're done being all cultural, hit the clubs, blag your way into the impossibly trendy Met Bar . . .

One assumes that the writer was perfectly aware that 'when you're done' is a crudely illiterate version of 'when you've done'. This amusingly exaggerates the shift in mood from 'cultural' interests to something earthier. 'Hitting' clubs or other high spots is established slang. The slang verb to 'blag' officially means to rob but the effect on us ordinary readers of seeing it used to mean something else is to make us feel out of touch with the latest trends. We recognize that it must be 'hip' to say 'when you're done' instead of 'when you've done' and hipper still to speak of 'hitting' clubs. So we must assume that it is hippest of all to talk of 'blagging your way' into a bar. If we really appreciate that we are not just trendy, we are positively funky.

Index

Words and phrases discussed in the text are indexed in *italics*; topics discussed are in roman type.